T0035761

Me and My Cat

Chicken Soup for the Soul: Me and My Cat
Amy Newmark

Published by Chicken Soup for the Soul, LLC www.chickensoup.com
Copyright ©2024 by Chicken Soup for the Soul, LLC. All Rights Reserved.

The publisher gratefully acknowledges the many publishers and individuals who granted Chicken Soup for the Soul permission to reprint the cited material.

Front cover courtesy of iStockphoto.com (©CagdasAygun)
Back cover and interior photo of cat over woman's shoulder courtesy of iStockphoto.com (©iprogressman), interior photo of man holding cat courtesy of iStockphoto.com (©Magui-rfajardo), interior photo of African American woman holding cat courtesy of iStockphoto.com (©Halfpoint), interior photo of couple holding cat courtesy of iStockphoto.com (©PeopleImages)
Photo of Amy Newmark courtesy of Susan Morrow at SwickPix

Cover and Interior by Daniel Zaccari

Publisher's Cataloging-In-Publication Data

Names: Newmark, Amy, editor.
Title: Chicken soup for the soul : me and my cat / Amy Newmark.
Description: Cos Cob, CT: Chicken Soup for the Soul, LLC, 2024.
Identifiers: LCCN: 2023949911 | ISBN: 978-1-61159-111-8 (paperback) | 978-1-61159-346-4 (ebook)
Subjects: LCSH Cats--Literary collections. | Cats--Anecdotes. | Cat owners--Anecdotes. | Human-animal relationships--Anecdotes. | BISAC PETS / Essays & Narratives | PETS Cats / General | HUMOR / Animals
Classification: LCC PS509.C37 C48 2024 | DDC 810.8/03629752--dc23

Library of Congress Control Number: 2023949911

PRINTED IN THE UNITED STATES OF AMERICA
on acid∞free paper

30 29 28 27 26 25 24   01 02 03 04 05 06 07 08 09

Me and My Cat

Amy Newmark

Chicken Soup for the Soul, LLC
Cos Cob, CT

Changing Your World One Story at a Time®
www.chickensoup.com

Table of Contents

❶
~Meant to Be~

❷
~Miracles Happen~

❸

~My Very Good, Very Bad Cat~

❹

~Who Rescued Whom?~

❺

~What I Learned from the Cat~

❻
~We Are Family~

❼
~Natural Therapists~

8

~Canine Friends~

9

~A Cat's Purpose~

Meant to Be

April Showers

Prayer requires more of the heart than of the tongue.
~Adam Clarke

"Winter storm on the way!" the radio blared. I glanced out the window. Dark clouds were already forming above our small subdivision in rural Illinois. Just then, I heard, "Mom! Mom!" In blew my three bundled-up boys and a crisp October wind.

"Mom!" cried five-year-old Robin. "There's a cat down in the ground!"

"Oh. You mean someone's cat's been buried?"

"No, Mom! Please! Come see! She needs help!"

Six eager hands pulled me outside to the curb. "Can't you hear it?"

Yes, I could — a very faint meow, floating right up from the storm drain!

Chat, almost four, squinted down into the darkness. "Maybe we could drop her a rope."

Two-and-a-half-year-old Jay started calling, "Here, kitty, kitty, kitty!"

By now a crowd of neighborhood children had gathered around. "This storm sewer drains across the street," one of the older boys explained. "If we go down to the opening and call, maybe she'll come out."

At the culvert opening, the children took turns shouting, "Kitty! Kitty!" Finally, when Jay called, out she came. Muddy, wet, bone-thin, with a woefully deformed tail. But alive.

"Whose cat is she?" I asked.

"No one's," piped up one of the girls. "Her old owners kicked her down there to get rid of her."

"Well, she's ours now," Robin announced. "'Cause Jay's the one she came out for."

Back at the house, we wiped the pathetic creature off the best we could. Then, looking around for something to feed her, I filled a bowl of milk.

She ignored the bowl completely and sat and washed herself all over. Now we could see that she was a longhair with striking black-and-white markings. Only when she was immaculate did she turn to the milk. Even then, instead of gulping it down, she sipped daintily, stopping to clean her whiskers from time to time.

"Look at that!" my husband Don exclaimed. "A real lady!"

And that's how Ladycat came to be with us.

Just in time, too. For all night long we were hit with wave after wave of pounding rain. By morning it had changed to snow.

But inside, our home glowed with the joy of a new playmate. For hours on end, Ladycat would play balls, blocks, and cars with three enchanted boys. She blossomed under this love. But two things about her sad past remained: her deformed tail (perhaps broken in that kick down the storm drain), and her need to go outside and hunt for at least an hour every night.

From then on, frozen days rolled into frozen weeks of 10, 20, and 30 degrees below zero. Then on Valentine's Day all three boys got chickenpox — Chat so severely, he went into a coma and had to be hospitalized. His brothers begged me not to let Ladycat out that night, in case something happened to her as well.

But the air that evening was spring-like, with just a little drizzle. "Don't worry, she'll be right back," I assured them.

Quickly, though, that drizzle turned into a wild rainstorm. And for the very first time, Ladycat did not come back. All night long, I listened for her. But I only heard the rain. Until it stopped and everything froze.

The next morning, Don's car slid all over the glass-slick road as he headed off on his long commute to work. But I couldn't call him to see if he got there okay. I couldn't even call the hospital fifteen miles away to check on Chat. Or turn on the radio. Or lights. Or heater. For under the weight of that ice, all the power and phone lines had snapped. Our furnace and water heater were inoperable. In fact, nothing worked but our gas stove. Soon it was so cold inside, the boys had to be bundled up in their snowsuits all day long. It was complete misery with those itching pox!

By evening, both boys had bronchitis. But sick as they were, they kept going to the window, looking and calling for their missing pet.

In the middle of the night, Don woke up in excruciating pain and a grossly swollen abdomen. Even though the house was freezing cold (it was 20 below outside and not much warmer inside), his whole body was afire.

"Don!" I gasped. "I think you have appendicitis!"

Normally I would have called the doctor or 911. But with the lines down, I couldn't even call my neighbors next door. Don needed to go to the hospital right away. But Robin and Jay were far too sick to take out into that frigid air. Don would have to go alone.

As quickly as possible, I packed him in ice, covered that with towels, threw a winter coat over his pajamas, and sent him out into the bitter night — praying he'd be able to make it to the hospital without passing out. Or ending up in a wreck.

By the next day, Robin, Jay, and I all had pneumonia. But so did almost everyone else for miles around. Only the most critically ill could be admitted to the local hospital. In fact, Don had to sit in a waiting room all that night — with a ruptured appendix, peritonitis, and double pneumonia — before they could even find a bed for him.

But finally, after a week, the power and phones returned. After two weeks, so did Don. And after three weeks, Chat did, too. But not our missing cat.

February blurred into March, one storm following another. The same with illnesses.

"It's all because Ladycat left," Robin sobbed one day. "Doesn't she love us anymore?"

"God knows where Ladycat is," Chat replied weakly. "I'm going to pray and ask Him to bring her back home to us for Jay's third birthday!"

On April 2nd, just a few days away? What an impossible prayer!

The last day of March was as white, cold, and dreary as ever. But the wind shifted. And on April 1st, the skies opened up.

"Look, children!" I cried. "April showers! It's raining cats and dogs!"

"Cats?" Jay cried. "Is Ladycat here?"

"She will be," Chat assured him. "For your birthday. God will bring her back."

Changing the subject, I asked, "So what do you want for your birthday tomorrow, Jay?"

"Ladycat. Just Ladycat."

That evening the rain finally let up. Then at the dinner table, Robin suddenly asked, "Who's at the front door?"

"Ladycat!" Jay shouted.

All three boys ran to the door, flinging it open. A biting wind roared in — followed by a tiny, mud-covered creature, barely able to move.

Don jumped up. "Quick! Get her some food!"

But as feeble as she was, the cat slowly, painfully cleaned herself all over. Only then would she eat. Ladycat was back.

The next morning we retraced her tiny footsteps in the mud — all the way to the culvert where we had first found her. Ever since the ice storm — that night she had disappeared — the opening had been completely frozen over. She had been down there the entire time, subsisting on mice and snow, until finally freed by the previous day's warm April showers.

Arriving home just in time for Jay's birthday.

Just as three little boys and God knew she would be.

— Bonnie Compton Hanson —

Eggnog with Pickles

Human beings, who are almost unique in having the ability to learn from the experience of others, are also remarkable for their apparent disinclination to do so.
~Douglas Adams

In the first few years after my mother's death, I was a little bossy with my widowed father. When he didn't seem to be moving on and enjoying his life, I decided he needed a pet. Dad had always taken an interest in my family's cats and dogs so I decided to get him a kitten.

I bought bowls and food, a litter box and litter, scratching post and catnip mouse, and a cat carrier. I wrapped everything and purchased a gift certificate for neutering and three veterinary visits. All I had to do now was select a kitten at the animal shelter and pick it up Christmas Eve morning. My kids jumped right on board with this gift for Gramps. "Great idea, Mom, he'll love it. Maybe we should get two!"

My husband Jim, a practical kind of guy who cares about actual facts, wanted to weigh the pros and cons. "Let's discuss both sides," he suggested. "On the one hand the five of you like this concept, but on the other hand, no one knows how Gramps will feel about the surprise." I assured Jim it would all work out. I knew what he really wanted was a firm guarantee that we wouldn't wind up with another animal. We already had three cats and a snooty Pekingese.

Jim had the last word: "Remember, all of you, this will be Gramps' cat. We have enough mouths to feed around here."

On the blustery, snowy day before Christmas, chubby, fluffy, gray-and-white Pickles (named by the volunteers at the shelter) planted himself on our family room couch. Except for the Peke, who took to his bed, all of our critters welcomed little Pickles and he soon joined in the cat festivities — batting tree ornaments and pawing at the bows on the packages under our freshly cut Scotch pine.

Surveying the cat chaos and the laughter of our kids, Jim's brow scrunched into those deep furrows that indicated considerable concern. "Don't forget, we're not getting attached," he said. "As of tomorrow, Pickles belongs to Gramps."

A beautiful, sunny Christmas Day dawned and shortly before noon Dad arrived. With Pickles hidden in my basement office and cedar logs crackling in the fireplace, we welcomed my father into our toasty family room and gathered around the tree to present him with the preliminary gifts.

"What's all this?" he asked. "You'd think I had a cat or something."

That was the perfect intro, as the kids marched into the family room with Pickles sporting a big red bow on his gray-and-white head.

"You have a cat now, Gramps," said my son Chris. "Merry Christmas."

Pickles took quickly to my father and at day's end the two of them left for home. I was elated that my father had a companion and new chores to add to his daily routine. The next morning I resisted the urge to call and check on the two of them. But I could imagine the scene — an adorable kitty and a dear old man playing and bonding. I decided to wait for our New Year's Day brunch for an update.

Then the doorbell rang. It was my father, cat carrier in one hand, and shopping bag in the other. I opened the door to a litany of complaints: "He's swinging on the drapes, scratching the furniture, scratching me, and that litter box is more than I bargained for. I can't keep him. I love you all for caring about me, but I really don't want a pet right now. Sure wish you had asked me first."

"You have to give him a chance to settle in, Dad," I said. "Oh, please try it for a few more days. He'll be such good company, you'll see."

Dad put his two hands on my shoulders and focused his warm, blue eyes on mine. His voice was gentle. "I need to find my own way, figure out decisions by myself and that includes pet ownership. Now give your old dad a hug."

Jim was first down the stairs. The kids followed right behind. I had my back against the front door, the kitten in his carrier at my feet, and the bag of supplies in my arms. Dad waved as he backed out of the driveway. Jim's sigh was deep and long and accepting.

"How about some eggnog for breakfast, Pickles?" he mumbled, picking up the cat carrier on his way into the kitchen.

— Carole Marshall —

Italian Lessons

The only sure thing about luck is that it will change.
~Wilson Mizner

"Wallet stolen — contained passport and credit cards." At the little police station hidden in a corner of the Stazione Termini, the main train station in Rome, I filled out the necessary forms while trying to hold back tears of anger, frustration, and humiliation. Oh, yes, we'd been warned. First by Rita, our Italian language instructor back in Indianapolis, and then over and over since we had arrived in Italy ten days earlier. Watch out for pickpockets! Guard your purse. And I had been careful. But they found me, a seasoned traveler, anyway, waiting for a train to the airport.

I felt so foolish. How could I have been so careless? The hotel welcomed us back, but it took several hours to cancel credit cards, notify our cat-sitter, and cover our two-day delay at our jobs. My husband, Jimmy, tried to console me with a reminder that since we were traveling standby with Delta Airlines Buddy Passes, we could board any flight with empty seats, but I just felt stupid, stupid, stupid! Later, even one of those long, delicious Italian dinners didn't alleviate my feelings of incompetency and humiliation.

The next morning we dressed in our traveling outfits and headed for the American Embassy to get my temporary passport, intending to make a mad dash for the airport if we finished in time.

"Tell me something about Indiana that is unique," the young

woman behind the counter said, looking up from my application. "I have to ask since you don't have a birth certificate with you."

Unique? My home state? "The Indianapolis 500?" I stammered.

She frowned. "Like a state park, anything like that? A famous mountain or beach?"

"I think the state bird is a cardinal. Or maybe not," I said, my mind a blank.

She must have decided an identity thief would have been better prepared, because ten minutes later we walked out with my new passport.

"Let's stay," Jimmy said as we waited to cross a busy street. "No one expects us home today."

"Really? Can we do that?" Suddenly I felt like a kid playing hooky. My depression began to lift.

It was a lovely day. We wandered all over the city, looking at sights we'd thought we would have to miss. Every so often, though, I had flashes of the embarrassment I was going to feel when I explained my carelessness to friends back home.

Our feet finally started hurting as we crossed a bridge near the block of ancient ruins where Julius Caesar was supposedly done in by Brutus. We headed toward a nearby bench. Several times during our stay we'd rushed past the ruins and even had remarked on the number of cats sunning themselves amid the broken columns fifteen feet or so below the level of the sidewalk. However, we'd never noticed the large hand-printed poster with a red arrow pointing down a flight of stairs near the end of the bridge. "Cat Sanctuary, Visitors Welcome." We couldn't resist.

At the bottom of the stairs was a small garden in front of an arched doorway that seemed to be built into the bridge abutment. Half a dozen cats were sunning themselves in the garden. It smelled like cat food. Okay, it smelled like cat urine, too, but not overwhelmingly. We obeyed the written invitation on the door and entered a large room lined with cages, all with open doors. From the information placards propped up on a long table, we learned the sanctuary serves over 600 cats, some feral, some abandoned. Once the cats are neutered and get shots and identification ear tags, they are free to roam, coming back to the room of cages for shelter and food. We bought a colorful picture book for our cat-sitter about a real-life, one-eyed cat that lived there. The woman who took our Euros told us to get Deborah to sign it and called over the writer, a slight woman with long, tousled hair and an energy force that was almost visible.

Deborah is American, intense, irreverent, and altogether delightful. She came to Rome for a visit sixteen years ago and never left. Helped start the sanctuary. She's passionate about taking care of the cats. The previous year they got 1,000 cats, adopted out 300.

The shelter survives on donations. It is occasionally threatened with closure by the city government because it doesn't have any legal right to be there. So far Deborah and her cohorts have won each skirmish by e-mailing to their list of donors around the world, which produces an enormous letter-writing campaign to the mayor and the threat of negative PR for the city.

Deborah spotted Jimmy's camera. "We're about to start a campaign," she said, "to show how we don't just help cats. There are many old people in Rome who spend way too much of their pensions on feeding homeless cats. Some give up food for themselves to do this. The sanctuary helps over fifty of them, giving them food or taking the cats in." She nodded at the camera. "We need photos for the posters."

An old woman, stooped over with osteoporosis, had entered the room. "Here's our model," Deborah said. "Carla has sixteen cats, lives in an apartment with no heat, and survives on her pension. She comes here for cat food and spends most cold days here helping with the animals and staying warm."

Deborah picked up two bowls of cat food and led us into the ruins. She set the bowls down and positioned Carla nearby as cats jostled each other for the food. The old woman leaned back to minimize her stoop and smiled into the camera. She was heart-wrenchingly beautiful. Jimmy and Deborah worked for over half an hour, snapping shots and then viewing them until they were satisfied. As I watched, it occurred to me: this was why we needed to stay in Rome.

"Of course it is," Deborah said when I told her. "I've had my passport stolen three times and there's always a reason. Can you e-mail the pictures as soon as you get home?" We parted with hugs.

I smiled all the way back to our hotel, all through dinner, and was still smiling the next day as we boarded the plane. Several years later, I still smile when I think about Deborah and her cat sanctuary. She e-mailed to let us know her campaign was a success, bringing in enough to assure the sanctuary another year of compassionate care.

Sure, I know the campaign could have happened without us, but we were there at just the right moment, and for two cat lovers from the U.S., it was a blessing to be part of something so splendid and noble, so universal. Now when I'm asked to name the best thing that happened to me in Italy, I always say, "Well, it started with getting my pocket picked."

— Sheila Sowder —

A Kitty, a Puppy, and a Pony

A person often meets his destiny
on the road he took to avoid it.
~Jean de La Fontaine

The Christmas season arrived, and as always, my mother asked, "What would you like for Christmas?"

"A kitty, a puppy, and a pony," I responded without hesitation. One could say I "placed my order."

My mom explained we didn't need another dog, as we already had one. Of course, I responded, "We do not have a puppy." She had no protest against the kitty, although she may have said something about the cost of vaccinations. As for the pony, it was a downright "no."

"Ponies are a lot of work," she said. "Not to mention they cost a small fortune."

A few days later, on a particularly cold December day, our friends called, begging us to take a kitten. Apparently, the mother had been killed. Once the kitten was in my mother's arms, she instantly gave in to those darling, green eyes hidden among black fur. He was cold and wet, and my mother's heart went out to him. She hand-fed him and tucked him inside her sweater until he was warm. Our friends named him Nicodemus, and there was no going back. I got my kitty.

A few weeks passed. Mom was coming home one evening when she spotted a stray mother dog and two puppies running in the road. She got out and tried to catch them, but only managed to catch one puppy. When she got the puppy in the back of the van, it snarled and snapped. I think the puppy thought it was much larger than it was. At last, Mom came home and brought the puppy in the house. The puppy was very scared, shaking and barking aggressively. It was rather snappish, so after lots of consideration, we named it Gingersnap. And there was my puppy.

At this point, I suppose my mom became a little afraid of a pony showing up. As a precaution, she bought a small pony figurine to give me on Christmas morning.

It seemed like forever until Christmas arrived. Finally, it did. I raced downstairs alongside my siblings and peered out the window. To my dismay, there was no pony. When I opened my stocking, I found the small pony figurine. Filled with disappointment, I looked into my mother's eyes. "I wanted a real pony," I said. It seemed as though my mother didn't understand.

"I would get one if I could, but ponies are expensive and require a lot of work," my mother responded sensibly. My heart sank.

A few days after Christmas, Mom was talking to the insurance man. I bet they had a normal conversation discussing each other's Christmases. However, seemingly out of nowhere, the man said, "I had the strangest thing happen to me! This pony showed up in my back yard and won't leave. Do you want it?" My mother about died laughing. Then she firmly said "no" and immediately hung up the phone.

— Rachel Katherine —

That Darn Cat

Cats are cats... the world over! These intelligent,
peace-loving, four-footed friends — who
without prejudice, without hate, without greed
— may someday teach us something.
~James Mackintosh Qwilleran

"Brace yourself," my brother warned as he hung up the phone. "Grandma is coming."

Don't get me wrong. We loved our grandma but when we heard that she and Gramps were coming for Christmas, we had mixed emotions. Gramps, a big, jovial fellow was always making us laugh. But Grandma, although tiny in stature, could be a grouch! She didn't mince words. "Nice girls don't wear tight dungarees." Now I wouldn't be able to wear my new jeans. "Only fools spend money on movies." There went our plans to see *A Magic Christmas*.

My brother and I quipped in unison: "When Grandma speaks, everyone cringes." Mom was not amused and warned us to be respectful.

Then we remembered Grandma's number one rule: "No pets in the house." Milot, our beloved cat would have to be banished to the basement. The basement wasn't heated. We glanced sadly at the gray and white Maine Coon, pregnant with her first litter. She was comfortably curled up on the counter in the kitchen — for now.

Mom had taken great pains to make everything perfect for the holidays. A bright, berry wreath hung on the front door. Live poinsettias adorned the windows. The vanilla fragrance and the soft light of scented candles created a calming effect. She smoothed out the festive red and green fabrics concealing the foldout tables and reminded us, "Mind your manners, don't talk with your mouth full, and use your napkin."

"What's a napkin?" half-joked my older brother, Dee.

The house was glowing. And so was Mom.

It was the first time all the relatives were coming to our new home. "Ooohs" and "ahhhs" were heard as each one entered. The grandparents were the last to arrive. We heard Gramps' old Chevy come to a screeching halt. I ran to the door as my brother removed the cat from the room. I gave Gramps a big kiss and turned to hug Grandma. She held me at arms' length, scrutinizing my face and blurted, "Too much rouge!" She meant "blush."

"Oh, Mama," Gramps jumped in protectively. "It's the cold that's making her cheeks so rosy."

My brother carried their overnight bag into the spare bedroom. They were staying a couple of days.

As Grandma's gaze took in the elaborate decorations, a "Humph!" escaped her lips. "Nothing better to do with your money, Mrs. Millionaire?" In the true essence of goodwill, Mom tactfully ignored the dig and welcomed her parents affectionately.

Everyone gathered in the tiny quarters. We spent a while catching up. Aunt Katherine got promoted. Adele announced her engagement. All good news except Grandma's arthritis was acting up.

Eventually, we took our places for the feast. Traditional American fare was tastefully arranged all around. There were even delicious side dishes from our grandparents' old country. The turkey took center stage. The parties at each table joined hands as the youngest, Cousin Mille, said her well-rehearsed grace. Things went without a hitch until she got to amen. Then an unexpected snicker arose from the kids' section, followed by increasingly louder chuckles and giggles. Soon boisterous laughter was in full swing. With a low moan coming from deep within, Milot, the cat was moving in slow motion, dragging Grandma's size 44 Double D bra behind her.

Mom's face was ashen. Grandma's mouth was open wide. Her complexion had taken on the color of the pickled beets on the platter in front of her. The laughter had come to an abrupt halt. An ominous silence ensued. My brother snatched the cat — which refused to let go of the brassiere — and whisked her out of sight. Mom threw us a harsh look and Grandma scolded, "An animal belongs in the yard; not in the house." Gramps grabbed a shot of Schnapps and practically shoved it under Grandma's nose: "Here, Mama. This will help your cold." Grandma slugged it down. And then another.

The Schnapps seemed to help because gradually the corners of Grandma's mouth turned up. She confessed, "That darn cat! She made me smile." Before long, we were all smiling and chatting, gladly putting the cat-and-bra incident out of our thoughts. The rest of the meal went smoothly. The supper was a huge success.

When all the dishes had been cleared, we gathered around the brightly lit tree and followed our custom of Christmas caroling. Aunts, uncles, cousins, brothers and sisters put aside any differences of the previous months. A feeling of contentment, gratitude and love enveloped us in a warmth not unlike a bear hug. For a few hours, harmony and accord prevailed; at least in spirit if not in our musical attempts.

Sometime later Mom noticed that Grandma was absent from this pleasurable and rare gathering. "Go find her," she urged.

I wandered toward the guest room. The door was slightly ajar. Without opening it further I peeked inside. Grandma was sitting in a recliner, her head bent over something. I looked closer. Milot, the cat was snuggled happily on her lap. Grandma's face wore a blissful expression. Her weathered hands gently stroked the cat's chin and behind her ears. "Pretty Milot. Whose kitty are you? Are you Granny's little darling? Yes, you are," Grandma purred. I don't know whose purr was louder.

Busted!

I sneaked away without being seen.

In February, when Milot had her litter, Grandma timidly asked for one of the kittens. She and Christmas spent the next seventeen years living together in peaceful contentment. And Grandma's disposition improved immensely.

— Eva Carter —

The Gift

Way down deep, we're all motivated by the same
urges. Cats have the courage to live by them.
~Jim Davis

One day a handsome black tomcat appeared at our back door. His coat had a white bib and four snowy paws, making him look like he was wearing a tuxedo. His tail was as crooked as a corkscrew.

My four-year-old brother Daniel and I had never had a pet. We both instantly fell in love with the gentle black and white cat. All that first afternoon, the three of us played together. When it got dark, we begged our parents to let our new friend come inside so we could feed him. Mom shook her head. "It might confuse him," she explained. "This cat looks too healthy to be a stray. He must have a home already."

But the next morning, the tuxedo cat was still there. He waited patiently by the front door like a butler at a mansion. "Yea!" said Daniel. "He wants to be our cat!"

It did seem like he was telling us something. He stuck around all day, playing with Daniel and me outside. When we went into the house, he jumped up on the barbecue and watched us through the window. The last thing I saw that night were his green eyes, staring in at me.

The next day, our parents warned us that we needed to try our best to find his owners. My mom helped me make a flyer that said "Found: black and white cat with crooked tail" with our phone number on it. I drew a picture of the cat on each one and we hung them around the neighborhood.

The second day, I named him Alley, as in "alley cat." The third day, our dad and mom let us put some food out for him. The fourth day, our parents broke down and we got to bring him inside.

Alley let me carry him like a baby, from room to room. Daniel built Lego castles all around him. He followed us all around the house and at bedtime he jumped on each of our beds while we got tucked in, as if he was saying good night to us.

Alley was a dream pet.

Our family woke up from the dream about two weeks after we adopted him. That was the day a big, tattooed man appeared at our door holding one of our "Found Cat" flyers. Before anyone could say anything, Alley strolled over to the man and rubbed on his leg. It was obvious that they knew each other.

"My name's Mark Johnson," he announced, casually picking Alley up. "I see you've met my only roommate, Dewey. He kinda wanders when I'm out of town. Can I offer you good people a reward for watching him?"

"No," Dad said with a sigh. "It was a pleasure to have him as our guest." The rest of us were completely silent. At the door, Mr. Johnson turned back and faced us kids. That's when he must have seen the tears in my eyes. "Wow. I'm sorry," he said. "I didn't realize you kids had gotten so attached. Hey, I only live a few blocks away. If you two would ever like to visit old Dewey..."

"His name's not Dewey!" Daniel yelled at the top of his lungs. "It's Alley!" He ran sobbing to his room.

Mr. Johnson's eyes widened. The full meaning of his visit had sunk in at last. He slipped out awkwardly. Over his shoulder was slung Alley. Alley's unreadable green eyes looked back at me all the way down the walk.

For days, I found myself staring out of the window at the barbecue as if Alley might suddenly rematerialize there. Daniel went through spells of bursting into tears. Our parents tried to console us by keeping our family schedule full and entertaining. They even talked about going to the pound to pick out another pet.

Then one day, I heard Daniel yell, "He's back!" We all hurried into the family room. Sure enough, Alley was there by the door nuzzling Daniel, his crooked tail lashing Daniel's legs.

He had found his way home.

My heart was jumping with joy. Then Dad said, "Daniel. Sarah. He can't stay. He's not ours, remember?"

Daniel and I both looked at him like he was crazy. "But Dad..." Daniel began.

"Do we have to tell that Mr. Johnson guy?" I asked, looking into my dad's eyes.

Dad nodded his head. Even though I could tell it made him sad to do it, he looked up the name and left a message on Mr. Johnson's machine. "Your cat is here again," Dad said. "Would you please stop by and pick him up?"

I felt like this would be the last time we would ever see Alley. I figured Mr. Johnson would lock him up in his house. For the rest of the day we played with him; making cat fortresses out of cardboard boxes, dangling strings around corners, petting him and feeding him treats. Alley went along with it all, just like he expected that kind of treatment and wanted nothing less.

When Mr. Johnson arrived at 8:00, I had made a decision. I waited in the hall behind Daniel and our dad, holding Alley in my arms. As soon as Dad opened the door, I said to Mr. Johnson, "I think he wants to live with us."

"Sarah..." Dad began.

But Mr. Johnson nodded at me, letting me know it was all right. Then he squatted down, so that he would be at the same level as Daniel and me.

"You know, Sarah, I think you're right. He seems to have made a decision. I think he must like kids," he said with a wink. He set down a small cardboard box. "I didn't come to take him. I just came by to bring you these." Inside were a bowl and several cans of cat food.

"You're letting us have him?" I asked, stunned. "Like a gift?"

"Well, kind of," he said with a shrug. A tattoo-scrawled arm darted out as he petted Alley. "Bye, Dewey. I'll miss you. But I have a feeling you'll be in good hands."

And, just like that, Mr. Johnson was gone. None of us ever saw him again.

From then on, the tuxedo cat was ours. In no time at all, he became a respected member of our family. He was a fierce hunter, yet he remained extremely gentle with us. Whatever room the family was in, Alley was there. Whenever Daniel and I were ready for bed, Alley popped in to say goodnight.

Sometimes I wonder what made our cat decide to stop being Dewey and want to become Alley. We will never really know, but it gave us all an example of what giving is all about. Because the truth of the matter was that Mr. Johnson hadn't given his pet away.

Alley had given himself to us.

— Sarah Strickland as told by Craig Strickland —

7

Conversion

*Are we really sure the purring is coming from
the kitty and not from our very own hearts?*
~Emme Woodhull-Bäche, translated

I have always been a "dog person." As far back as I can remember, there were dogs in my house. Not cats, dogs. So when two coworkers found a tiny gray kitten eating out of the Dumpster near our office building and asked me to take him in, I agreed, reluctantly. "Only temporarily," I proclaimed, "I'm a dog person." My coworkers nodded their heads knowingly and handed me the warm little bundle.

The kitten was three months old when I brought him home. Weighing in at barely three pounds, he rode peacefully in the passenger seat, atop my gym bag, and waited patiently while I went into Wal-Mart, befuddled in front of the cat items trying to decide what to buy. I knew I would need cat litter and a pan, some cat food, maybe a toy or two. I made my purchases and returned to the car to find his small gray face with green eyes soften at the sight of me. Something inside me shifted a little bit.

Don't get attached, I told myself, it's only temporary.

I took him to the vet the next day, calling him John Doe. I announced loudly in the waiting room that I was in possession of a cat in need of a permanent home. Meanwhile, I tried not to notice the warm feeling I got as I felt John Doe purring in my arms.

Several months went by with no responses to my "Cat Needs Good

Home" posters. Since he had started responding to my calls (as much as cats will respond), I officially named him Bonaparte. I thought it was a funny name and I wasn't keeping him anyway.

At some point during those months, Bonaparte started sleeping with me at night. He had a curious habit of laying down in such a way that his body always touched mine. When I shifted, he stood up, waited for me to get settled again, then lay down against me again.

I had never known cats could be so affectionate.

He performed the usual kitten antics that caused me to scream with frustration. He brought the curtains in my bedroom down so many times that I started telling friends that he was redecorating. His sudden bursts of energy that caused him to race frantically around the house in pursuit of invisible bugs left me shaking my head in amazement. He yowled every night by the front door to go out — until I got him neutered. He woke up at five every morning and parked himself on my chest; paws folded neatly under his body, staring at me intently until I finally woke up and drowsily stroked him.

Then there was the constant purring that never ceased to delight me.

When he was two years old and I had long since fallen in love with him, Bonaparte became deathly ill. He spent three months in and out of intensive care at the vet's office, and he required a feeding tube for most of that time. One night, when I had to take him to the emergency clinic, I slept by his cage because I didn't want him to wake up and not find me there. I took him to a specialist one hour from home, where he stayed for almost a month. I drove there every day to visit with him, cuddle him and brush him because he was so sick he had stopped grooming himself. The vets were grim about his prognosis. I remember standing in the hallway one morning, sobbing, begging them not to give up on him.

See, there were these cold nights that I had to get through without his warm body snuggled up against mine. The hole in my heart left by the loneliness was tremendous.

The vet finally determined that a risky surgery had to be attempted, although there were no guarantees for Bonaparte's survival. It was his last and only chance. Miraculously, Bonaparte came through, recovered and was able to come home a few weeks later.

Today he is six years old, and over the years I have brought home two other stray cats. Bonaparte worked his magic on them just like he worked it on me. They were unsure, insecure and frightened, yet practically melted in his presence. He grooms them, lays against them while they sleep, or touches noses with them as they pass in the hallway. His heart is so big that it spills out and touches the cold, hidden places in other hearts.

Somehow Bonaparte found that place in my heart. He found it before I even knew what was happening. And every night when he climbs into bed with me and arranges his body so that every part of him is touching me, I feel my heart fill with love all over again.

— Kelly L. Stone —

8

Babblers Anonymous

People who love cats have some
of the biggest hearts around.
~Susan Easterly

During my college days, I began cultivating myself to fit the image I held of an aspiring author. I fancied myself a connoisseur of language and shuddered at others' misuse of it. Most of all, I scoffed at people who spewed drivel at babies or, even more loathsome, at pets. Although neither babies nor pets were part of my life, I felt quite certain that when they were, I would be a role model for mothers and animal lovers everywhere.

Then one day my friend Marcia called and asked if I would take in a stray cat. "He's cold and scared," she said. "He's been living on my neighbor's garage roof. Someone dumped him from a car."

Cats are sensible animals, I thought. I had always admired their regal bearing and independence. Besides, Charles Dickens, H. G. Wells and Mark Twain had all owned cats. I imagined a cat curled at my feet as I typed, perhaps inspiring my creativity to new heights. I invited Marcia to bring over the stray.

As Marcia approached my apartment, I heard rather than saw the cat. He protested loudly until she set the carrier on my living room rug. The moment she opened the door of the carrier, a skinny black cat streaked out, raced into the bedroom, jumped into the bathroom and bathtub, leapt out, then charged back into the living room and onto my lap.

"I've got to run," Marcia said, grabbing the carrier and stepping outside in one smooth move. "Yell if you need anything."

By this time, the cat was kneading his paws on my stomach in frantic rhythm, much like a boxer jabbing a punching bag. "You're not shy," I said wryly. Although the cat was bony, his coat shone blue-black in the lamplight. His mustard-yellow eyes blinked at me momentarily before he resumed his activity.

"I guess I need to call you something." I choked on my words. Listen to me, I thought. I'm talking to this animal as if he understands.

"Ralph," I continued, despite myself. "Ralph is a nice, no-nonsense name." No cutesy Boo-Boos or Fluffys for me.

That night I set down the rules of cathood. Ralph would not be allowed on my bed. He would sleep on the rug in the living room. He would learn to respond appropriately to simple, one-word commands. For my part, I would speak to him like the intelligent animal he was.

After a two-night cycle of putting Ralph on the floor and awakening to find him beside me in bed, I gave in on that rule. I told myself that this was for my good rather than his, because his purring relaxed me, and his warm, fuzzy body felt wonderful against my back.

As the week wore on, we seemed to understand each other perfectly. I made sure not to speak to Ralph other than as master to animal. Then one morning, I accidentally stepped on his tail. Such a pitiful wail! I scooped him up and held him close.

"Oh, Mommy's so sorry!"

I looked around. Who said that? Oh, no! It was happening. I was beginning to talk like one of them.

Over the next few days, I desperately tried to curb my maternal feelings. I decided to squelch the Mommy business first, but nothing else seemed appropriate. Master was a bit much. Kathy? No, too familiar — I would lose my authority. "Mommy" best summed up my role. So grudgingly, I became Ralph's mommy... but I promised myself I would make no further concessions.

Then one night Ralph was sick on the carpet. After cleaning up, I hugged and stroked him.

"Poor baby," I cooed. "Him was sick."

Him was sick! I envisioned my English professor tightening a noose around his neck. As Ralph napped, I reviewed my worsening condition. I could no longer deny the facts. I was rapidly becoming a pet owner-babbler.

During the next few weeks, I resolved to control every word that came from my lips, but the unthinkable happened. Such aberrations as "You is a widdle baby boy" flowed freely, as though the evil spirit of grammar atrocities possessed me every time I looked at Ralph. Worse yet, he seemed to expect such talk.

One night I decided to go cold turkey. I placed Ralph on my lap so he faced me. "Now," I began, consciously resisting the babble, "you're a sensible, intelligent animal. You want an owner who treats you as such, don't you?"

Ralph's eyes never moved. I read understanding there, encouraging me to go on. "Henceforth, I will treat you with the dignity and respect such a noble cat deserves."

Ralph's mouth was opening. So intent was his stare that for one insane moment, I thought he would speak. He yawned in my face.

"You silly, pweshus baby," I said, laughing and cuddling him to me.

Now the rules are gone. I never had the authority anyway. Only love and the babbling remain. Does anyone know of a Babblers Anonymous?

— Kathleen M. Muldoon —

Lucky to Be Alive

Wherever there is a human being, there is an opportunity for a kindness.
~Seneca

aria, a gentle, soft-spoken woman of seventy, had always managed to view the world with a child's sense of wonder. She greeted the dawn of each new day with the brightness of the sun itself and found joy in the smallest of things: a dove perched on her birdfeeder, the fresh morning dew, the sweet scent of jasmine in her garden.

A widow, Maria lived alone in a run-down neighborhood in Deerfield Beach, Florida. One day while out tending the small garden in front of her modest home, Maria had been injured in a drive-by shooting. The bullet had pierced her skin with a ferocious bite and lodged itself in the old woman's right thigh. Crying out in agony, she had dropped to the sidewalk. When the mailman found her unconscious nearly an hour later, her injured leg had been bleeding profusely. She'd made it to the hospital just in time and later, the doctor had told Maria she was lucky to be alive.

Returning home, Maria didn't feel so lucky. Before the shooting, the elderly woman had always been grateful that she was healthy for her age. Now just getting the daily mail required a Herculean effort. In addition, her medical bills were mounting alarmingly, straining her meager income. And although she had watched the neighborhood deteriorate, somehow things had seemed safe in the daylight — but not anymore. For the first time in her life, Maria felt frightened, alone and vulnerable.

"I feel defeated," she had told her friend Vera. "I'm just an old woman with nothing to do and nowhere to go."

When Vera came to pick up Maria for her checkup at the medical center, she hardly recognized her old friend. Maria's soft brown eyes held a haunting sadness and her face was gaunt and haggard. All the curtains were drawn and her hands shook with fear as she hobbled out onto the front porch, a cane stabilizing her injured leg.

They were a little early for Maria's appointment, so to try to cheer up Maria, Vera took a longer, more scenic route. They were stopped at a red light when Maria suddenly shrieked. "Look at that cat! It's trying to run across the street!"

Vera looked up to see a small black-and-white cat bounding into the middle of traffic. Both women screamed as they saw one car, then another, and finally a third, hit the cat. The cat lay motionless, its small body flung into the grass. Cars slowed, but no one stopped to help.

"We must save that poor creature," said Maria. Vera pulled over, got out of the car and went to the hurt animal. Miraculously, it was still alive, but badly injured.

"Take my jacket and wrap the kitty in it," said Maria. Vera carefully put the cat on the seat between them. It looked up at Maria and gave her a plaintive, barely audible meow.

"Everything will be all right, my little friend," Maria said tearfully.

Finding an animal clinic, they went inside and told the receptionist what had happened.

"I'm sorry," she said, "but we cannot accept stray animals."

It was the same at the next clinic. Finally, at the third clinic, a kind veterinarian, Dr. Susan Shanahan, agreed to help and quickly started working on the cat.

"This little guy is lucky to be alive," she told Maria and Vera. "If you hadn't been there for him, he never would have made it."

The vet took Maria aside. "The cat's injuries are very serious," she said. "He has severe head trauma, crushed paws and a cracked collarbone. He'll need a lot of expensive medical attention. Today's bill alone will cost at least $400."

Maria gasped. But taking her worn cloth wallet from her handbag, she gave the doctor all the money she had after paying her bills — $50.

"It's all I have right now, but I promise I will pay you the rest over time. Please don't put that kitty to sleep," she pleaded. "I'll take him home. We need each other."

Sensing how important this was, Dr. Shanahan kneeled and took Maria's hands in hers. "I could get into trouble with my boss for doing this," she said gently. "You see, I really shouldn't have helped the cat in the first place, but, don't worry... I will personally pay for this."

While the cat was at the clinic, Maria went to check on him every day. She spoke softly to him and gently stroked his chin with her little finger. As the days passed, the cat began to purr and the sparkle returned to Maria's eyes.

The day arrived for the cat to come home. As excited as a little girl on Christmas morning, Maria smiled brightly as she walked into the clinic to pick him up.

"What have you decided to name the cat?" asked Dr. Shanahan.

Cradling the cat in her arms, Maria answered happily, "I'm going to call him Lucky, because together we have found a new life."

— Christine E. Belleris —

A Cat Named Turtle

Since each of us is blessed with only one life,
why not live it with a cat?
~Robert Stearns

I didn't grow up with cats. Or with dogs. We once harbored the dalmatian of a vacationing aunt and uncle. If all had gone well, we'd have gotten our own dog.

But all did not go well. My brother refused to clean up after the dog, and soon we were permanently critter-free. Not that my mother minded. Having been scratched by a cat when she was little, she feared anything that moved too quickly on too many legs. My father, a city boy, had no experience with animals and less interest in them.

But I married a cat lover. In his meager walk-up flat in New York City, Roy had enjoyed the company of several marvelous felines, one of them a waif from the subway. I listened to his fond recollections in the same way I heard his tales of some other experiences: They were interesting, even compelling, but nothing I thought I'd ever experience myself.

And then we moved to Vermont and found the cats on our land. Or they found us — and it was really their land. They were feral, having lived in the wild for who-knows-how-long. We extended a hand literally and figuratively to newly named Mama Cat, Honey Puss, Herbert and Sylvester, giving them food on the deck, shelter in the carport and veterinary care for the occasional ailment. Now we realized we should have neutered them, too.

We first saw Turtle trotting along behind her mother, in a parade that included several chubby kittens making their way from the blackberry thicket, across the driveway and into the pine trees. She reappeared briefly a year later, unmistakably the same tortoiseshell. The year afterward, she visited often. I named her when I didn't quite like her; she was nervous, pushy, eating Honey Puss's food. Turtle seemed a good name for a tortoiseshell, especially one who didn't yet have my affection.

I was already reading about feral cats. The universal opinion was that unless a feral cat becomes used to people very early in life, taming the cat is virtually impossible. But nobody told Turtle, who grew ever more comfortable with us. She'd fall onto her back with a thud, inviting us to pet her lovely white belly. She'd linger on the deck with our guests, on summer evenings, sampling one lap after another. Then, as soon as everyone had gone, she'd trot off into the darkness.

Could we bring her inside? Roy's on-again-off-again allergy to cats suddenly returned. But she wouldn't want to come inside anyway, I proclaimed.

Or would she? My office, on the second floor, looks out upon our hillside. Many times I'd put down my work to gaze out the window, and I'd see Turtle staring at me, her wide golden eyes and her dear, crooked little face — haphazardly splotched in black and tan — not twenty inches from my own face. Often I heard her talking to me before I saw her.

We were having a new wing constructed, and she found another route to my office one day, staring at me through the side window. Her muddy paw prints on the roofing paper led from my window to the builder's ladder at roof's edge. I was impressed.

She built a nest for herself in the developing new wing, settling into an open carton where the carpenter had tossed his sweaty t-shirt. She was so comfortable here that she barely lifted her head to greet us when we came looking for her. Roy started getting allergy shots.

With the new wing enclosed, Turtle was again outside. But the next time she looked in at my desk, Roy opened the window screen, waited for her to climb in and carried her downstairs. She was purring loudly. She walked through the living room, poking into all the little places: a cupboard, the bottom of a small bookshelf. She seemed oblivious to us, and indeed we were as dumb as chairs. After a few moments, Roy took her outside.

Later that day, she was sitting near him on the deck, when he got up and moved toward the kitchen. She reached the door ahead of him and scrambled inside. She didn't mind being taken out again. I didn't mind either. She might want to be inside (I now conceded the possibility), but did I want her? Wouldn't a feral cat, even a friendly one, shred everything to tatters? Wouldn't she scratch us at the slightest provocation? Wouldn't she yowl all night?

The deciding moment arrived after I'd been away for a few days. Turtle had stayed at the bend in the driveway for most of my absence. But barely fifteen minutes after my return, she was at the kitchen door! When Roy opened the door to bring her some food, she pushed past him into the kitchen and headed straight for me. No curiosity about the house this time. No interest in the food. She jumped into my lap, readjusted her weight and purred — the kind of purring you could hear from twenty feet away. She missed me! She missed me! That was it. I was ready to share my house with her.

Very soon it was also Turtle's house as she figured out the best spot on our bed (between us, lengthwise) and the sunniest corner of our living room. She had a lot to learn. How to sprawl across my in-basket. How to awaken us for her breakfast. How to keep the house free of the tiny mice that sneak inside every autumn, when the cold air ruffles their rodential dispositions. How to launch a steady stream of complaint at the snow. How to stand guard at the bathtub until I could be meowed safely from the water. How to settle her weight on precisely the document I might be reading from, or typing from, or writing on. The litter box? A snap. She managed that in half a day.

I had a lot to learn, too. And to unlearn, from my mother's prejudices. But with Turtle's help, this cat was soon my dear companion, gentle and wise, considerate and affectionate. Roy was delighted to see how I loved her and how she loved us back. She became the subject of several chapters in the book I wrote on feral cats, and I wish she could have understood the gifts and letters she got from adoring readers. Roy however was convinced she understood everything we said, or even thought; he was sure she could read our minds. Once, he was only thinking of her, and was startled to hear her sudden purring from a nearby chair.

She knew plenty, our Turtle. In parts of the British Isles, it is considered a good omen when a tortoiseshell cat comes into the house. The tortoiseshell is considered special. But Turtle was special beyond all other specialness. The sweetest pussycat we've ever known. And the smartest. Never a pest. Never seeking attention when we were heavily preoccupied with work or chores. But there in a flash whenever a lap became available, whenever a head hit a pillow. She was very special. I knew it, Roy knew it, and Turtle knew that we knew it.

She lived with us for ten sweet years, until kidney disease claimed her, and she is buried just up from the bend in the driveway, under a stone that has her coloring. We see the stone from our kitchen.

I bless the day that she decided to chance it with us. She knew so much more than I did, about the important things. She knew enough to make that running leap that day into my house, my lap, my heart.

— Ellen Perry Berkeley —

11

The Cat Lady

The cat is domestic only as far as suits its own ends.
~Saki

have lived in my neighborhood for twenty years. It seems to me that I've spent at least ten of those years looking for a lost pet, either mine or one I'd seen listed in the newspaper's lost pet column.

Recently, I was at it again, going door-to-door looking for one of my own lost kitties, a little black cat named Nicholas who'd slipped out the door before I could stop him. I made my rounds, visiting with all the neighbors, describing Nicholas. Familiar with this routine, everyone promised to keep an eye out and call me if they spotted him.

Two blocks from my house, I noticed a gentleman raking leaves in the yard of a home that had recently been sold. I introduced myself and presented my new neighbor with the plight of the missing Nicholas, asking if he had seen him.

"No," he replied, "I've not seen a little black kitty around here." He thought for a moment, looked at me and said, "But I know who you should ask. Several of my neighbors have told me that there's a woman in the neighborhood who's crazy about cats. They say she knows every cat around here, probably has dozens herself. They call her 'The Cat Lady.' Be sure to check with her."

"Oh, thank you," I said eagerly. "Do you know where she lives?"

He pointed a finger down the street, "It's that one."

I followed his finger and started to laugh.
He was pointing at my house!

—Patti Thompson—

Miracles Happen

12

All Shapes and Sizes

Watching a peaceful death of a human being reminds us
of a falling star; one of a million lights in a vast sky that
flares up for a brief moment only to disappear
into the endless night forever.
~Elisabeth Kübler-Ross

watched as Dad's strength faded before my very eyes. He was in a hospice house as Alzheimer's disease continued its relentless assault on his brain. After more than five years of its debilitating effects, the progressive malady finally managed to rob him of his desire for food and water. Without those vital necessities, my brothers and I knew Dad's time with us was coming to an end. His six-foot-two body weighed less than 140 pounds.

I left Dad's room around 10 p.m. that March evening and headed home, exhausted. My forty-ninth birthday was coming in three days, but there was no cause for celebration. The only thing that kept going through my mind during the drive was how lucky I was to have had Dad around for forty-nine years.

I fell into bed and immediately went fast to sleep. Around 1 a.m. I was awakened by a noise coming from my kitchen. The sound aroused my suspicions enough to get me out of bed to investigate. I grabbed the baseball bat that I kept by the bedroom door as I cautiously crept toward the kitchen. However, I found nothing out of the ordinary, only my cat playing with a plastic bag. She was usually asleep at the foot of my bed at that hour, so I wondered why she was up. I checked all the doors and windows and decided my imagination was running away with me since I was so tired, and the noise obviously had been made by the cat.

I fell back into bed, but sleep wouldn't come. My mind kept replaying the doctor's words when he said the end was very near, so I decided to go back to the hospice house and wait out the night in Dad's room.

I arrived around 2:30 a.m. to find Dad sitting upright in bed as I slipped quietly into his room. He smiled when he saw me, and I fought back tears because he had not recognized me in more than two years. However, there appeared to be a glimmer of recognition as I walked to the side of the bed and he reached for my hand, his blue eyes twinkling. I felt my throat tighten.

"How ya doing, Dad?" I asked, even though I wasn't expecting an answer because he had not spoken an intelligible word in over a year.

His smile grew bigger as he motioned for me to sit in the chair beside his bed, another feat from his plaque-ridden brain that caught me off guard. I sat down and he continued to hold my hand as he motioned to the ceiling with his other hand, pointing for me to look up. I did as he asked, but I saw nothing. He kept pointing.

"What do you see?" I asked.

"Mama," he replied, again pointing and wanting me to see her, too.

Hearing the clarity of his voice in that one-word answer both shocked and surprised me since all his words had been locked inside his head for so long, thanks to the ugliness of Alzheimer's.

I couldn't see anything on the ceiling, but I wish I could have because he obviously was looking into the face of his mother, who died in an accident when Dad was only six years old. That accident also claimed his father's life.

I believe a thin veil separates us from heaven, and at that point the veil was lifted. He saw his mother just the way he remembered her that November morning of 1923 as she waved goodbye from the car window. Less than two hours later, he and his siblings were orphaned when a Southern Railway train slammed into the side of their vehicle in Pelzer, South Carolina.

For another hour Dad pointed upward, smiling and nodding for me to look up. It saddened me to think that I couldn't share in the wonderment he saw as he gazed upward, but I was delighted to participate in his enjoyment of the moment. I was amazed at his burst of energy, even though he never spoke another word. I could tell he was revisiting a happy time in his life, perhaps a time where he was a carefree lad running barefoot through the meadows or catching tadpoles at the old farm pond. It was the time before his six-year-old world shattered and he and his brothers and sister had to learn to fend for themselves and depend on each other for survival.

Soon exhaustion overtook him and, still clutching my hand in his, he leaned back against his pillow and closed his eyes. He never opened them again. I held his hand until after the sun came up, reminiscing about happier days we had shared. The doctor on duty said he had lapsed into a coma. As I watched his chest rise and fall and his breathing become labored, I whispered into his ear that it was all right if he was ready to go. He breathed his last breath around four o'clock that afternoon. He was buried on my birthday three days later.

Even though these events took place thirteen years ago, that night is a precious memory that's still fresh in my mind. One thing that sticks out is how exhaustion had overtaken me that evening, yet the cat, which normally slept with me, had woken me from a deep sleep with that plastic bag. If that had not happened I could not have shared those wonderful final moments of Dad's life with him.

I firmly believe angels take on many forms and come in all shapes and sizes. They don't always come to us in a mist wearing wings and halos, and they don't always spell out their mission. Sometimes we have to observe and listen and be open to receiving their messages. I believe my cat was commissioned that night as Dad's angel, summoning me to his room.

Because of those special last moments, I know Dad is in a safe, loving place today where he has no symptoms of Alzheimer's. I am also certain in my heart that he has reunited with "Mama," and that thought alone gives me much to smile about.

— Carol Huff —

From Princess to Queen

Impossible situations can become possible miracles.
~Robert H. Schuller

On a bright, crisp September day, I started my shift at the Mansfield, Massachusetts animal shelter. My heart sank as I stepped from my car and heard a faint meow coming from a dilapidated cat carrier sitting on the steps.

Terrified eyes stared at me as I opened the carrier and took her in my arms. Immediately, she buried her face into my chest, her body trembling. This beautiful dilute calico was skin and bones, but she managed a muffled purr as if she knew I was there to help.

The veterinarian estimated her age to be around twelve or thirteen. Although she was dehydrated and malnourished, she could return to her normal weight with proper care and daily fluids. Unfortunately, she tested positive for feline leukemia virus, which can be contagious to other cats even if they are vaccinated against it. The disease is generally transmitted by a cat bite, with no known cure. With proper care, though, cats can live normal, happy lives. But how was I to relay this to the Humane Officer? Technically, we were not yet a no-kill shelter (although we were working on it). Even though I pleaded, begged and offered to scoop dog poop for an entire week, the officer regretfully deemed her "unadoptable." She would have to be euthanized.

The only alternative was for a volunteer to adopt her.

My cats were updated on all their shots, but I had made up my mind I was not going to put them through the stress of learning to live with a new animal. Plus, I had already agreed with my husband that we had reached the animal limit. Nevertheless, I took her home and quarantined her in my shed.

The upcoming cold weather concerned me, but my husband installed a wood stove that he insisted was for him. He, too, had sympathy for this emaciated waif. The first few nights were difficult; I could hear her haunting meows inside the house. I spent as much time as I could with her between my job as a pet sitter and my time volunteering at the shelter.

As time went on, she seemed to accept her fate and waited every morning for me by the door. The accommodations weren't the Taj Mahal, but it was the best I could do at the time. She ate voraciously and soon looked quite healthy again. Between my husband and me, she was fed well. This cat was becoming spoiled and walked around the shed as if she owned it. She became a little princess, so "Princess" she was named.

Nine long months passed, and Princess was still a resident, even though I tried and tried to find her a home where she could be the only cat. I prayed daily to the St. Francis of Assisi statue placed above her crate. But it didn't appear that a new home was to be, so we simply accepted her fate.

Summer arrived. Every year, one of the shelter volunteers hosts a party. That year, it was my turn. About thirty volunteers and their guests enjoyed barbecuing and sharing animal stories while the kids romped in the pool. Of course, everyone wanted to see "the cat in the shed," so Princess received more than her share of attention.

Jody, the Sunday morning volunteer, arrived and introduced me to her fiancé, Eric. We chatted for a while, and Jody excused herself to get a bite to eat. Since the activity around the shed had quieted down, Eric asked if he could "check out the tenant."

I was totally unprepared for what happened next. Princess dashed over to him as she did to others, but there was obviously something special about this man. With innocent eyes, she gazed up at him, rubbing against his leg, and refused to leave his side.

He scrutinized her a little closer and then scooped her up in his arms. "This is my cat," he said calmly, never taking his eyes off her.

I replied, "Oh, I know. I have a cat like this, too, with all the light colors and the…"

He interrupted. "No, no, you don't understand. *This* is my cat." The words rang in my head until I finally grasped what he said.

Evidently, he and his family had moved, and somehow the frightened feline had become disoriented and ran away. Having contracted the virus from her mother, she was strictly indoors and had never seen the outdoors. Of course, the family was devastated and placed ads, posted flyers, and even visited the animal shelter, but she hadn't arrived yet, dropped off by that kind stranger.

"Oh, by the way, what's the cat's name?" I asked, still in shock. He grinned and replied, "Queenie because she walked around the house like she was royalty." Does that sound familiar?

Queenie's family came for her the next day. It was a bittersweet moment. I cried, but I would be seeing her again very soon. Eric and Jody travel often and would now need a pet sitter. Could I start next week? In fact, the day of my party, Eric was supposed to be away, but the event had been canceled. How serendipitous was that?

So now when I see Princess — I mean Queenie — basking in the warmth of her cozy bed, I know my prayers were finally answered.

It took almost a year for my miracle to happen, but it was worth the wait.

— Suzanne Gill —

14

Coming Home

Hope is faith holding out its hand in the dark.
~George Iles

Rushing out the door with backpack, kids' bags, and a time clock ticking in my head left me too frazzled to notice another passenger quietly jumping into the back of our Dodge Ram.

Robby faithfully did his duty as the eldest. "Mom, everyone is buckled up. We can go now." And off we went.

With a sigh of relief I crossed Interstate 59, relieved that I wouldn't be late for my classes at USM. Finishing my degree while raising three kids got a little wild some days, but I knew that when I finished and started teaching it would be well worth the effort. I was happy that my husband Glen R. would be home Friday to give me some help.

Smiling contentedly as the kids laughed, I pulled into the babysitter's yard and started to unload the crew.

Melinda let out a squeal. "Mama, Kitty Karen just jumped out of the back of the truck! Quick, go get her!"

"Sweetheart, don't worry, she won't go far! As soon as I get home this evening we'll find her. Kitty Karen will be okay." I comforted the kids, whose frightened big eyes looked to me for assurance.

Glancing at my watch, I quickly kissed my babies goodbye and hurried to pick up my carpoolers on the way to school. Although I enjoyed my classes, I was glad when the time came to scoop up the kids and head home. Little did I realize that the morning's events would come back to haunt me.

"Mom, look at my picture! It's all of us! Look, there is Daddy. See his beard."

"That's great, Robbo. Ryan, what did you make today? Jeri, thanks so much for letting them paint. They really love it. I guess we had better find Kitty Karen and head home. Did you guys see her when you were outside playing? No? Well let's pack up. I'm sure she isn't far."

Melinda sat in the front and helped me scour the neighborhood. As we looked and looked with no sign of Kitty Karen, I got a sinking feeling in my stomach.

Where in the world could she be? I prayed, "Lord, please help us find her. The kids will be sick if she's lost." I was really worried, but I didn't want the kids to know.

We drove around the same streets over and over, but no beautiful fluffy white cat with jeweled eyes of blue and green came running. My heart sank lower and lower as I berated myself for rushing off to class instead of looking for her right when she got away.

I tried to keep everyone's spirits up as the stars twinkled in the evening sky and we gave up looking for the day. "We'll surely find her tomorrow, guys! It's going to be okay. Don't cry now. We'll ask God to take care of her for us tonight."

After dinner and bath time, our bedtime prayers were filled with pleas to keep Karen safe and help us find her the next day. Unfortunately, we said those same prayers the next night, and the next, and the next. Days turned to weeks. We searched and searched, but no Karen.

I started looking less and less. Finally, I faced the realization that our prayers would not be answered. I tried to keep the children busy with activities and distracted them when they wanted to talk about Karen and pray for her return. I didn't want them to have to learn the hard lesson that prayers are not always answered in the way that we would like. They were too young for this harsh reality.

One day flowed into the next. With three kids, a husband, and a dog, it was never boring! Thankfully the kids prayed for Karen less and less. I dodged the bullet of having to explain to them why God didn't hear their prayer and answer.

A year sped by and out of nowhere Melinda said, "Mama, let's pray for Kitty Karen to come home."

What in the world would I tell her after all this time?

"Melinda, let's pray that Kitty Karen has found a good new home. We can pray that God will help us find a different cat that needs a home, too. How about that?"

"No, Mom," Melinda declared with conviction. "I am going to pray that Karen comes home!"

"Okay, sweetie, but you know it has been a long time and Karen may have another home by now."

Melinda looked at me with her big, brown eyes and said, "Mama, you know God can do anything!"

"Yes, honey, He sure can. Let's pray."

The next morning, around ten, I was washing dishes and heard a faint scratch on the front door. Almost afraid to hope, I called Melinda and we opened the door together. There stood our Kitty Karen. Her once beautiful white hair was matted with dirt and her paws were sore and bleeding, but she was home.

— Jan Penton Miller —

15

Butterscotch

Everything that occurs in your life is part
of God's plan to wake you up.
~Leonard Jacobson

Ronnie is disabled and lives in an efficiency apartment on the other side of town. I used to take care of him when I was a nursing assistant, and we remained good friends even after I left the field.

One evening last week, I visited Ronnie. As I got ready to leave, we noticed his precious tabby cat Butterscotch, always the center of attention, was nowhere to be found. We called and searched for him to no avail. Ronnie asked me to check the back screen door to see if perhaps Butterscotch had slipped out unnoticed. As I looked out the door, the yellow-and-white striped Butterscotch ran across the yard and through the alley. I hollered back at Ronnie that Butterscotch did get out and I was going after him.

I did the fastest walk I could manage on two bad knees in pursuit of Butterscotch. Each time I called him he would stop, turn and look at me as if to make sure I was following him. And just as I got close enough to nab him, he would take off running a few more yards ahead of me. By the time I got across the large parking lot, I was praying, "Dear God, I know you are so busy, but if you could just please stop Butterscotch I would really appreciate it! Besides, my knees are killing me!" As we both neared the end of the parking lot, I saw the fence separating me from the dark brush and busy roadway. This would mean the end of my pursuit.

"Butterscotch, please, just stop!" I hollered one more time. He turned around, looked me right in the eye, and then vanished over the fence. I was out of breath and knew that Ronnie would be devastated! He had raised Butterscotch from a kitten. I couldn't delay letting him know. I called Ronnie. "Ronnie," I breathed into my cell phone, "has Butterscotch ever run away like this before?" I was mustering up the courage to tell him his beloved Butterscotch was gone.

"You know, as soon as you left, I called one more time for Butterscotch and he came right up behind me. He never left the apartment," Ronnie replied. "I have been looking for my eye glasses so I could see to dial the phone to let you know."

"Oh, thank God!" I exhaled and took a huge sigh of relief. "Okay, I'll be back at your place in a couple of minutes." I stopped for a second to wipe my tearing eyes and offer a brief but sincere prayer of thanks to God for sparing Butterscotch.

One thing I have always tried to do when things like this happen is determine what God's purpose might be. You know, you run late for work in the morning because you can't find your keys only to discover that you missed being in an accident by a few cars. That's how I try to deal with the negatives in life. All I knew was that I was hurting all over from semi-running to catch a cat that wasn't even the right cat. And, I had a long walk ahead of me back to Ronnie's apartment.

Halfway back, a voice called out from the darkness. "Miss! Miss! Can you help me Miss! Miss! Please, help!" From the shadows, a figure of a huddled man appeared seemingly out of nowhere. As I got closer, he continued his plea. "Miss! Miss! Please help!" I made my way quickly over to the man and put my arm on his shoulder. He immediately turned his head away and vomited.

"Sir," I said, "what's the problem?"

He turned back to me, sweating and his breathing labored. "I think I'm having a heart attack. I got some bad chest pains, I can't stop throwing up. I can't get anyone to answer their door. I don't have a phone. Can you help me?"

I immediately called 911, gave our location, and relayed his symptoms, pulse and respirations to the operator. I stayed with the man until help arrived, trying to keep him alert, calm and breathing. The man, whose name I later learned was Gerard, was having a heart attack right in front of me! The ambulance arrived in a few minutes and rushed Gerard to the hospital. According to the first responder who thanked me for assisting, I probably helped save Gerard's life.

I have always firmly believed that things happen for a reason. I may not always know immediately what God's plan is, but if I pay attention and let Him take the lead, He will show me. So the next time you lose your keys when you are running late, pause for a second before letting the frustration consume you. It could be God's way of slowing you down or delaying you so you avoid an accident. Or, like me, what seems like an inconvenience actually puts you somewhere you are needed to make a difference in someone else's life. When you allow God to take the lead and trust that He has a plan, that's when true miracles can happen.

As I made my way back to Ronnie's apartment, the reality began to set in. I actually helped save a man's life! It was surreal. I paused for a moment at the screen door. Lo and behold, the "real" Butterscotch was there to greet me, his outstretched paws gently plucking at the weave of the screen in eager anticipation.

"Ronnie," I said, overwhelmed by the chain of events, and scooping up Butterscotch for a warm hug, "you are not going to believe what just happened."

— Michele Dellapenta —

16

Namesake

Miracles are not contrary to nature, but only
contrary to what we know about nature.
~Saint Augustine

Our dogs announced the doorbell before it rang. But I had a hot water bottle against my newly injured rotator cuff and, therefore, no interest in getting up.

When my husband, Harry, answered the door, I heard him say, "What's that?"

Our neighbour's voice was strained. "Our dog found him in a snow bank. I don't know if he's still alive." With curiosity now overpowering the pain, I went to investigate and found Lee Anne heavily gloved and holding a lifeless, three-month-old kitten. I took him from her, but quickly realized he bordered on being frozen. It was December 18th; it had been a very cold Canadian winter, and no one knew how long the kitten had been out in the snow.

"Thanks, Lee Anne, I'll take care of him," I said, not at all convincingly. I laid him across my hot water bottle and searched for signs of life. His eyes and nose were clear and his coat fine, but as my hands tried to coax him back to our world they found skin stretched across bone. The emaciation was almost total; there was so little muscle it was a mystery how he could have moved at all.

I checked for reflexes: my finger produced no gagging when extended down his throat. I tapped the inside corner of his eye: there was no blink. The kitten was much closer to dead than alive. He had no visible respiration but occasionally a ghastly rattle emanated from his throat so I knew he had one tiny toe still on Earth.

"Harry," I sighed to my long-suffering husband, who'd only tolerated animals until he fell in love with me, "if this kitten has any hope of survival, it's at the vet clinic with a warm IV installed."

He didn't miss a beat. "I'll start the truck."

On the way, I stretched the kitten over the hot water bottle, rotating him periodically in a desperate attempt to warm his little body. Always the realist, I wondered about the cost since he was a feral kitten who probably would never tame down anyway, even if he lived.

The clinic receptionist was one I didn't recognize. "I need a vet; now!" I insisted.

"They're all gone," she said, looking upset.

"What about a technician?" I pushed, knowing that without help, this kitten had very little time and certainly none to spare.

"They're gone, too," she admitted.

The next ten minutes seemed an eternity. Finally two of the technicians, Kate and Katy, returned.

"Come on, Diane," they said, motioning me into the back, "let's see what we can do."

An oxygen mask was quickly fitted over his little face. Then we discovered that he was so cold the thermometer wouldn't even register. He wasn't receiving enough oxygen because whatever respirations he had were too shallow. So the techs installed a tube and started bagging oxygen into his lungs.

Still, there was no change. We surrounded him with hot water bottles and took his temperature again. He remained the same.

"Can we get a warm IV going?" I asked.

The "Kates" looked at me. "Are you sure you want to?" they asked. I knew what they were thinking; the charges were really going to run up and he wasn't even my cat.

"Yeah," I grimaced. "It's Christmas. We have to do what we can."

Three consecutively smaller needles later, a vein was finally mined. The IV bag was heated and the frozen kitten started receiving the fluids.

And still, nothing changed.

Eventually, having done all they could, the Kates had to resume their work, leaving me with the comatose kitten. In spite of continually looking for signs of returning life, I found none. It certainly seemed hopeless.

Two hours after we'd arrived one of the vets returned to the clinic. Once she understood the situation she grabbed a stethoscope, and after listening carefully, she sadly shook her head.

"I'm afraid he doesn't have a chance," she concluded. "His heart isn't even beating; it's fluttering. And it's barely doing that."

I remained silent; *but it's Christmas*....

It had been two and a half hours with no improvement and it was now clear to me that human effort was not going to be enough to revive this kitten. Although I'd always had a spiritual focus and was interested in its many aspects, I'd never seriously contemplated the reality of angels. However, I'd just begun reading Doreen Virtue's teachings regarding angels and had been consciously living with them in a new way.

"Well," I thought, "here's a good test!"

I found my eyes searching the ceiling. "Raphael (the Archangel of healing)," I whispered. "I need your help, please. This kitten needs saving and while you're at it, this needs to be paid for because he's *not* my cat!" I then glanced around to make sure no one had heard me.

Within seconds, the little chest rose deeply and fell, rose and fell again.

"Hey, look at this!" I shrieked.

Kate, Katy and the vet quickly rushed over. The kitten was now chewing on the intubation tube so they quickly removed it. Weakly and with much shaking, the little guy lifted his head. Kate opened a can of food and popped it under his nose to stimulate him. As we watched in amazement, our tiny patient reached out and began to eat. In stunned silence, big smiles grew on every face.

"Thanks, Raphael," I whispered.

"I guess I can take him home, eh?"

I tucked him under my jacket and summoned my husband to retrieve us. Not even a little surprised, Harry simply grinned. He was used to my little miracles with animals.

I paid the bill; it was only $107 because the techs alone were involved. The clinic very generously charged me only for the supplies used.

The kitten was indeed wild and hissed often. So I kept him under my warm sweater for the rest of the day, taking him out occasionally to scratch his head and help him to understand I wasn't a threat.

"This little guy needs a name," I said to Harry.

He raised an eyebrow, wondering why I had not yet seen the obvious. "Raphael," he shrugged, not bothering to add, "of course!"

After having dragged this young life back from the other side, it was an obvious decision that Raphi join our family.

A few days later, Lee Anne came over and gave me $55 to help with the vet bill. And then I received a Christmas card from my older brother and his wife. Enclosed was a $50 check made out to "The Nicholson Rescue Team." $105 of the $107 had now been paid.

Raphi ate ravenously until he filled out into a beautiful, healthy tabby. Although definitely feral, he is playful and loving and seems to show only one major scar from his early life. All our cats are "inside-only," but they are allowed out on our deck. Raphi is happy enough to go out in the warm weather, but the moment the temperature dips in the later fall, he cannot be enticed outside. He'd much rather coil into a tight ball, safe and secure and close to the warm fireplace.

— Diane C. Nicholson —

Dr. Christmas

Miracles don't just happen, people make them happen.
~Misato Katsuragi

"Angie, you have to understand," my mother pleaded, tears in her eyes. She reached for my hand, which I promptly pulled away.

Oh, I understood all right. My very own mother was a murderer. I stared at her in disbelief as she tried to justify her reasons for killing my best friend. It was too much for my nine-year-old brain to comprehend.

"Angie, please don't look at me like that," she said softly, her voice breaking up, "Teeger was very sick. He had a bad bladder infection. The operation was too expensive and the veterinarian couldn't guarantee that it would work anyway. I had no choice but to have him put to sleep. It's better this way. He's not in pain anymore."

Teeger was a big, fat, roly-poly, orange cat who I loved like no other. And now he was gone. I wanted to close my eyes and make it all go away. This would be the worst Christmas ever.

"You didn't even let me say goodbye," I finally choked out.

Teeger had come into my life at a time when I really needed a friend. It was shortly after my dad had moved out for good. I was the only kid in my class whose parents weren't together, so there was no one I could talk to who would really understand what I was going through. I had a hard time making friends as it was, since I was painfully shy. Moving once a year didn't help. Being overweight also didn't help. My mother saw how much I was struggling, but she didn't know how to make it better. She did, however, know how to cheer me up. Enter Teeger.

Teeger and I had bonded instantly. He was a lot like me, actually. Shy... chubby... loved Cheezies. He had a playful side — but only when no one was looking. If you caught him chasing his tail, for example, he would stop and pretend that he was just cleaning himself or doing something equally sensible. What I loved most about Teeger, though, was how special he made me feel. He preferred me over everyone else he knew and he wasn't afraid to show it. He made me feel like the most important person in the world.

As the years went on, my bond with Teeger grew even stronger. When I was home, he followed me wherever I went. He sat beside me on the piano bench as I practiced for my upcoming lesson, occasionally putting a paw on the piano keys to remind me that he was there. He slept at my feet every night. He licked away my tears when I told him about the kids at school who made fun of me or about how much I missed my dad. He was my best friend.

One fateful morning, I woke to find that Teeger was not beside me and I immediately knew that something was wrong. I jumped out of bed and ran from room to room, frantically calling his name. I checked every nook and cranny in our little farmhouse, but Teeger was nowhere to be found. For two more days I searched like this, refusing to accept the possibility that he might actually be gone. On the third day of searching I was in the basement, looking for the hundredth time, when I heard a faint "meow" coming from up above. I looked up and suddenly saw those familiar green eyes and orange fur. Teeger was in the furnace duct!

I called for my mom, who ran down the stairs as fast as she could, and I pointed out the unlikely hiding spot where Teeger had been this whole time. We instantly got to work. It took a while, but I finally got him down. And then panic set in. He didn't look like the Teeger I knew. His fur was matted, his stomach bloated, and his eyes seemed quietly desperate.

"Angie," Mom said quietly, "I think Teeger is very sick. Sometimes cats go off into hiding when they know they are going to die."

I could not accept this. I had already decided long ago that Teeger was a miracle cat and he would live forever.

"He's not going to die," I said firmly. I held him close, comforting him as he had done for me so many times. "You're going to be okay, buddy," I told him over and over. "You'll get better, I just know it. You can't leave me yet."

Mom looked at me sadly and promised to take him to the vet right away.

Looking back, I understand why my mother didn't talk to me before making the decision to have Teeger put to sleep. How could she possibly have said no to a teary-eyed, inconsolable girl begging her to save her best friend? I likely would have told her to keep my allowance and to take back my Christmas presents so we could afford the operation. She might have taken a third job just to pay for it, even though she was exhausted working the two jobs she already had just to make ends meet. No, she really didn't have much of a choice at all. I understand that now.

In the weeks that followed, my mother did her best to try to cheer me up. She sang. She baked. She decorated the house for Christmas, going "all out" like she always did. But this time there was no cheering me up. I didn't want to get into the Christmas spirit. And besides, I wouldn't get what I wanted for Christmas anyway… my best friend back. No one could give me that. Or so I thought.

And then I got a phone call that I would never forget.

"Angie, the phone's for you," my mom said, handing it over to me with a puzzled expression on her face. "It's the veterinarian. He asked specifically for you."

"The veterinarian?" I echoed, equally puzzled. I had never even met him before. Why would he ask for me? Hesitantly, I picked up the phone.

"Hello?"

"Hello, Angie," a deep voice greeted me. "I… well… I wanted you to be the first to hear what I have to say. Your mom told me that Teeger was very special to you. So… in the spirit of Christmas… I gave Teeger the operation for free."

Could it really be true? Was Teeger alive this whole time? It was a miracle! A Christmas miracle!

"I'm sorry that I didn't call sooner," the veterinarian continued, "but I wanted to make sure that Teeger was completely better and stabilized before I called you to let you know. He's ready for you to pick him up now. I think he misses you."

It seemed an eternity before I was able to blurt out the words, "Thank you! Thank you so much!" Tears of joy streamed down my face and I had my shoes on before I could even explain to my mother what was going on.

When we got to the animal clinic, the veterinarian was waiting for us. I immediately ran over and hugged him, thanking him over and over again. He looked over at my mother and blushed, unsure of how to handle my display of emotion. He brought out Teeger, who immediately began purring so loudly you'd swear that a car with a bad muffler had just driven through the office. My heart felt like it was about to burst with happiness.

Thanks to that wonderful man, I got to spend twelve more years with Teeger by my side. And I got to learn at an early age that the true spirit of Christmas has nothing to do with spending money or getting gifts; it's about giving to others from the kindness of your heart with no expectation of getting anything in return. And I learned that sometimes... just sometimes... angels come disguised as veterinarians who make Christmas miracles happen and little girls' wishes come true.

— Angela Rolleman —

18

The Cat and the Christmas Star

*I would maintain that thanks are the highest form
of thought; and that gratitude is happiness
doubled by wonder.*
~G.K. Chesterton

Tears fell from my eyes onto the poster board below and mixed with the ink from the felt marker I was using to write "Missing: Gray tabby cat with white paws and green eyes."

Linda, my missing cat, had shared a close relationship with me ever since I had adopted him about two years before. Despite the fact that I had given him a female name (after an exam, our vet mistakenly told us he was female and we didn't find out the truth until much later), he didn't seem to mind. And even now, when we had taken him from his familiar South Carolina neighborhood and moved him to Virginia, he seemed to bear it well. Linda continued to faithfully greet me every day when I returned home from school. But my younger sister had recently adopted a kitten, and Linda hadn't taken this change well. The image of the hurt look he had given me after meeting the kitten was still etched vividly in my memory.

One night soon afterward, he didn't come home for his evening meal, and none of my repeated calls throughout the neighborhood brought him running. The cheerfulness of the Christmas decorations on the houses failed to excite me the way they usually did. I went to bed reluctantly, certain he would turn up first thing the next morning. But I was wrong. And after two days, I started to panic.

Frantically, I dialed the local animal shelter, but no cats fitting his description had come in. So, with my family's help, I'd made and distributed the posters and even found a local radio station willing to announce Linda's disappearance and plead for his return. Every day after school, I spent hours either on foot or bike scanning the neighborhood for him and calling his name until my voice was hoarse. Every night in bed I asked God to bring him home.

By the time Christmas Eve had arrived, Linda still had not. He had been missing for eight days. After spending the church service and our Christmas Eve dinner distracted by my sadness and anxiety, I glumly went to bed where I dutifully prayed once more that God would bring Linda home. Then exhausted, I fell into a deep sleep.

Several hours later, my clock radio blinked 11:59 P.M. I suddenly awoke. It was rare for me to wake in the middle of the night; I'd always been a sound sleeper. But as I lay in the darkness, I was fully awake and consumed with a desire to get up and look at the stars outside.

For several years, I'd had a personal Christmas Eve tradition of scanning the sky for the brightest star, which I liked to imagine was the "Christmas star." Whether it was actually the North Star that led the ancient wise men to baby Jesus in the manger, I didn't know. But I enjoyed viewing it anyway, and usually looked for it before I went to bed on Christmas Eve. As I lay there wondering why I was awake all of a sudden, I realized that I hadn't even bothered to look for it this year.

Eagerly, I leapt from my bed and peeked through the blinds on my bedroom window, but I couldn't discern any stars. Then a thought came to me with surprising strength. Try the front door. Now.

The thought of opening the door to the icy wind outside didn't excite me, but somehow, I felt, I had to find the Christmas star. So I unfastened both locks and swung the door open. Shivering in my nightgown, I scanned the sky until a silvery white dot came into view. The Christmas star! At that moment, I knew that no matter where Linda was, or if he ever returned, God still cared for me.

I stared at the star for a moment, then reached for the door to pull it shut, looking down to the front stoop as I did so. And then I saw him — Linda — thin, shivering and reeking of gasoline. He sat quietly before me. His green eyes searched mine, as if to say, "I'm sorry. Will you take me back?"

Immediately, I scooped him up. But before I closed the door, I stood with Linda in my arms to gaze once more at the Christmas star. Then I said a prayer of thanks to the God who watches over all his creation — from the most distant star to the purring cat I held closely.

— Whitney Von Lake Hople —

19

The Cat Who Needed a Night Light

Courage is not the absence of fear,
but rather the judgment that something
else is more important than fear.
~Ambrose Redmoon

On a warm August day, a dainty little cat named Dolores was receiving a special award: the American Humane Association's William O. Stillman award for bravery. The association gives the award to people who risk their lives to save animals from danger, and to animals who face down danger to save the lives of people. Either way, the winners are heroes, whether they're take-charge, fearless sorts of people, or extroverted, devoted pets like Dolores.

Dolores hadn't always been an extrovert. And she hadn't seemed very devoted to anyone, either. In fact, she'd been what most people call the quiet type. When she first came to live with her owner, Kyle, Dolores rarely had anything to say. And most of the time, she didn't like being touched.

Kyle didn't know why Dolores was so standoffish. And he didn't understand something else about her: why she always became upset whenever the lights were turned out. But Kyle didn't care. Something about the cat's quiet, unassuming manner appealed to him. So, at night, he just left all the lights on in the apartment where he and Dolores lived, even when it was time to go to sleep. And if Dolores wanted to keep her distance — well, he could respect that. Maybe, if he was patient, Dolores would someday decide to come to him, to talk to him, to be friends.

So for the next year, Kyle loved Dolores for exactly who she was. He let her keep her distance, and he didn't ask for more than she could give.

Then, one May evening, everything changed. The night started like any other. And, at evening's end, Kyle checked — as usual — to make sure all the lights in his apartment were on. Then, he went to sleep.

Sometime later he woke with a start. Something was jumping on his head! Paws were scratching his face! And, when he opened his eyes, his apartment was no longer brightly lit; instead it was filled with black smoke. But he could see who was doing the jumping and scratching: Dolores.

The little cat was all Kyle could see. But she was enough.

Together, the two made their way to the only available exit from the apartment — the back door. Kyle felt his way along the walls. At the same time, he felt for Dolores with his feet and followed her. Finally, the pair reached the back door. Kyle pulled on the knob to open the door, only to have the knob fall off into his hand. The door remained firmly shut.

Making his way to the door had taken every bit of strength and oxygen Kyle had, and he collapsed to the floor. But, once again, he felt those insistent paws scratching his face. Kyle mustered his last bit of strength to hurl himself against the door, break it down and run outside to fresh air and safety. Once there, he looked around for the cat who'd saved his life.

She wasn't there.

With sickening clarity, Kyle realized that Dolores was still inside the apartment. He ran to one of the firefighters.

"My cat's still inside my apartment!" he exclaimed. "Can you find her?"

The firefighter promised to try.

Now all Kyle could do was wait. He knew Dolores's chances weren't good, but still — maybe, just maybe, she would be found alive.

An hour or so later, the firefighters brought the blaze under control. And one firefighter brought Kyle a bundle wrapped in a towel. Kyle held his breath. Inside the bundle was Dolores — eyes seared shut, hair singed, but alive.

The firefighter explained that Dolores had collapsed just inside the door and that a fireman had stumbled on her when he entered the apartment. After removing her from the apartment, paramedics gave the cat CPR and oxygen before bringing her to Kyle.

The fire changed Kyle's life dramatically. He'd lost all his clothes, furniture and other possessions, and had to go live with his mother for a while. His cat had changed, too.

The once-quiet Dolores was now a talker who meowed and purred almost constantly. Even more surprising was her new desire to be touched and cuddled — preferably while she was lying on Kyle's lap.

Now, just four months later, Dolores was being recognized for her bravery. But Kyle knew he'd gotten a bigger prize. He'd never asked for more than Dolores could give — and then found she was willing to give him everything she had.

— Susan McCullough —

My Very Good, Very Bad Cat

20

The Ghost of Turkeys Past

Just because something is traditional
is no reason to do it, of course.
~*Lemony Snicket,* The Blank Book

For years, our family Christmas feast has consisted of a standing rib roast with all the trimmings, paired with an abundance of side dishes and desserts. But it wasn't always that way. Before the Christmas of 1970, we served a big roast turkey on both Thanksgiving and Christmas. Only the desserts changed — from pumpkin pie in November to mincemeat pie and Grandma's special butter rum cake in December.

The tradition changed that fateful Christmas in 1970 when the turkey was set out to brine. Grandma had always done this. Mom did this. So, I followed the tradition and did it. The sink was filled with cold, salted water and the bird was placed in it to soak.

The bird for that Christmas was a beauty — huge, almost thirty pounds. My father had paid a fortune to a local turkey farm to get us the biggest, best bird possible. It would be a true feast for all. The cookies, pies, cakes, and puddings had all been made. The candied yams were ready for the oven and the cranberry sauce was chilling in the refrigerator. All that was left was to brine the turkey a few hours, then pat it dry and refrigerate it while I made the stuffing to get it ready for an early morning oven. Due to its huge size, it needed to be rotated in the brine because it was too large to actually soak the whole bird at one time. The brine only came halfway up the body of the bird as it soaked, breast down in the sink.

I was just about to go in and turn the bird in the brine when a scream from the kitchen changed my plans entirely. My three girls came running out shrieking that the bird's ghost was there and the monster was going to get them! Their father and I ran into the kitchen to see that the "dead bird" soaking in the sink was hopping all over the place and splashing water everywhere.

My husband approached the bouncing bird with caution and made a grab for it. It slipped from his hands, as heavy as it was, and bounced onto the floor where it continued to do a jig across the tile.

The girls continued to scream while our two Collies started barking and jumping at the naked, dancing bird. I managed to push the dogs and now hysterical children back into the living room and held them at the doorway while their father continued to try to control the giant bird. Finally, it hit a corner between the sink and refrigerator and got wedged in. It continued to bounce up and down, breast side down, until finally something started poking through the back of the bird.

A smear of black appeared through a small hole near the spine of the fowl. Then a set of whiskers and a paw appeared. Our little cat Johnny had actually climbed into the open cavity of the bird and was happily chewing his way out. His little black and white head popped out through the hole in the back of the giant bird and he looked straight at us as he continued to gnaw off another chunk of raw turkey.

Of course, we could have removed the cat, washed the bird out (which was now stuffed with cat hair) and salvaged the dinner plans with none of the guests the wiser, but somehow, none of us wanted to eat turkey after that. I called my dad and told him what had happened. He made an emergency run to the local butcher and came over with two large standing rib roasts, enough to feed the crowd.

Thus began the new family tradition that my children now follow in their own homes with their own families. Johnny is long gone, but to this day, everyone who is still around to laugh about it remembers the day the turkey jumped out of the sink. And to this day, we still have turkey on Thanksgiving, but we always have roast beef on Christmas.

—Joyce Laird—

21

The Bubble Bath

There must be quite a few things a hot bath won't cure,
but I don't know many of them.
~Sylvia Plath

The tub in our new house beckoned to me. It wasn't just any tub, though. It was the likes of which I'd never owned before. Never even dreamed of owning. It was a marvelously decadent Jacuzzi tub big enough for two, with jets and all. And it existed in our new house for me to use whenever I wanted!

I couldn't believe our good fortune. We'd been able to purchase our dream home for less than market value, which included this grand tub.

Granted, there was a reason for the bargain price. The previous owners hadn't taken very good care of the home. It needed a lot of repairs.

But they were mostly cosmetic and superficial. A little new carpet, some paint, and we'd be able to enjoy our beautiful dream home.

What was a little elbow grease? When we'd made the offer on the home, I'd been in the process of prepping and painting our Jacksonville house for our move to Nashville. I was an experienced DIYer. I could handle shaping up the Nashville house too.

Or so I thought.

Our new house was only six years old, but the previous owners had been very hard on it. It turned out there was a lot more wrong with it than stained carpet and scuffed walls.

Sometimes we had water pressure in our shower, sometimes not.

The air conditioning worked sporadically. The dishwasher backed up on its first use and flooded our kitchen. One of the banisters had a disturbing jiggle, as if it was going to give way each time we grasped it. The roof leaked — a slow, gradual leak in our master bedroom that resulted first in a faint, almost imperceptible stain. We weren't even really sure we had a leak until a heavy rainstorm sent a deluge onto our carpet. The lawn sprinkler system exploded the first time we tried to use it and shot a geyser ten feet in the air until we could find the shut-off valve — an hour later.

Basically, everything we touched seemed to break, crumble, or collapse on us. We felt like Tom Hanks and Shelley Long's characters in the movie *The Money Pit*.

I'd wanted to take a bath from the very first day we moved in, but I had waited. It was going to be my treat after I completed all of my painting projects. (Which I thought would only take a week or two. I hadn't counted on the other repairs the house needed interfering with my painting schedule.)

Plus, with everything else that had gone wrong with the house, I feared my precious Jacuzzi tub wouldn't work either. I didn't dare touch it.

For weeks I only looked at it admiringly. Then one day the temptation proved too great. My arms and back ached from a hard day's work in the yard. I was sunburnt. I smelled. I was in desperate need of some solace.

Even if the jets didn't work, I could still soak in the tub — provided the floor held and I didn't go crashing into the living room.

Apprehensively, I turned on the water. I half expected the stopper not to work. But when the tub filled without leaking, I dared to press the on button. There was a pause, then came a rumbling grumble, a sputter, and those jets started spewing!

I let out a triumphant cry. After nothing but calamities, something was finally working right! And what a something it was. My big, beautiful, beloved tub! Calgon take me away!

I lit a candle, grabbed the bubble bath, and slid into the tub. I squeezed the bottle generously, not sure how much to use in such a large tub. Certainly more than a regular tub. I figured a third of a bottle ought to do it. Then I sat back, closed my eyes, and relished the massaging water jets.

For two minutes I knew heaven.

Then Mr. Meow, our ever-demanding feline, leaped onto the tub's ledge and meowed for attention. I promised him I would pet him as soon as I was done. But that wasn't good enough for him. He came closer, mewing louder. Something tickled my chin. I knew he was flicking me with his tail.

"Stop it," I admonished him, keeping my eyes closed. This was my time. He wasn't going to wreck it.

He tickled me again. With eyes still closed, I swiped at my face to try and catch him in the act. I knew his tricks. I might be able to resist his pathetic cries, but there was no defense against the powers of his tail. He'd use it to taunt me relentlessly until I paid him the attention he sought.

I simultaneously got whacked on the head and tickled on the chin. Either he was becoming incredibly talented or...

I opened my eyes and saw Mr. Meow's butt towards me, his tail swishing, but not to torment me. He was staring intently at the bubbles, engrossed in swatting them.

"Oh no!" I shouted, not at the cat, but because the bubbles had multiplied at an alarming rate. They were now threatening to spill over the tub and onto the floor!

Frantically, I searched through the field of foam for the off button to the jets. But before I found it, I saw that in his quest for a better bubble-batting spot, Mr. Meow had repositioned himself near the candle. His tail now swished mere millimeters from its flame. No sooner had I comprehended the possibility of his fur catching fire than it did.

I jumped up, grabbed him, and doused the flames with my hand. My rescue was rewarded with a hiss and a nice gash across my belly before Mr. Meow squirmed free and jumped to the floor. Which was now a sudsy swamp, thanks to the bubble waterfall cascading over the tub's edge. He left a nice trail into the bedroom as he ran away.

I leaned over the tub to hunt again for the off button. I managed not to tumble head first into the tub as I shut off the jets. Then I rinsed myself off in the shower, bandaged my wounds, and headed downstairs for the mop and bucket.

So much for a nice relaxing soak.

Well, at least my dream tub had worked, but I learned relaxation was not necessarily synonymous with bubble bath. Just like renovations, it also required effort.

That first attempt at a bath was a disaster. I have since mastered the art of relaxing in my beloved tub. It requires flameless candles, locking Mr. Meow out, and using bath salts instead of bubbles.

— Courtney Lynn Mroch —

22

The Telltale Meow

*One reason we admire cats is for their proficiency in
one-upmanship. They always seem to come out on top,
no matter what they are doing, or pretend they do.*
~Barbara Webster

Recently, while cat sitting for my neighbor's two felines, I had
quite the scare. As I doled out kibble, I heard a loud meow that
seemed to be coming from behind the stove.

Of course, I was startled. Heart racing, I opened the stove
and saw that it was empty. Quickly, I searched the small condominium
for the cats. I could only find one. Panic set in. Could Diesel have
crawled behind the appliances? Was he trapped or hurt?

I hurried across the hallway to retrieve my cell phone and dialed
Mary, the owner. Her voicemail kicked in and announced that her
mailbox was full. Shoot! What to do?

It occurred to me to call the fire department. Wouldn't they be
willing to help a lady who was looking out for the welfare of a beloved
pet? I called the non-emergency phone number and explained my
situation.

"Well, I suppose we could send a firefighter out to see if he can
help. We haven't any emergencies at the moment."

Diligently, I began to look in every nook and cranny for M.I.A.
Diesel. Having a cat, myself, I was aware that they could hide in the
oddest of places. "Diesel. Kitty, kitty. Come on, Diesel, I have a treat."
As I continued to hunt, I felt lightheaded and nauseous. "Dear Lord,

please let him be alright," I prayed.

"Meooow," I heard again. The sound was definitely coming from the kitchen wall. That poor cat had been stuck in there at least fifteen minutes since the last time I heard him. I ran to the spot and, with a closed fist, began to tap the wall. I heard nothing.

My investigation was interrupted by the knocking on the front door. "Come in!" I shouted.

Two extremely fit and handsome firemen entered. *Stay focused,* I chided myself.

Introducing themselves, I realized I was clad in pajamas and slippers that weren't a pair. *Stay focused!*

I explained the situation quickly as my panic returned. "He must be stuck!" I cried.

"Meooow!"

"Goodness, it sounds like he's in the wall!" exclaimed blond Rob. *Stay focused! This is a serious situation!*

"I suppose we can open the wall," Rob continued. "This is your condo?"

"No, I'm cat sitting. I live across the hall."

"We'll need to contact the owner before we do any damage."

"She isn't answering her phone, and her voicemail is full."

"Hmm. Does he know his name? I'm a dog person. I must admit I know little about cats."

"Yes, but cats rarely come when called."

Gorgeous Tim piped in, "Maybe we can shake his food bowl. Perhaps he'll try to come for food."

The three of us stood facing the oven as kibble sounds emanated from the bowl. We heard nothing. "Dear Lord," I prayed again aloud. "Please let him be alive!"

The sweet Lord answered with, "Meooow!" but this time it was coming from behind us.

Rob turned and asked, "How many cats does she have?"

I turned, too. Sitting not three feet behind us were Diesel and Mitsi. "What? She has two, these two," I sighed as I pointed. "Who is trapped in the wall?"

We looked at one another. Tim shrugged his shoulders, and Rob said, "Hmm. This is the damnedest thing. Are you sure she only has two?"

"Positive." I turned again. Was the furry pair smirking? Honestly, I am quite sure they were.

Silence.

"Meooow!"

Rob began to laugh as he reached for the clock mounted above the stove. Twelve cats on a round disc were positioned as the décor on this timepiece.

Rob turned the minute hand slowly until it reached the feline at quarter past.

"Meooow!"

— Kathleen Gemmell —

23

Cat Warning System

Tree decorating with cats. O Christmas tree,
O Christmas tree, your ornaments are history!
~Courtney VanSickle

Quimby was picked up as an emaciated stray and eventually made his way into the shelter where we found him one hot July afternoon. By Christmas, he had fully assimilated into domestic life. As the sole pet in our home, the recipient of all snuggles, cuddles, and chin-scratches, I'm sure he thought life couldn't get any better.

Then the Christmas tree came.

Per our usual tradition, I popped in our DVD of *Christmas Vacation* to get in the spirit. And as Clark Griswold wrestled in the wilderness to get the family tree, I hauled our own heavy boxed tree up from the basement.

As soon as the basement door opened, Quimby rocketed off the couch to investigate. The basement was strictly off limits to him, and on the rare occasion he managed to sneak in, he was immediately shooed back upstairs.

But this time, he dug in and refused to go away. I tried simply closing the basement door as I worked downstairs, but the curiosity was just too much for him to bear. He pressed his face against the bottom of the door and began yowling pitifully to me in the basement.

Well, I'm a big softie, so I thought that maybe if he watched what I was doing, he would calm down a bit.

That turned out to be an incorrect assumption.

I pulled box after box of Christmas décor out from our storage closet under the stairs. Tail flicking, Quimby's excitement grew with each one.

He started by pawing the newspaper wrapping off the big wreath we used for the front door. Delighted to find a wiry evergreen shrub underneath, he latched onto one of the shiny, plastic presents glued onto the wreath and proceeded to start dragging the wreath back upstairs.

"Drop it!" I snapped at him from the bottom step. His bright green eyes dilated as if he'd just taken a whiff of catnip. "Drop. It." I repeated. And he did — right after he yanked the sparkly present off the wreath, and shot off to go play with his prize.

Okay, I thought, *one plastic present isn't so bad in the grand scheme of things.*

The respite lasted long enough for me to haul the rest of the boxes upstairs before Quimby came back for more.

I managed to get all three sections of the Christmas tree up and centered in the tree stand. I was able to fan out and rearrange the branches. I had just started stringing the lights when Quimby skidded under the tree, using the satin tree skirt as a slide. I would soon learn our hardwood floors were the perfect sledding venue. Quimby would get a running start, leap onto the tree skirt, and skid as far as the skirt would take him.

We had brought the outdoors to him in the form of a wonderfully colorful tree with lots of shiny baubles, and he couldn't get enough of it.

Then he started taking ornaments off the tree. My husband and I would turn our heads or step away just long enough to come back and see the tree shaking, immediately followed by the unmistakable cadence of four little feet running down the hallway.

Following him, we'd invariably find him huddled in the middle of a guest bed. He would be curled up as tightly as possible, eyes huge, and his little nose tucked into his paws as he watched us enter the room. One of us would hold his shoulders while the other gently moved his paws away from his belly to discover what he'd taken. He loved snatching one ornament in particular: a silver pinecone covered with glitter. Quimby would steal it every time we put it back on the tree.

We had made peace with the fact that Quimby loved to slide under the tree, and aside from that one silver pinecone, he didn't seem to be taking any other ornaments. But then, he started chewing on the tree. He would get a mouthful of fake pine and chomp away. Short of taking down the tree, we had to figure out a way to keep this cat out!

Quimby didn't realize it, but he was about to help us create a new Christmas tradition.

We knew he would scale or squeeze through any gate we put up around the tree, so we had to come up with a more creative solution.

My husband laughed and said, "I think I've figured out something that might work." A half-hour later, he returned from the local drugstore and held up a large pack of silver bells. He opened them and threaded them along the bottom branches of the tree.

"Watch this," he whispered.

Nonchalantly, we walked away from the tree, pretending to ignore Quimby. Then, we watched him from the corner of our eyes as he quietly inched closer to the tree, before latching onto a low-hanging branch for an evening chew.

Then a handful of bells chimed.

Quimby froze. He tried again — only to be met by a mass tinkling of bells.

"Get out of that tree!" we both said in unison to him. It worked. He shot off.

He tried several times over the night to go back to the tree, but each time the bells rang, we scolded him to get out of the tree. Each time, he would take off like a rocket down the hallway. Thirty minutes would pass, and he'd try again — only to be foiled by ringing bells.

We've celebrated three Christmases with him since then, and each year it's become a tradition to add more bells in various sizes. The entire bottom third of our tree is now nothing but a twinkling mass of silver bells.

Every year, as we sift through all the newspaper-wrapped ornaments and prepare them for hanging, we giggle when we come upon one of the sets of bells. And as each one is unwrapped, Quimby flops under the tree and huffs loudly in defeat, watching us thread the bells through the bottom branches.

True to tradition, Quimby still regularly tests the cat warning system and freezes immediately once the bells ring.

And every holiday season, we still grin when we hear a bell ring. It might be true that somewhere an angel just got her wings, but in our house every time a bell rings, the cat is back in the tree.

—Kristi Adams—

24

Solved

After scolding one's cat, one looks into its face and is
seized by the ugly suspicion that it understood every
word. And has filed it for reference.
~Charlotte Gray

"Where on earth have they gone to?" my mother asked as she eyed the half-empty Christmas tree.

"I haven't the foggiest," I said, "but there's definitely less than yesterday."

And the day before that… and the day before that…

Decorations had been disappearing for a while. Most of the lower branches were now bare. No matter where we looked in the house, though, we couldn't find a trace of them.

It was as if they had vanished into thin air.

As we pulled on our coats, we pondered the mystery. It was the day before Christmas Eve. We had some last-minute groceries to collect, so we were about to head out to the local store.

"Who do you think the culprit is?" my mother asked, heading outside. "Faye or Cassy?"

Both of our little felines had shown a keen interest in the tree, it was true. They did every year. Twinkly lights and the fabric "cat-safe" decorations fascinated them. But while Faye was a gentle observer, content to look and not touch, Cassy had to be monitored. Her paws constantly twitched toward the branches like a mischievous toddler's. So, naturally, she was the prime suspect. But after being told once to leave the tree alone, she hadn't reoffended.

Nevertheless, we had checked the cat beds and their other usual hideouts to be sure. Alas, no decorations.

The entire situation was a mystery.

I shrugged. "Maybe it's neither of them. Maybe it's Dad playing a prank."

Even to myself, I sounded doubtful. It just wasn't his style. But aside from the cats, there was no one else in the house.

"Or perhaps we have a ghost." My mother smiled. "Maybe two or three — the ghosts of Christmas Past, Present, and Yet to Come. And they'll show themselves tomorrow night to tell us the true meaning of Christmas, as well as to return our missing decorations."

"Bah, humbug!" I said, doing my best Scrooge impersonation.

As my mother was climbing into the car and I was locking the front door, I happened, by chance, to turn and look through the bay window in which our Christmas tree stood.

And there, right in front of me, was Cassy.

Mouthing a decoration.

"You little scamp," I muttered.

As I watched, our little tortoiseshell ever-so-stealthily lifted the decoration from the branch, cradling it in her teeth, and then turned and carefully slotted it down the narrow gap between the radiator and the wall, just below the windowsill. Then she let it go.

Moving to the window, I tapped my nails faintly on the glass. Quiet as the noise was, Cassy snapped to attention, her face the perfect picture of: *Oh, busted!*

"What are you doing, Little Miss?"

She sat perfectly still for one frozen second… and then bolted.

"Mum!" I called out. "I think I've solved the case."

Sure enough, when we went back inside, there they were: the missing decorations. All nine were lying in a heap down the back of the radiator. We couldn't help but laugh.

— Nemma Wollenfang —

Does That Come with Sides?

A cat will do what it wants when it wants,
and there's not a thing you can do about it.
~Frank Perkins

grew up in a family of five children, all perfectly spaced three years apart. On top of that, my father was a veterinarian, so we always had at least a dog and a cat, if not also a gerbil, hamster or rabbit.

My mom did her very best to keep the house and us kids under control, which was especially difficult around the holidays. But she was an expert hostess, and she always planned and executed holiday meals perfectly.

One particular Thanksgiving, Mom had set the table a week in advance, putting a king-sized sheet over it so that dust and pet hair wouldn't settle onto the beautiful china and crystal. She made a list of all the dishes she would be preparing, changing it until she was satisfied with the spread. She was also an excellent time manager and had baked the pumpkin and apple pies several weeks in advance and frozen them.

Her Thanksgiving routine had been meticulously crafted over the years, and she stuck with the same agenda every year. It began, of course, with the turkey. It was usually at least twenty pounds, and she would dress it and truss it the night before, and then get up early in the morning to put it into the oven for slow roasting. Then, she would take a break to have a cup of tea, eat breakfast, and scan the newspaper.

Afterward, she would finish prepping the side dishes and rolls.

As she whizzed around the kitchen, my siblings and I were prohibited from staying there longer than the time it took to eat a bowl of cereal and take on our chores for the day. My dad made the floral arrangements fresh from his garden, taking up most of the kitchen table. He had prize-winning mums for a burst of autumn color on the table and hutch.

By mid-afternoon, everything was prepared, and the aroma of roasting turkey with butter, rosemary and garlic filled the air. Only then could my mother retreat to her bedroom to get ready for our company. Just before our guests were due to arrive, she pulled the turkey out of the oven to baste one last time, tented it with aluminum foil, and placed it on the kitchen counter to cool. She said this would make it juicier before my dad began carving. This also gave her time to increase the heat of the oven for the side dishes and gave her a break from the kitchen to return to her guests.

My final job before dinner was filling up the crystal goblets with ice water. When it was time, I left the living room and headed back down to the kitchen. And, oh, what a sight awaited me. Our cat, Funny Girl, had managed to climb up on the counter where the turkey had once been resting, and I saw nothing but her tail sticking out from the tented aluminum foil! On the floor below her, our German Shepherd, Samantha, was licking up the bits of turkey that had dropped on the floor. I ran and lifted the foil to discover that more than half of the turkey had been eaten. Funny Girl stared directly at me, cool and aloof, before jumping down off the counter and sauntering away.

"MOOOMMM!" I yelled again and again.

"Adrienne, why are you yelling?" she asked, rounding the corner.

However, before I could even say, "Funny Girl ate your turkey," I could tell by the horrified look on her face that she already knew. Then, she did something I had rarely seen her do. She broke down and cried. "My dinner is ruined," she said as tears streaked down her cheeks. "I can't believe that darn cat." I tried my best to console her by wrapping her in a hug. We clung together for a moment as I tried to blot her tears with a napkin. I asked if we could still serve the remaining half of the turkey, but when we saw the cat hair where she had sat atop the carcass, we knew that it was inedible.

"Mom, at least we have the side dishes," I offered. They were all still browning in the oven. That's when she burst out laughing. The tears were gone. She knew that there was nothing left to do except move on and deal with the problem. She removed the sides from the oven and the salad from the refrigerator.

"Adrienne, go get your father — quietly!"

My dad came into the kitchen and surveyed the damage. "Well," he said, "at least we have the sides." Gratefully, my mother broke out into another big laugh as she plated what was left of our meal. Dad threw the turkey into the trash outside and went to offer more drinks and wine to our guests. "It won't hurt to get everyone a bit more relaxed before we tell them that there's no turkey this Thanksgiving!"

Finally, I felt like I could laugh, too, as I helped my mother finish getting dinner on the table.

That was truly the most memorable Thanksgiving, especially for Funny Girl, who spent the rest of the evening locked in my parents' bedroom, vomiting up her feast… all over my mother's side of the bed!

— Adrienne Matthews —

26

The Cat in the Bag

Mirth is God's medicine.
Everybody ought to bathe in it.
~Henry Ward Beecher

Aunt Faye and her cat Sophie were inseparable. In fact, though Aunt Faye never had any children, Sophie was like a child to her.

I have to admit that the cat was amazing. Sophie always knew when Aunt Faye wasn't feeling well. In fact, Sophie even knew when Aunt Faye's feet were cold at night. Because that cat would snuggle up at her feet in bed, Aunt Faye used to call Sophie her "bed warmer." My aunt was sort of hard of hearing, so when anyone came to the door of her apartment, Sophie ran to the door to alert her.

Good old Sophie the cat was getting on in years. My aunt would call me from time to time to ask me to drive Sophie and her to the veterinarian. In fact, I think she took better care of Sophie than herself. If Aunt Faye didn't feel well, she wouldn't go to the doctor; she would just take an aspirin. But should Sophie sneeze or cough with a hairball in her throat, we were on our way to the vet almost immediately.

So it came as a bit of a shock when Aunt Faye called me crying hysterically. "Sophie is dead! My little Sophie is dead!"

Between sobs, Aunt Faye explained. "You know I don't sleep so good at night. So the doctor gave me some sleeping pills. I didn't like the way they smelled so he told me to put a drop of vanilla extract into the bottle to make the pills taste like candy. So this morning when I was cooking in the kitchen, Sophie got into my bedroom and accidentally knocked over my bottle of sleeping pills. They must have smelled good to her because she ate almost every last one of them. The empty bottle was on the floor next to her."

Aunt Faye was still crying uncontrollably. "You know how long my Sophie and I have been together?" Not even waiting for my answer she said, "We've been together for twelve years. Yesterday, I even bought her a new cat food. They said this cat food was softer for older cats... her teeth have started to fall out like mine. Do you know how much Sophie meant to me?"

I sympathized with her.

"Now what can I do?" she sobbed.

"Look Aunt Faye, there isn't much you can do. Put Sophie's body in a paper bag, and place it in the garbage can in the basement. The sanitation department will take her away."

"What?" she screamed. "My Sophie in a garbage can? She was like my child. Since your uncle passed away, she's been my closest friend for all these years. I can't just put her in the garbage!"

"Okay," I said. "I'm working very late tonight so I won't be able to get over to your house. However, if you'll feel better about it, take a taxi to your veterinarian and ask him to have Sophie taken to the animal cemetery. I'll provide the money for the plot and the burial."

The tears continued. "Will I be able to visit her from time to time?"

"Sure. I'll take you to the pet cemetery any time you want to go."

"How can I take Sophie to the vet? Her carrying case fell apart a few years ago."

"Put her in your old suitcase. It's not too big and Sophie will fit perfectly."

"Will there be a funeral?"

"No, dear. The vet calls the people from the pet cemetery. They'll put Sophie in a little casket and take her to the cemetery."

"Okay," she muttered with a broken heart. "It will be dignified?" she asked.

"Yes, it will," I said.

That was it. I felt bad for her, but there was nothing more I could do.

About six o'clock that evening, Aunt Faye called me at my office. "Arnold, I have something to tell you." Strangely, I sensed excitement in her voice.

"What now?" I asked. "Did you go to the vet?"

"I did just like you said. I put Sophie in my suitcase. I was standing by the bus stop waiting for a cab, so I figured, why spend money for a taxi when I could certainly take the bus? So I put the suitcase down next to me and started to look into my purse to see if I had the exact change. While I was looking in my pocketbook, some teenage boys came up behind me. One threw me to the ground and grabbed my suitcase with Sophie inside!"

"Oh no, Aunt Faye! Did you get hurt?"

"Just a few scratches. Nothing serious. I yelled for the police, but nobody came. So what could I do? I figured this was the way my relationship with Sophie was supposed to end. So I went home."

"I don't believe this!" I said, trying to hold back my laughter. "Can you imagine the expression on those kids' faces when they opened the suitcase and found a dead cat?"

She started to laugh. Aunt Faye was actually laughing!

"Wait, wait — that's only part of the story. Sophie came home! She really wasn't dead! I only thought she was dead because she was lying so still when I found her in the bathroom this morning. Being jostled back and forth in that suitcase must have finally roused her. When I got back to the house, she was waiting at my door!

"Arnold, thank you for all your help. I prayed for Sophie to enter heaven, and she came back to me."

The next time I went to visit Aunt Faye, she had a little sign on her front door that read, "This is heaven."

— Arnold Fine —

27

A Mother's Love

God could not be everywhere, so he created mothers.
~Jewish Proverb

I am a New York City fireman. Being a firefighter has its grim side. When someone's business or home is destroyed, it can break your heart. You see a lot of terror and sometimes even death. But the day I found Scarlett was different. That was a day about life. And love.

It was a Friday. We'd responded to an early morning alarm in Brooklyn at a burning garage. As I was getting my gear on, I heard the sound of cats crying. I couldn't stop — I would have to look for the cats after the fire was put out.

This was a large fire, so there were other hook and ladder companies there as well. We had been told that everyone in the building had made it out safely. I sure hoped so — the entire garage was filled with flames, and it would have been futile for anyone to attempt a rescue anyway. It took a long time and many firefighters to finally bring the enormous blaze under control.

At that point I was free to investigate the cat noises, which I still heard. There continued to be a tremendous amount of smoke and intense heat coming from the building. I couldn't see much, but I followed the meowing to a spot on the sidewalk about five feet away from the front of the garage. There, crying and huddled together, were three terrified little kittens. Then I found two more, one in the street and one across the street. They must have been in the building, as their fur was badly singed. I yelled for a box and out of the crowd around me, one appeared. Putting the five kittens in the box, I carried them to the porch of a neighboring house.

I started looking for a mother cat. It was obvious that the mother had gone into the burning garage and carried each of her babies, one by one, out to the sidewalk. Five separate trips into that raging heat and deadly smoke — it was hard to imagine. Then she had attempted to get them across the street, away from the building. Again, one at a time. But she hadn't been able to finish the job. What had happened to her?

A cop told me he had seen a cat go into a vacant lot near where I'd found the last two kittens. She was there, lying down and crying. She was horribly burnt: her eyes were blistered shut, her paws were blackened, and her fur was singed all over her body. In some places you could see her reddened skin showing through the burned fur. She was too weak to move anymore. I went over to her slowly, talking gently as I approached. I figured that she was a wild cat and I didn't want to alarm her. When I picked her up, she cried out in pain, but she didn't struggle. The poor animal reeked of burnt fur and flesh. She gave me a look of utter exhaustion and then relaxed in my arms as much as her pain would allow. Sensing her trust in me, I felt my throat tighten and the tears start in my eyes. I was determined to save this brave little cat and her family. Their lives were, literally, in my hands.

I put the cat in the box with the mewing kittens. Even in her pathetic condition, the blinded mother circled in the box and touched each kitten with her nose, one by one, to make sure they were all there and all safe. She was content, in spite of her pain, now that she was sure the kittens were all accounted for.

These cats obviously needed immediate medical care. I thought of a very special animal shelter out on Long Island, the North Shore Animal League, where I had taken a severely burned dog I had rescued eleven years earlier. If anyone could help them, they could.

I called to alert the Animal League that I was on my way with a badly burned cat and her kittens. Still in my smoke-stained fire gear, I drove my truck there as fast as I could. When I pulled into the driveway, I saw two teams of vets and technicians standing in the parking lot waiting for me. They whisked the cats into a treatment room — the mother on a table with one vet team and all the kittens on another table with the second team.

Utterly exhausted from fighting the fire, I stood in the treatment room, keeping out of the way. I didn't have much hope that these cats would survive. But somehow, I just couldn't leave them. After a long wait, the vets told me they would observe the kittens and their mother overnight, but they weren't very optimistic about the mother's chances of survival.

I returned the next day and waited and waited. I was about to completely give up hope when the vets finally came over to me. They told me the good news — the kittens would survive.

"And the mother?" I asked. I was afraid to hear the reply.

It was still too early to know.

I came back every day, but each day it was the same thing: they just didn't know. About a week after the fire, I arrived at the shelter in a bleak mood, thinking, Surely if the mother cat was going to make it, she'd have come around by now. How much longer could she hover between life and death? But when I walked in the door, the vets greeted me with big smiles and gave me the thumbs up sign! Not only was she going to be all right — in time she'd even be able to see again.

Now that she was going to live, she needed a name. One of the technicians came up with the name Scarlett, because of her reddened skin.

Knowing what Scarlett had endured for her kittens, it melted my heart to see her reunited with them. And what did mama cat do first? Another head count! She touched each of her kittens again, nose to nose, to be sure they were all still safe and sound. She had risked her life, not once, but five times — and it had paid off. All of her babies had survived.

As a firefighter, I see heroism every day. But what Scarlett showed me that day was the height of heroism — the kind of bravery that comes only from a mother's love.

— David Giannelli —

28

Moving Together

You enter into a certain amount of madness
when you marry a person with cats.
~Nora Ephron

was on a hillside whipped by wind, soaked in dew, beyond disgusted, all because of that wretched cat. I'd only opened the door for a moment. I'd been groggy with motel sleep, eight hundred miles from our last night's bed, so I wasn't thinking clearly.

I had been in the rented box of a room, and I needed something real to look at for a few moments. But when I opened the door there was nothing but sky and highway — gray on gray with scrub bush in-between.

I closed the door just as Lisa was coming turbaned out of the bathroom.

This was the big trip, her return to Winnipeg from Montreal where she had what she repeatedly called "the best year of my life."

My mail and phone campaign had coaxed her to return. Now, packing hopes, memories and her smoky tortoiseshell cat into my station wagon, we were heading back west together. She had been reluctant to leave, dawdling for sips of café au lait, strolling down the boulevard of St. Denis to sigh au revoir and kiss her friends on both cheeks as they eyed me with deepest suspicion.

It was a little later that we discovered the cat was missing from the motel room. "I only opened the door for thirty seconds," I pleaded.

"That's all it takes," she snapped.

That's all it took to feel like a complete failure. Eternal vigilance, the price of loving a woman with a cat.

Moreover, it was no ordinary cat. Not when it had been raised by Lisa, the social worker. Its every response had been scrutinized. A nap in the pantry was a sulk, a scratch on the hand was a plea for attention, a walk out the window onto the second-story ledge was a suicide attempt and cause for Lisa to cancel our date.

"I should have seen it coming," she'd said. "Chloe's been alone too much."

And how would Lisa analyze this blunder during our very act of moving together? A cat's jealous rejection? A dark flaw in my character? This could affect our future together. I had to find that cat.

We called out in cat sounds along the bushes. I prodded the underbrush. It opened into a jungly ravine. Where would I go if I were a cat?

"She's gone!" Lisa cried into the wind. "I just know she's gone! I loved her so much!"

If only I had a reputation for being reliable — for locking doors and mailing letters, finding my car in a parking lot — but I didn't.

Ashamed, I stared into bush and vines thinking how Chloe was really just a vulnerable creature, frightened of the car, anxious in the cage. She just wanted some peace. I could empathize. A quiet rabbit hole, soft leaves. She could sleep for days. And so could I.

But we were late. We had to meet the movers. We had family waiting and friends taking time off work to help. We had jobs.

I crashed into the ravine. Never mind the branches and nettles. Scratches were good. Blood could draw sympathy.

Could that cat really want to linger in this wilderness? She was a consumer cat, supermarket-wise in the ways of Kat Chow and Miss Mew. What did she know about hunting mice and sparrows?

Then I stumbled through the tangles and discovered another world. It was a housing development — streets with names like Buttercup Bay and Peony Drive and children on skateboards staring at my muddied clothes.

"Hi, kids." They looked suspicious. "I lost my cat." They stayed frozen. "I'll give you fifty bucks to find her."

Sudden acceptance. "Wow! Was it black?"

"She's smoky tortoiseshell grey. She has a hot-pink collar with toy sunglasses attached."

"I saw her!" hollered one of them. "She was right here. I knew I should have grabbed her!" The boy was furious with himself. Never again would he let a cat get away. He'd pack his garage with them for years to come. The kids scrambled into full alert.

I found Lisa and told her Chloe was spotted up the hill from the motel. She suddenly came to life. "That tramp!" she said. "What's she doing way up there?" Where there is anger, there is hope. Where there is hope, there is action. We put up reward posters, knocked on doors, phoned the local vet and police. As the day wore on, we left a reward if she was found later, hired someone to drive her to the airport, arranged plane fare and a flight cage.

We finally ate. The fast-food franchise overlooked the development. We watched children on skateboards and bikes cruising the lanes below. Some were checking shrubs, trampling a flowerbed. It was comforting.

We were both pretty quiet. Lisa finally spoke, "She was a good cat."

"Lisa, it's not over."

"She can live here okay. As long as she finds someone to care about her."

"I wish we could find her," I said. "I'd give more than money."

Lisa lowered her eyes. "I've been bargaining in my head. 'Give me back Chloe and I'll be better to my mother. I'll do volunteer work.'" And then she added, looking straight at me, "And I'll stop blaming you."

My secret thought welled up. "I've been making all this into a test. Lose the cat, lose Lisa. Find the cat, keep Lisa. I'm almost ready to give up everything — the move, the house, whatever. I guess I can't handle tests."

Lisa cupped her hand as if she were speaking to me through a microphone. "This is not a test. I repeat. This is not a test." We smiled to each other. "I'm not coming back for you," she said. "I'm coming back for us."

Dusk was settling in. The hills were gray — smoky, tortoiseshell gray. Chloe was nowhere, but it felt as if she were everywhere.

We were already packed so it didn't take long to clear the motel room. I only had to call the radio stations and leave an announcement about Chloe. Lisa took out the last bag.

That was when Chloe appeared. She simply walked out from under the bed, blinking in the light. She had been asleep inside the box spring all that time. It seems there was an opening we couldn't see. Lisa shrieked. The cat fled back into the mattress but we pulled her out. Then we left in a run.

As we pulled out of the motel driveway, we saw a pack of kids heading up the hill towards us. They probably had cats with them. At least two or three. We didn't stop to check. We already had everything we needed.

— Sheldon Oberman —

29

The Education of Jeeves

I had been told that the training procedure with cats
was difficult. It's not. Mine had me trained in two days.
~Bill Dana

t's inevitable whenever cat lovers get together that the topic of litter boxes comes up — the merits and drawbacks of various brands
of kitty litter, the best locations for the boxes, the problems certain cats have using the litter box and of course the debate over
whether those new electronic self-cleaning models are really worth
the price. It is an awkward moment for me, for I have nothing to
say to my fellow feline fanciers on this subject, except to mention as
humbly as I can, that my cat, Jeeves, is toilet-trained.

This announcement always causes a stir. Some people laugh, while
others scoff. After insisting that it's true, I explain that Jeeves uses — and
flushes — the toilet like any other civilized apartment dweller. I ignore
the head-shaking and envious mutterings, for it is a privilege and a
joy to live with this refined gentleman of a cat.

I must admit, though, there were times while Jeeves was being
taught this marvelous feat, when my husband Tim and I realized that
training a cat is not as simple as it seems.

One of those moments came in the final stages of Jeeves's mastery
of the toilet. It had been a long, involved process. We'd started by
setting the litterbox on top of the toilet, and then in various stages,
we'd graduated to putting a spare toilet seat over the litterbox. It was
a simple matter to eventually remove the litterbox completely — the

cat recognized the toilet seat and voila!

Now we were attempting to introduce the ultimate nicety: learning to flush. We tied a string with a small empty film canister on the end of it to the toilet handle. The small canister was punctured all over and inside it we placed kitty treats. When the cat pulled on it, thereby flushing the toilet, he received a treat. This was straightforward enough, and Jeeves was really getting the hang of it.

It was a Sunday morning. Tim and I were sleeping late, a luxury for us on our constantly busy schedule, when we were awakened by a noise. As we slowly surfaced from sleep and our brains began to register what we were hearing, we realized it was the sound of the toilet flushing—and flushing—and flushing. Over and over again, the toilet gurgled and whooshed. Tim staggered sleepily from bed and made his way to the bathroom to investigate what we assumed was faulty plumbing.

Instead, when he opened the door, he saw an imperious Jeeves, paws wrapped around the film canister, pulling the string again, looking for all the world like a monarch using the royal bell pull to summon a servant to his bedside.

"Ah, there you are, my good man," he seemed to say. "Now, where's that treat of mine?"

My husband dutifully fetched a treat and the porcelain Niagara Falls was finally silenced.

Back in the bedroom, Tim recounted to me what had just happened. Up till this point, we had been feeling pleased with how successfully we were training our cat. It was then we sensed the hollowness of our victory.

The cat was doing what we wanted him to do, yet it was clear that somewhere along the way, we'd lost the upper hand. I began to wonder if we'd ever really had it.

To this day, it remains a mystery just who has been conditioned to do what, but one thing is certain: Cat training can be a very tricky business.

— Debbie Freeberg-Renwick —

30

The Thanksgiving of The Incident

The moment may be temporary,
but the memory is forever.
~Bud Meyer

Our son Hyrum, his wife Cara, two small children, and one huge dog, Diesel, spent four days with us over Thanksgiving. Though my husband and I greeted them eagerly, our cat, Harley, was not as welcoming. She gave Diesel a disdainful sniff and stalked off.

"Harley's accustomed to being an only child," I joked.

Everyone laughed.

We continued to laugh at our pets' standoffish attitude toward each other until it happened: The Incident.

At sixteen years old, Harley had diabetes, which caused her to have "bathroom accidents" in various places throughout the house. One such accident left a steaming pile on the living room rug. Usually quick to spot such messes, I missed this one, too involved in playing with my grandchildren to notice.

When Diesel wandered into the family room, reeking of a foul odor, I jumped up, ran into the living room, and saw what I had feared: He had rolled in the pile of poop and spread it all over the rug, furniture, and everything else.

My cry of dismay alerted other family members. My daughter-in-law tried to catch Diesel, but he took the excitement as a signal to run through the house, slinging feces with every step. The grandchildren joined in the ruckus.

We were a household in chaos.

"Diesel, come here," Cara commanded.

Diesel skidded to a stop. The sudden movement caused more bits and pieces of excrement to fly from his quivering-with-joy body.

As for me, I was on my hands and knees cleaning up what would send most hardened crime-scene professionals into shock.

Cara took Diesel to the downstairs shower to shampoo his feces-matted fur.

Several hours and loads of laundry later, the family, including a chastened Diesel and an unrepentant Harley, gathered in the family room.

"We'll look back and laugh at this at some point," my husband said.

I wasn't so sure, but I knew that The Incident would be forever seared in our memories.

—Jane McBride—

Who Rescued Whom?

Nurse Buddha

When watching after yourself, you watch after others.
When watching after others, you watch after yourself.
~Buddha

n my dreams, a turquoise Buddha circled my bed, round and round, week after week. It wasn't a particularly pleasant dream nor was it a nightmare. It was more of an informative one, urging me to understand something I knew nothing about.

As the dream continued to appear each night, I felt the need to discern its meaning. I knew nothing about Buddhism, but what I discovered was indeed poignant considering where life had deposited me recently. I learned a turquoise Buddha signifies limitless heights of ascension, embodies the duality of living and dying, and is associated with purity and healing. In other words, this was indeed a message, one that I needed to pay attention to.

I had been diagnosed with stage 2 lobular breast cancer. A double mastectomy was followed by radiation and weeks of chemotherapy. During my second round of chemo, a friend told me I needed to stop thinking about myself and get another pet. I was taken aback by her careless remark. Not only did I have every right to feel sorry for myself, but my beloved cat had passed away just six months earlier. Yet her words kept nagging at me until I sensed she might be right. I did need something to care about, to bring myself back to life, because I had begun to realize that mine wasn't over quite yet.

I spent hours at the local animal shelter one afternoon getting acquainted with each cat. If this was to be my companion, hopefully for a good number of years, I needed to be sure our personalities matched. I found myself standing in front of the last cage and asked the attendant about the cat wedged into the back corner.

"Oh, that's Buddha," she told me. "He's been here a while. He's about three years old, and I gather he had been abused. The lady who brought him in said her boyfriend was going to kill him."

Was this a coincidence, synchronicity, or a miracle? How many cats named Buddha would one find in a shelter on this particular day? He wasn't turquoise; he was a pale orange color with wary, copper-penny eyes. The cat was definitely uncomfortable being held, and the attendant told me if I adopted him, I'd never see him because he would probably hide all the time to protect himself. I could certainly understand that.

From the very first day he came home, Buddha stuck to me like flypaper. He did have issues, and when I removed a clothes hanger from the closet, he would charge at me. But after only a few days, a mutual trust began to surface from deep within us.

Three weeks later, it was time for another round of chemo. Most people don't realize it's not the day after treatment that's hard; it's the next one that does you in. When I awoke that morning, I found all the new toys I had bought for Buddha were surrounding my bed as if a protective castle wall had been erected.

I got through my treatment with the help of Buddha the cat — and perhaps Buddha himself. And even now, if I have just a cold, I wake up to find a delightful assortment of fish, mice, bouncy balls and twirly things arranged around my bed.

I have not had a dream of a turquoise Buddha in more than ten years.

— E.M. Corsa —

32

A Resolution Gone Awry

It is impossible to keep a straight face
in the presence of one or more kittens.
~Cynthia E. Varnado

One steamy July afternoon in central Arkansas, I was working on an important project in my home office with a dear friend and colleague. My trusty printer was churning out a time-sensitive report when it simply stopped. After fifteen minutes of trying to coax, cajole and tickle the device back into operation, we conceded defeat and left to get some lunch and buy a new printer. Upon our return, my heart froze to see the cul de sac teeming with fire trucks, a web of hoses, and heavily-suited emergency personnel sprinting toward my house.

Despite having spent much of my life crafting prose, I still stumble for adequate words to describe the sick, sinking feeling of seeing your home, business, and belongings going up in flames along with photographs and memories collected over a lifetime. But the panic that filled my stunned heart in that awful moment was for the nine cats that shared my home after being rescued from situations of abuse and abandonment.

Responding to an early security-system alert, the amazing firefighters arrived in record time, but the chemical-laden smoke had already taken its toll. I examined, cuddled, and kissed each cat goodbye, immensely grateful that they had passed gently, without injuries or burns. A dog-lover EMT and the fire chief, who professed a cat-loving wife, assured me they had only taken a couple of breaths before passing. My fur babies had all been found in places they frequented during the day — snuggled on my bed, cupped in a cat tree, nestled on a window sill, and one was even discovered in his favorite hidey-hole behind a 1911 H.P. Nelson upright piano.

Only animal lovers really understand the incredible impact that the loss of one beloved four-legged family member can have on your heart, mind and soul. The loss of so many dearly loved critters sent me reeling.

After staying with another great friend for a couple of weeks, I was relocated to a furnished apartment; rebuilding the house would take months. Overwhelmed by indescribable grief, I made the absolute resolution not to even consider taking in more animals (which friends immediately began to offer) until after returning home, if then. I simply did not have the wherewithal to deal with myself, much less anyone or anything else! The jagged holes in my heart needed time to heal.

The weeks that followed were incredibly rough. It was a time when a maze of critical decisions loomed — securing a contractor, negotiating city permits, maneuvering through cumbersome red tape and over complicated insurance hurdles, replacing everything from toothbrushes to computers, reconstructing tax records, and trying to salvage my business. It was also a time for reassessing my workaholic lifestyle.

One evening, about a month after moving in, I was ensconced in writing a mystery novel (another resolution) when a falsetto "meow" sounded from outside the apartment door. Was it my mind playing tricks again? More than once I had heard, seen or felt the brush of one of my departed furry roommates. The meow grew louder and more insistent. Curious, I opened the door.

Sitting on the doorstep was a kitten with an exotic black coat and alert amber eyes. A neighbor walking by scooped him up and began petting him. When I remarked how cute her kitten was, she explained that he had been born under a bridge in the apartment complex and scrounged around for food. This kitty-loving neighbor was quick to offer an extra litter box if I was interested in giving him a home. My immediate reaction was a facetious "that's all I need!" After all, my resolution had been well reasoned and remained firm.

As if they had conspired like some pre-coordinated team of flimflam artists, she put the adorable kitten down. Without hesitation or respect for privacy, the little guy sauntered past me into the apartment with a master-of-the-manor air. He took a brief self-guided tour, sniffed here and there, and then curled up on the couch; apparently the residence had passed his inspection. For the first time in what seemed like forever, I genuinely laughed. Not giving me a chance to object, my conspiratorial neighbor appeared with a litter box and enough food for a few days. Wondering when someone had emblazoned a big "SUCKER" on my forehead, I thanked her and closed the door, resolved to just let him stay until a real home could be found. It is mind-boggling how easily one can become steeped in sheer denial!

That night, as I slid between the sheets of the still unfamiliar bed in the still unfamiliar apartment, the feisty little furball plopped onto the bed, yawned dramatically, and nestled by my side. Those who have never shared a snooze with a critter or two may not relate, but that was the first night since the fire that I actually slept. Stubbornly determined not to open myself to more animals — to more pain — I had refused to admit how desperately I missed having a warm fuzzy cuddled close.

Needless to say, the cat community knew the precise prescription for healing far better than I. Over the next few days, the kitten's hilarious, playful antics drew laughter and affection, in spite of the awful grief tugging at my heart and constant self-reminders he was only visiting for a few days. The name Starlight (Star for short) seemed perfect because that night he brought some light back into my life.

Star grew into a sinewy, sleek black panther-like cat with intelligent eyes the color of sun-kissed bronze. Actually, cat is a misclassification for Starlight; he's really more like a dog. He craves attention, knows no boundaries, greets workmen at the door, sports a relentless shoe fetish, harasses his fellow felines, and even plays fetch if in the mood. He adores wrestling rubber bands, races up and down the stairs, darts outside anytime the door opens, suddenly appears everywhere I don't want him to be, holds onto the broom while I'm trying to sweep, rolls in catnip or whatever else happens to be on the floor, and upends every open vessel containing liquid. In hindsight, a better name might have been "Star, Stop It!"

In the five years since the fire, we have been through a lot, Starlight and I. We returned to the house, managed to keep the business alive, replaced belongings as best we could, brought the mystery novel to the final edits before it's submitted in hopes of publication, and made a lot more resolutions. Star helped me through a massive, albeit untraditional, healing of spirit. The memories of the kitties that passed in the fire now spark only warmth in my heart and winsome smiles. Every single day, I appreciate the serendipitous nature of the Universe that sent me hope in the form of a little black furball.

So take a little advice from my furry friend: no matter how bleak things may become or how fixed your resolve may be, open the door whenever opportunity knocks. It just might be a star to light your way.

— Nancy Sullivan —

33

Fleas and Thank You

I think that someone is watching out for me.
God, my guardian angel, I'm not sure who that is,
but they really work hard.
~Mattie Stepanek

I owe my life to a flea. If I am honest, I'm sure it was more than one flea. I just like how it sounds to say I owe my life to a flea. It makes me stop and think about how you never know what seemingly insignificant detail could end up being extremely consequential. As it turns out, the existence of those nearly imperceptible fleas played a major role in one of the most consequential events of my life.

Cats get fleas. Having owned several cats over the years growing up in small-town Missouri, this was simply an accepted and acknowledged fact of life. Through those years, we had always been relatively lucky. The few times when fleas were apparent, simple flea treatments from the store had been more than adequate to handle the problem. Thankfully, in 2017, that pattern was broken.

My cat, Boomerjax, was scratching at fleas more than he ever had in the two years since I brought him home from the shelter. It had been about the right amount of time since the last treatment, so despite the increased scratching, I didn't assume anything was different. I ran to the store and bought the same flea treatment I had used on him previously.

A few days after applying the treatment, I noticed he had not improved at all. In fact, he seemed to be even more aggravated. A closer look showed his skin was red and irritated. Not wanting to take any chances, I called the vet's office and made an appointment to get Boomerjax some help.

December 6, 2017 felt like any other day. I ran a couple of errands, watched some TV, read for a while, and then started thinking about getting Boomerjax into his carrier to take him to the vet. As with most cats, it usually took a great deal of time and effort to accomplish this task. To my surprise, on that day, Boomerjax did not put up much resistance. At first, I simply attributed the cooperation to the level of misery caused by the fleas. Looking back, I like to believe it all worked together as part of a bigger plan. I had planned for it to take a while, but now we were running early due to the cat's unusual cooperation. I decided to load the carrier in the car and leave for the vet anyway.

The waiting room offered the standard distractions: TV, magazines, and random strangers with their pets. My distraction of choice was playing a mindless game on my cellphone. When Boomerjax was called to the exam room, I quickly grabbed his carrier and exited my game. What I didn't realize was that I had not simply closed the game app; I had silenced the phone entirely. The vet was very kind with Boomerjax and concluded that he was suffering from an allergic reaction to the saliva in the flea bites. I was given some medicine to put in the cat food, and all seemed right with the world.

Before starting the drive home, I pulled out my phone to send a message to my sister about Boomerjax's diagnosis. To my surprise, the display showed I had four missed calls and two voicemail messages. My surprise turned to shock with the first voicemail. It was the first time in my life I had a message begin with the caller identifying himself as a member of the police department. He asked me to call back as soon as possible. With nervous fingers, I managed to push the button to do just that. After confirming my identity, the officer informed me there was a fire at my house.

As I got closer to home, I found the roads blocked in every direction; I had to be cleared to get through. When I saw my home, I was confused. It looked fine. I was expecting a pile of ashes or at least some visible sign of destruction. One of the firefighters took some information and warned me that the interior did not fare as well as the exterior. When it was finally safe for me to enter, I was walked through the scene. The fire marshal explained exactly what he believed had happened, including the timeline of events.

Due to the materials and design of my century-old house, the fire, which started in old wiring, was contained in the wall until it built up enough pressure to explode through. The full-sized filing cabinet and large freezer that I assumed had been moved by the firemen had, in fact, been blown across the room by the force of the explosion. The fire marshal explained that the build-up of the fire inside the wall would have made enough noise for me to hear from anywhere on the first floor, especially right before exploding through the wall. He felt confident that, had I been home, I would have heard the noise and been investigating — placing me in the immediate path of the explosion. Given the intensity of the force, heat, and flying debris, there would have been little chance of survival.

When the discussion turned to the timing of events, I really understood the important role every small detail can make. The explosion happened shortly after I had left for the vet with Boomerjax. In fact, the first 911 call reporting the fire had come in during the time that I had put aside for wrestling Boomerjax into his carrier. If he hadn't uncharacteristically cooperated, I would have been home and looking for the source of the noise in the wall. And if he hadn't developed an allergy to flea bites for the first time, after our prior successful treatments, we wouldn't have been heading to the vet.

Therefore, I owe my life to a flea, or more accurately to an infestation of fleas.

Amazingly, three years later, Boomerjax has never had fleas again. He's a good boy.

— David L. Bishop —

34

A Cat, Six Kittens and a Wheelchair

Not all angels have wings.
Sometimes, they have whiskers.
~Author Unknown

I didn't care for Ike at first. Nobody did. Named after Ike Eisenhower, "Grumpy" suited him better. I suppose I'd be grumpy, too, if I sat in a wheelchair all day long.

As a community nurse on the Alaska Highway in northern British Columbia, I often encountered taciturn patients, but Ike took the cake. It was the dead of winter. Snow swirled around, sneaking into my boots as I lurched through snow drifts toward the dilapidated pewter-gray shack on the outskirts of town. Ice crystals pierced my face like needles in the forty-degree-below-zero cold. The front door hung askew, a result of permafrost heaving the foundation. A large crack split the door frame. Wind whistled eerily through the house. Thick frost covered parts of the living room walls in spite of a pot-bellied stove puffing away in the corner. I could see Ike sitting at the kitchen table, a sour look on his bearded face.

How can anyone live like this? I wondered.

I had to treat him for bedsores on his heels caused when he carelessly threw his legs around like wooden posts.

I looked at the alligator head on the TV.

"Where'd you get that thing?" I shuddered.

"Aah, an Indian friend of mine came with me to Florida last year and we bagged it... not bad, eh?" He grunted, waving me off. Ike was like that, adventurous... unusual... didn't let a little thing like paraplegia stop him.

"Meow."

"Was that a cat?"

"Hmmm." Conversation was difficult with this taciturn man. He wanted his dressing to be done and for me to get out of there — a silent but direct attitude.

"How did you break your back, Ike?"

"Oh, I was building a house for my family up at the 'half way' [a place farther north in the wilderness]... it was supposed to be our dream house... had my boy with me... I was stupid really... sat on a rafter and fell off to the basement... broke my back... Jim took the truck... he was only twelve... and drove it to the neighbors twenty miles away... the closest... hardly a road except a dirt track. They got me out to Edmonton by Air Ambulance but there was no hope... so here I am... wife left me a year later."

Rehabilitation helped him cope as a paraplegic but no one helped him cope with being abandoned by his family. He disliked women, especially pesky snoopy community nurses.

"Meow." A plaintiff cry came from underneath the floorboards.

"Ike, that is a cat under your house — we've got to get her out."

"She's been there a couple days now — drives me nuts... ever since the blizzard blocked her escape hole. She can freeze under there for all I care!"

"You can't just let her freeze to death or starve... that's cruel."

"Why not?... no darn good to anyone... just a pest."

"Well, your dressing can wait. I'll see if I can dig her out."

"Yeah sure, you care more for a cat than for your patients."

The snow, like whipped cream, was piled high on the side of the house. I grabbed a shovel and started throwing the snow aside to reveal a hole to the crawl space. I peeked into the cavernous blackness. I could see green eyes peering out at me, but no way was she going to creep out.

"Well, she'll come out now when I'm gone." I finished his dressing.

"She's scared to death... she'll come out," Ike griped. "Then what?"

"Well, you can feed her for heaven's sake. I'll bring you some cheap cat food tomorrow."

Ike didn't answer but rolled his eyes toward the ceiling.

The next day I placed a huge bag of cheap cat food on the table in front of him.

He said little as I did his foot dressings. When I returned the day after that, during a Chinook warm spell, I found Ike with the back door open. A rusty tin pie plate sat on the back step overloaded with dry cat food. A very pregnant, beautiful, long-haired calico cat sat there munching away, quite content.

"Aha, so your heart isn't so hard after all."

"Well, she'll be having a bunch of kittens soon and what am I going to do with those?" He grinned sheepishly. He tried his best to be gruff but couldn't.

By spring, Ike was the proud father of six kittens and a cat. Wild things they were, bouncing all about. They kept their distance, too, but approached gingerly to grab food from Ike's hands and scramble away.

"They'll only come so far, and they won't come for anyone else," he said proudly.

For the next three months, Ike faithfully fed his menagerie and seemed softer, more pliable, less grumpy.

But all kittens grow up. One day, Ike declared he couldn't possibly keep all seven cats.

"I phoned a farmer friend, and she'll take the kittens if I can catch them. This is all your fault so you have to help me."

He handed me a pillow case in which to place the kittens. I leaped about, slithering on the icy stoop, arms akimbo. Ike laughed uproariously as the kittens scampered about, just out of my reach.

"I ought to get more pay for this," I grumbled.

Eventually with a lot of stealth, I got all kittens into the pillowcase, ready for transfer to the farm.

"What about Kitty?"

"Nah, I'll keep her and get her fixed... she's kinda attached to me by now."

"Sure." Kitty owned the place now.

As for Ike... well, he wasn't so bad after all. In fact I got kinda attached to him, too. Even though his coffee was lousy, I always had a cup with him as we laughed and talked about all kinds of things. As far as I know, Ike is still sleeping with his beloved Kitty. And the community nurse still visits and brings Kitty all kinds of treats. It's part of the job description, after all!

—Arlene Alice Centerwall—

35

Smokey

A Guardian Angel walks with us sent from above, their
loving wings surround us and enfold us with love.
~Author Unknown

M y daughter had her parenting cut out for her. Only two days after my grandsons Josh and Jarod, identical twins, were born, my daughter brought them home from the hospital. The babies weighed only about four pounds each, and my daughter had dressed them in Cabbage Patch nightgowns, the only clothes she could find to fit them.

For the next five days, we all pitched in. The household revolved around these two tiny creatures. They ate every two hours, and we spent virtually the entire day in some stage of feeding them: making bottles, emptying bottles, cleaning bottles, changing diapers, preparing more bottles. After the twins had sucked down the last of their 8:00 P.M. bottles and we had changed them and tucked them into bed, we would head to the kitchen for a cup of coffee and a much-needed break. What we needed was a full-time, paid staff. What we had was Smokey, the family cat.

Smokey had been fascinated with the twins since the day they came home. He spent more time at their side than we did, watching them curiously or napping near their beds. We watched him cautiously at first, making sure he didn't hurt the babies, but though he never left their side, he never got too close to them. He seemed a loyal caretaker.

One evening, though, we briefly doubted our trust. We were

unwinding in the kitchen when Smokey let out a blood-curdling howl, like an animal killing its prey. We raced into the twins' room, and the sight that greeted us filled us with terror. Smokey was almost sitting on Josh, the smaller twin, butting the baby's little body with his head and literally rolling him around the crib. As we ran to save Josh from what we thought was serious injury or worse, Smokey suddenly lay down and started softly mewing, almost moaning. That's when we discovered that little Josh wasn't breathing.

I immediately started CPR while someone else called 911, and an ambulance raced Josh to the hospital. It turned out that both boys were highly allergic to milk. Their bodies had reached their limit in milk intake, and because Josh was smaller, he had gotten sick sooner. Mercifully, Josh had not been without oxygen for very long. Smokey had realized that Josh had stopped breathing and alerted us just in time. Josh would be fine. In fact, the doctor said Smokey had definitely saved Josh's life.

Over the following months, the family settled into an amiable routine. Then late one night, Smokey jumped into bed with my daughter and son-in-law and started to bite and scratch them. More annoyed than puzzled at the cat's strange behavior, they got up to shut him into the bathroom for the night. But Smokey dodged their grasp and darted upstairs to the twins' older brother John's room. When my daughter followed in the chase, she found John so ill that he couldn't move or call for help. "My chest," was all he could say. When he underwent emergency heart surgery, the doctors found that his aorta was almost totally blocked.

Smokey, the hero-cat, now holds a special place in our family. He may have been content to be your typical family pet when the house was half-empty, but as it filled up with children, he decided he better promote himself to a mothering position. When it comes to raising a houseful of kids, Smokey figures it doesn't hurt to have some extra help.

— B. A. Sutkus —

Good Neighbors

The cat has nine lives: three for playing,
three for straying, three for staying.
~English Proverb

The old house behind ours was deserted now. My neighbors, the elderly couple who had lived there for many years, had died within a year of each other. Their children and grandchildren had gathered, grieved and gone.

But looking out my kitchen window one morning, I saw we still had "neighbors." Two white cats had made their way up the back steps of the old house to sit in the sun on the back porch. Their favorite overstuffed chair was gone. Everything was gone. Even from my kitchen window I could see they were pitifully thin. So, I thought, no one is going to claim the cats. They've been left to starve. They'll never leave that old place. They're as shy as their owners were.

I knew they'd never even been inside a house. Even during bitter cold winters, they lived outside. Once, when the female cat had kittens, a dog had killed them. After that the mama cat had her kittens in the attic of the 100-year-old house, entering through a hole in the tin roof. Several times the kittens fell down into the small space between the walls. Once my neighbor told me, "We worked most all afternoon, but we finally got the kittens out. They would have starved to death."

I sighed, looking at the hungry cats sitting on the back porch. A familiar battle began inside me. Part of me wanted desperately to run to the cats. Another part of me wanted to turn away and never look at the starving cats again. It was frustrating to be a forty-year-old mother and still want to pick up stray animals. When I reached twenty-five, then thirty, then surely by thirty-five, I had assumed I would outgrow my obsession with abandoned animals. Now I knew that it was only becoming worse with the years.

Sighing again, I wiped my hands on my apron, grabbed two packages of cat food and headed for the old house. The cats darted beneath the porch as I approached. I crawled part of the way under the house, which sat on concrete blocks, and called, "Here, kitties." I saw four slanted, bright eyes gleaming at me. I could see it would be a long time before I would be able to become friendly with these neighbors.

For several months, I fed the cats this way. One day the mother cat came cautiously toward me and rubbed her face against my hand for a brief moment; then fear sprang into her eyes and she darted away. But after that she met me at the fence at five each day. The other cat would scamper away and hide in the bushes, waiting for me to leave. I decided the white male was probably the female cat's son. I always talked to them as I put out their food, calling them by the names I had given them — Mama and Brother.

One day as Mama rubbed slowly against my leg with her eyes almost shut in contentment, she purred for the first time. My hand didn't reach out, not yet, but my heart did. After that she often rubbed against me and allowed me to stroke her — even before she touched the food. Brother, reluctantly and stiff-necked, allowed me to touch him occasionally; but he always endured my affection, never fully receiving it.

The cats grew fat. One day, I saw Mama kitty on my patio. "Mama kitty," I whispered. She had never come into my yard before. My own cats would never permit that — and yet, here she was. "Good for you, Mama," I said to myself. Suddenly she leaped up into the air, and I thought for a moment that she was choking. Then she seemed to be chasing an object rapidly across the patio. For perhaps the first time in her life, Mama kitty was playing. I watched her toss an acorn into the air and leap after it. My cats came lurking toward the patio door to try to hiss Mama kitty away. She only looked at them and continued playing with the acorn in the sun. Brother sat on the fence, as usual, waiting for supper.

That summer Mama kitty had kittens again — in the attic. She came to my back door to get me. The Realtor had given me the keys to the empty house in case of emergency. I went to the house with the cat and crawled somewhat reluctantly into the dark attic, ignoring the spiders, dust, heat and rattling sounds that I suspected were mice. Finally, I located the three kittens. Brother stood guard over them. I brought the kittens down and fixed a box for them in the empty front bedroom of the old house. Mama kitty wasn't too content with my moving her kittens, but she let them stay — for a while, anyway.

A week later, human neighbors showed up! Unexpectedly, another family moved into the house. Their moving frightened Mama kitty and she returned her kittens to the only safety she knew — the dark, terribly hot attic.

I quickly went over to introduce myself and explained to the family who had moved in about Mama kitty. They gave me permission to go into their attic and rescue the kittens. But I discovered Mama kitty had moved them to another spot. The old attic was a maze of hiding places, and I couldn't find them.

Three times I went back to look, apologizing to the new tenants each time. Three times I was unsuccessful. Back at home, I would look out my window at the tin roof of the house. I could see the heat rising off it. The outside temperature stood in the upper nineties. The kittens couldn't possibly survive.

I couldn't let it go; I felt it was my duty to watch over those cats. One morning as I lay in bed, I prayed, "Lord, I'm asking you to get me those kittens out of that attic. I can't find them. I don't see how you can get them out. But just please do it. If you don't, they're going to die." Silly, maybe, but it didn't feel silly to an animal lover like myself. I hopped from my bed and ran to the back door, half expecting to find the kittens there. They weren't there — no sign of Mama or Brother either. Nevertheless, I expected to get the kittens.

I was worried that I was wearing out my welcome with my new neighbors, but I wanted to go over one last time to look for them.

When the wife answered the door to find it was me with the same request yet again, she said, without enthusiasm, that I could go up in the attic. Once I got up there, I heard them meowing!

"I'm coming. I'm coming!" I called out, my heart pounding with joy.

The next moment I couldn't figure out what had happened. I seemed to be falling. Plaster broke loose. I wasn't in the dark, hot attic any more, but dangling into the kitchen. I had forgotten to stay on the rafters and had crashed through the ceiling. I climbed back up onto a rafter, only to fall through again in another place.

Thoroughly shaken, I climbed back down. In the kitchen my neighbor and I looked at the damage. I was horrified, and it was clear that I wasn't making the best impression on this woman. Not knowing what else to do, I grabbed her broom and began sweeping. More plaster fell on us and we coughed in the dust. I apologized over and over, babbling that we would have the ceiling fixed. I assured her I would be back over to talk with her husband. She nodded, silently, with her arms folded, and stared at me with seeming disbelief. I hurried home, humiliated.

That night at supper, when I told my family what had happened, they all stared at me silently, the way my new neighbor had. I was close to tears, partly because of the plight of the kittens and also because of my own stupidity.

The next day I went back to the neighbors' to speak to them about the ceiling. I arrived during a meal. The couple's children were eating with them. They all stared at me as they continued eating. I was introduced as "that woman who goes up in the attic all the time and fell through yesterday." I smiled at them all.

The husband looked up at me, still chewing, and said solemnly, "Get my gun, Ma."

For one horrible moment, my heart froze. Then he broke into a little-boy grin. "Forget it. I'm a carpenter and the ceiling needed repairing, anyway."

I smiled back at him and added, "I came to tell you that I won't be going in your attic any more — ever."

"Okay," he grinned, and I thought I heard his wife sigh.

Who Rescued Whom? |

The next afternoon, our family sat in the living room reading the Sunday paper. Only I wasn't reading, I was praying behind my part of the paper.

"Lord, it seems more hopeless than ever now. But I have no intention of giving up on this request. Give me the kittens, please."

As I prayed, I imagined the kittens in a dark, obscure corner of the attic. I knew almost for certain that Mama kitty had moved them again. Then I imagined a large, gentle hand lifting them up and bringing them down into light and cooler air. I saw it in my mind, over and over, as I prayed. Suddenly, I thought I could actually hear the kittens' tiny, helpless mews.

Silly, I told myself. Your imagination goes wild when you pray.

Jerry put down the sports page; the children looked up from the comics. We all listened quietly, almost without breathing. "Mew, mew, mew." It was real!

The doorbell rang and we all ran for it. I got there first and there stood my neighbor, cobwebs in his hair, dust on his overalls, and the impish little-boy grin on his lean face. We all looked down and there, cradled in his hands, were the kittens.

"Lady, you won't have to look any more for 'em. I found 'em for you."

This time Mama kitty let her brood stay where I put them, in our small storeroom, just off the carport. We found excellent, cat-loving homes for the fat, playful kittens. And I found a permanent solution to the attic/kitten problem. I had Mama kitty spayed.

That was over a year ago. Brother still sits cautiously on my backyard fence, cold and often hungry. I keep trying with him, but he's obviously still skeptical about my neighborly good will.

Not Mama kitty. Now she comes right into the kitchen to eat from my other cats' dishes! She rubs against my leg when I let her in. On cold nights she sleeps curled up in a kitchen chair. And often she sits and watches me type. At first, my cats hissed, growled and fumed. Eventually, they just gave up and accepted Mama kitty.

Now when I look out my window at that old house, I have to smile. It's good to see lights on in the kitchen and children's toys in the yard. The new occupants and I have become pretty close. It's not hard to break the ice — once you've broken the ceiling.

— Marion Bond West —

37

The Cat and the Cat Burglar

I have studied many philosophers and many cats.
The wisdom of cats is infinitely superior.
~Hippolyte Taine

I lived in New York City for many years. As a professional dancer and dance instructor, it was the logical place to pursue my career. The city had its many good points — fine museums, great theater, wonderful food and terrific shopping, but it also had its downside — high prices, crowding, noise and crime. The crime bothered me the most. As a single woman, I felt particularly vulnerable. I considered getting a dog for protection; I had grown up with German shepherds and loved them. But the idea of cramming a big dog in a tiny apartment didn't feel right. So, like every other single woman in New York, I had a few deadbolts on my door, and in the streets, I watched my back.

One day, I huddled under an awning on St. Mark's Place with a group of other people who had been surprised without an umbrella by a sudden cloudburst. A scruffy-looking guy, a street person standing in the small crowd, held up a tiny kitten and said, "Anybody give me ten bucks for this cat?"

The kitten was beautiful. She had a fawn underbelly with a chocolate tail and back, and a deeper cocoa mask with pure white whiskers. I was immediately intrigued. But a kitten didn't fit in my watch-dog scenario. I wrestled with myself internally for a few moments before digging into my purse and scooping out all the cash I had on me — seven dollars and a few coins. I needed a dollar for the subway home, so I said, "Will you take six dollars for her?"

He must have realized that this was his best offer, or else he was so desperate that he just took whatever he could get, because we made the exchange and he left.

I named my new roommate Seal because her whiskers looked like a seal's. She seemed happy in my small apartment, and I enjoyed her company immensely.

One night, after I'd had Seal for about two years, I woke up in the middle of the night to a loud noise. Loud noises are not unusual in New York, even at 2:00 A.M., so I settled back down and attempted to sleep again. Immediately, Seal jumped on my chest and started stomping on me with all four feet. This was not kneading or playful swatting, and I realized Seal was trying to alert me to something. She jumped off the bed and I followed her. We both crept in the dark toward the kitchen. I watched Seal and when she stopped at the doorway to the kitchen, I stopped too. Keeping her body hidden, she poked her head around the corner of the doorway, and I did the same.

There we saw the figure of a man outlined against the frame of the broken window.

He was in my kitchen.

I refrained from emitting the high-pitched and therefore obviously female scream that was welling in my chest. I made myself inhale an enormous breath. Exhaling, I imagined the opera star, Luciano Pavarotti, and a sound like "WHAAAA" blasted out of me. I think I was planning on saying, "What do you think you are doing?" But I didn't need to. Even to myself, I sounded like a linebacker, and that guy was out the window and crawling like the human fly along the brick wall of the airshaft outside my kitchen as fast as his burglar legs could carry him.

After that night, I felt more confident about living in New York City. I kept a bat near my bed and practiced grabbing it and using it from every angle I thought might be necessary.

Seal and I became a team. I found myself trusting her more and more. If I heard a noise, I'd look at Seal. If she seemed curious or concerned, I'd investigate it. If not, I'd ignore it too. She became a source of security for me.

Seal is still around. She's eighteen years old and still spry. I have a bigger place now and I'm toying with getting a German shepherd, but not for protection. Seal and I have that one handled.

—Laya Schaetzel-Hawthorne—

38

Bumpus

There is no such thing as "just a cat."
~Robert A. Heinlein

The big, Maine–coon-type cat was found by firefighters on Father's Day 1996, his long orange fur matted and scorched. He lay, barely alive, in the charred remains of the wildfires that plagued Alaska that year. Even though he must have been in great pain, the cat purred the moment he was touched. When the vet first saw the badly burned cat, he began to cry. He had never seen a living animal with such extensive injuries. The fire had claimed his rear feet and all his front toes. The vet was afraid this latest fire victim might not live long.

But the cat was a survivor. Bumpus, as he came to be called, seemed unaware of the odds against him. Once he began to heal, Bumpus struggled persistently to learn to walk again. Eventually, to everyone's astonishment, the cat succeeded.

Bumpus became a favorite with the rescue volunteers who helped the clinic staff care for him. After facing so much ruin, devastation and death left in the wake of the fires, the presence of this friendly, spirited cat boosted morale and helped the rescuers continue their work.

One of the volunteers, a woman named Sharon, fell in love with the big orange cat. When she was finished in Alaska, she couldn't face leaving him behind, so when Bumpus was well enough to travel, he came home to live with her in Missouri.

Besides doing emergency rescue work, Sharon volunteered at

her local humane society. Her specialty was fostering sick or injured kittens in her home and nursing them back to health.

Not long after Bumpus came to live with her, Sharon took in a litter of badly wounded kittens who required special medical attention — two of them eventually needed to have a leg amputated. After the surgery, one of the two-month-old kittens, a female named Minus, came home from the vet, charged out of her carrier and jumped right up on the bed. She didn't even seem to notice she was missing a front leg.

But her brother, Cheerio, named for the circular patterns on his solid orange coat, was traumatized by the operation. Unlike other amputees Sharon had fostered, Cheerio seemed depressed at having lost a limb. He cried constantly, and when he tried to walk, Cheerio always fell and ended up doing a somersault. He took his frustration out on the carpeting, biting and growling at anything around him. At other times, he hid under the bed, refusing to come out.

When Sharon saw how depressed Cheerio was — even his eyes were dull — she worried he might sicken and die. She had to do something, but what? Her eyes fell on Bumpus, serenely grooming himself in a sunny spot on the floor. He's been through this, she thought. Maybe he could help.

Sharon had isolated the injured kittens in one room in an attempt to keep them less active. When she opened the door to the kittens' room for Bumpus, he made a beeline for the crying kitten, quietly talking to him the whole way. He walked right up to the kitten and, wrapping his furry front paws around Cheerio's damaged little body, held him like a child holds a doll. Then Bumpus began rubbing his head against Cheerio's head and licking the kitten's face. Immediately the crying stopped — and the purring began. The little three-legged kitten, who could not warm to the love of a human, immediately responded to the love of another orange cat — a larger version of himself — who had suffered in this way, too.

Over the next few days, Cheerio and Bumpus became inseparable. Though Cheerio didn't want his littermates around, he stuck close to Bumpus. Often when Sharon looked in on them, she found Bumpus and the kitten curled up together on the bed — the same bed that

Cheerio had refused to jump on, hiding under it instead.

Thanks to Bumpus's therapy, Cheerio regained his cheerful disposition and eventually went to live with a devoted new family.

Since then, Bumpus has become Sharon's secret weapon. Any time she has a problem with a kitten, she sends the big cat in and waits for the inevitable miracle.

Bumpus works his magic on people as well. Sharon often takes him to visit children in the pediatric oncology ward at a local hospital. The children are deeply affected when they see what the fire did to Bumpus and witness how his strong will to live has helped him. They reach out eagerly to pet the big, brave cat. And his purring presence seems to quiet their fears.

Sharon doesn't wonder how Bumpus does it, because she's always known. This wonderful cat possesses an enormous quantity of the healing spirit — more than enough to share.

— Janine Adams —

39

Dharma

The cat does not offer services. The cat offers itself.
~William S. Burroughs

Nearing the lake on that warm September morning, I heard a tiny mewing sound. My first inclination was to ignore the cries. I've been through enough lately, I thought;
I can hardly take care of myself.

Three months earlier, at age thirty-seven, I had been diagnosed with breast cancer. Because the cancer was in more than one place, the doctor had recommended a radical mastectomy. It was scheduled for later that same month. I still remember the shock and denial I felt when I overheard my husband Gary telling someone on the phone, "She's probably going to lose her breast." Those words seared through me like a knife. No. No! I silently cried to God, I'm too young for that.

A few weeks later, while I was recovering from the mastectomy, the surgeon called with more bad news: "The cancer has spread to your lymph nodes. Chemotherapy offers the best chance for survival." All I could do was sit there stunned, thinking, Oh God, I'm going to die.

I was terrified of dying. Many of my friends draw comfort from their beliefs about the afterlife or reincarnation. But I had trouble blindly believing in things I couldn't see or touch. I wanted proof. I prayed for God to show me the truth about death.

With the fear of dying in my heart, I decided to go on an aggressive clinical trial that included a combination of high-dose chemotherapy and a five-year follow-up with a hormone blocker.

The chemotherapy wiped me out completely. Even with the antin-ausea drugs, I was sick every time. Two months into the treatment, it was all I could do to get dressed and keep a little food down every day. In addition to working, my husband was doing his best to care for the house and me. Wonderful as he was, it was hard on both of us. I was irritable and lonely most of the time. This short walk to the lake was my first time outdoors in a while.

Meow! Meow! The insistent pleas continued.

No, I really can't care for an animal right now, I thought as I passed by. Suddenly, ear-splitting shrieking and squawking filled the air. Four blue jays were dive-bombing the bush where the mewing sounds were coming from. Shooing the birds away, I ran and looked under the bush. Standing on wobbly legs was a tiny three-week-old orange tabby, with bright blue eyes, mewing his little head off. Gathering him up into my arms, I headed to the lake in hopes of finding his owner or else convincing someone to take him home.

The wind whipped all around us as the shaking kitten cuddled close, still scared to death. We sat together by the lake trying to find him a home. Asking a number of people and finding no takers, I decided to take him home temporarily until I could find him a home of his own. Still feeling exhausted from the chemo, I spent most of the day on the couch with the little kitty curled up on my chest purring. Later that evening, as my husband was leaving to go to a meeting, I asked him to take the kitten with him. "Try and find him a good home," I said, placing the kitten in a box. Little did I know, my heart had already been stolen.

An hour later, I beeped my husband. "Have you found him a home yet?" I asked.

"I was just giving him to someone," Gary replied.

"Don't," I said without hesitation. "Bring him home. I need him."

When Gary and the kitten returned home, the little orange tabby curled right back up on my chest like he'd never left.

For the next week, while I was bedridden, Dharma and I were constant companions. He just loved snuggling, sometimes trying to get right up under my chin. He didn't even notice my lack of hair or uneven chest. It felt good to love and be loved so unconditionally.

I chose the name Dharma because in India it means "fulfilling one's life purpose." Cancer-recovery research has shown that finding and following one's bliss or purpose supports the immune system and increases chances of survival. For me, I hoped this would include two deep-seated desires: writing and being of service to others. Dharma's name reminded me of that intention and so much more.

Arriving home from my biweekly doctor visits, I immediately picked him up like a baby and carried him around the house with me. I even carried him to the garage while I did laundry. We were inseparable. With Dharma around, I wasn't so needy and grouchy with Gary. And, boy, did Dharma purr loudly! It was so comforting to hear and feel the love he expressed so freely.

As he grew, fighting, biting and clawing furniture became his favorite pastimes. We have a fenced-in backyard, so when he got too wild for me, I would let him play out back with other neighborhood cats.

Dharma also loved chasing butterflies. Last spring, I planted purple Porter's weed specifically to attract them. The whole backyard, with its multitude of colorful butterflies, was one big playpen for Dharma. I don't think he ever caught any, but I spent countless afternoons sitting on the back porch watching Dharma live his bliss. So free. No cares. My spirit soared as I watched him live his life so fully, and I decided it was time I do the same.

Late that December, I scheduled my final reconstructive surgery and let my office know I would be back to work in February.

Then, three days after my final surgery, the unthinkable happened. Escaping from the backyard, Dharma was hit by a car and killed instantly. My life, too, seemed to end at that moment. I was devastated and no one, not even Gary, could console me. I sat there on that same couch where Dharma and I had shared so much love and cried and cried for hours. Why, God, why? I asked in desperation. I wanted to turn back time and never let him outside. With all my might, I willed it not to be so. And still it was so.

Finally, Gary asked, "Do you want to see him?" Although I had never wanted to see a dead animal in the past, I answered, "Yes." Gary then placed Dharma in a towel in my arms, and I held him and wept. We decided to bury him in the backyard by the Porter's weed.

While Gary dug the hole, I held Dharma one last time, telling him all he meant to me and how much I loved him. I thought back on all the gifts he brought me in just the short time he was with me: unconditional love, laughter, a playful spirit, a reminder to live fully and a sense of my life's purpose.

My husband said, "You know, I believe Dharma was sent by God to help you through a very rough time. Now that you're through the worst of it, it's time for Dharma to move on and help someone else."

"Do you really think so?" I asked, wanting so badly to believe it was true.

"Look at the timing," Gary said. "You hadn't been to the lake in months and the one day you venture out, you find Dharma blocks from our house in dire need of help, and in rescuing him you get rescued as well. All of his gifts can't be a coincidence. There's definitely a reason he was put in your life when he was and also taken out when he was. He was your little angel."

"Thanks," I said, letting my husband's healing words wash over me.

Watching Dharma lying so peacefully in my arms, I got the much-needed answer to my prayer about death. I realized that he would go on in me forever, the same as I would in the lives of everyone I touched. I believe Dharma gave his life so that I might know peace. When Dharma died, I awakened spiritually. I am no longer afraid of death. Through Dharma, God showed me there is nothing to fear. There is only peace. And love.

We buried him at the foot of his butterfly bush and on his headstone I wrote, "Dharma — My Little Angel." Now, whenever I sit on the back steps, I see Dharma chasing butterflies for all eternity.

— Deborah Tyler Blais —

Chapter
5

What I Learned from the Cat

The Paws in Our Plans

Some people have cats and go on to lead normal lives.
~Author Unknown

After five years of dating, including four years of sharing a flat and the affections of a little cat called Figuero, it was time for us to make it official!

Neal's proposal came over an ice cream cone, simple and sweet. Smiling so wide I could only nod my acceptance, I became his fiancée and was soon wearing the engagement ring of my dreams — gemstones and diamonds.

Together, we threw ourselves into wedding plans, sharing each decision regarding the ceremony, the guest list, the menu. Like every couple, we wanted our wedding to reflect who we were as a couple. The cake would be vegan. The reception at an historic hotel. The bouquet and boutonnieres would contain not only orchids and roses, but also the joyful greenery of carrot tops, dill weed, and parsley.

But one of the most lasting decisions — our wedding date — we left up to our cat. The beautiful, long-haired tabby was the light of our young lives, an integral part of every day since his unexpected arrival one cold winter night. From his frostbitten ears to his elegant sweep of tail, he exuded personality and immediately warmed our hearts.

He woke us up each morning, taking quite seriously his role of Alarm Cat. He greeted us each evening, waiting none too patiently to share dinnertime. He cuddled between our knees at night, ensuring sweet dreams all around.

If he couldn't be at the wedding, we decided, he could at least have a part in the plans.

We looked at the calendar and chose three dates in the autumn. Then came Figuero's turn.

Neal wrote each date on a separate scrap of paper while I held Figuero in my arms. Crumpling each scrap into a ball, Neal tossed them randomly onto the kitchen floor one at a time. Loving nothing more than a crumpled bit of paper, Figuero watched with great interest, as if sensing the extra importance of this particular game.

The first piece he walked over to, we had decided, would be the date of our wedding.

As soon as I set Figuero down, he trotted over to the paper ball that had landed in front of the stove. With his big paw, he gave it a little swat of approval.

I scooped him up again, squeezing him with excitement. Neal smoothed the paper out and, with our heads together, the three of us read the date that would be special for the rest of our lives: October sixth.

Neal and I have been married nearly twenty-five years now, sharing fifteen of those years with our little man, who lived to the ripe old age of twenty-one. On every anniversary, I remember the way Figuero helped make our wedding special. I think about the joy he added, not only to that day, but to every single one we knew as a family.

A gift that goes beyond the years, his legacy is our lifetime of love.

— Kate Fellowes —

41

Accountability Partner

Authors like cats because they are such quiet, lovable,
wise creatures, and cats like authors
for the same reasons.
~Robertson Davies

Nothing motivates a writer like an accountability partner. Right now, mine sits on my desk two feet from my elbow. From her spot, she has a lovely view out my office window to woods across the street. The sun gleams on her black fur, and I pause in my writing to admire her.

"Do you have any idea how beautiful you are?" I ask Naomi.

She blinks her round yellow eyes. "Meow," she says, which might mean "certainly," but more likely, "Get back to your writing." Or maybe, "Finish that story so you can read it to me."

Naomi, as foreman of our morning routine, is a harsh taskmaster. When the first summer light slips through the vertical blinds of the bedroom, she pads up my chest and presses her nose to mine. Never mind what time I got to bed the night before. "Mrrow."

I open one eye. I've been known, after a particularly late night, to tell her, "Not now, Naomi."

She answers by leaping off the bed and playing with her toys in a shoebox nearby for two or three minutes, jangling bells and scratching cardboard boxes. Then she springs back up. "Rrrrrrrow," she insists in her raspy voice.

I snake one hand out from under the covers, and stroke her

cheeks and the length of her back. This is my miracle kitty, seventeen years old and an eighteen-month cancer survivor. I can't possibly be cross with her. "Okay," I murmur, slip out of bed and tie on my robe.

"Meow, meow, meow." Naomi runs down the hall to stand outside my office door.

"Can I brush my teeth first?"

"Rrrrrow." Evidently not. Naomi stalks through the door and over to my desk. She's a drill sergeant disguised as a seven-pound feline. She's also right. The house will be quiet for another hour or two before my retired husband gets up. It's a perfect time to work on the story circling in my head.

I sit at my computer, and she leaps up to the water and food bowls I've put to my right. With a different accountability partner, one might offer coffee and donuts. My gift to her is an unlimited supply of kibbles and fresh water.

I'm tempted to start with e-mails. You know, warm up the brain. She glances at my computer. Can she actually see my inbox? She paces the length of my desk. "Meow, meow," she scolds in her imitation Siamese cat voice.

"You're a slave driver, you know." I stroke her silky cheeks. She's such a smart cat. I can do e-mails along with laundry when my husband is up. He'll be offering to make oatmeal, wanting to review plans for the day, suggesting a walk or a hike. Now is my opportunity for uninterrupted writing time.

When I am steadily working, Naomi jumps from the desk and takes up residence on the heater grate. Understandable. It's one of those damp, gray mornings in Portland. I've worked fifteen minutes when she gets up, arches her back in a cat pose perfect for a yoga calendar, and settles into the empty file-folder box near my chair. A few weeks earlier, I'd used the last of the folders and set aside the box for recycling. Naomi stepped delicately into it and snuggled down. The box is hers now. She especially favors it for morning naps.

She turns her head lazily toward me. "Meow," she says. I think she means, "Isn't this nice? You working away, me keeping you on track?"

It is nice. The ideas come easily, and my fingers dance on the keyboard for an hour. Then a story that started out charming turns into drivel. I'm not sure what to do next. Rethink the plot? Add a bit of spicy dialogue? "This is so not working," I tell Naomi, stretching my arms in front of me, fingers curled together.

She lifts her head to look at me. I see no sympathy in her eyes.

"I need a break," I tell her and head into the kitchen. Maybe if I spend a few minutes with the newspaper and a cup of tea, ideas will come to me.

As quickly as I'm out of my chair, Naomi is out of her box. She scolds me with a haughty flick of her tail and walks from the room. The word "quitter" reverberates in the air.

"I'm only going to take five minutes," I call over my shoulder as I retrieve the newspaper. I plug in the electric teakettle, spread the newspaper on the dining-room table, and open it to the crossword puzzle. Naomi sits alert on a chair beside me. "Every writer should do crossword puzzles," I explain to her. "Keeps the mind sharp."

"Rrrrrrr." She flattens her ears.

"What a commando." I fill in a couple of words that quickly come to mind, then abruptly hit a snag. I look at Naomi. "8 across, 'carries things too far.' What do you think? 'Provokes'? That isn't quite right. 'Exaggerates'? Too many letters. 'Overdo'?"

"Mrrrow." She isn't helpful.

"I'm going with 'overdo.'" As I'm penciling in the word, Naomi leaps on the table and walks onto the paper, crinkling it with every step. She sits squarely on the crossword puzzle and lifts one hind leg to begin her morning ablutions.

"I had three more minutes to relax." There's a slight whine in my voice.

She lifts her other hind leg and continues to clean herself.

I think of the advice a writing teacher gave me in a workshop recently. "When you hit an obstacle, stay with it. The bigger the obstacle, the greater the triumph. Stay with it, and you'll get a major breakthrough."

He didn't mean a blank in a crossword puzzle. He meant that issue I'm having with my story. "Okay, sweetie. You win." I sigh and chuck Naomi under her chin, take my cup of tea, and return to my office and my story. If Naomi can fight cancer, I can fight writer's block.

She follows me in and jumps on my desk with a throaty whir. "This is where we belong, isn't it?" she seems to say.

"Here's to a major breakthrough. And to the world's best accountability partner." I lift my teacup to her and catch her eye.

She stretches out a paw, softly touches my forearm, and purrs her agreement.

— Samantha Ducloux Waltz —

42

Violet and Diesel Shelter in Place

If you are a host to your guest,
be a host to his dog also.
~Russian Proverb

When I walked through my dining room this morning, there was nine-pound Violet the Cat sprawled across the table in the sun. She had perfected her sprawl so that she could now touch all four placemats at one time — one with her head, one with her tail, one with her right front paw, and the last with her left back paw. I understood her feeling of accomplishment. She had been practicing this position for months.

Violet loves these placemats the way other cats love catnip-stuffed felt mice. Her morning ritual is to lie on one and suck the corner of another one for at least half an hour before anyone else in the house wakes up. At the same time, she does that thing only cats do — kneading bread with her paws in the air, and purring like she has sleep apnea with her eyes half-shut. Non-cat people find this disturbing. And no, I never set the table with Violet's placemats.

Violet is just over a year old. My husband and I adopted her from the SPCA when she was twelve weeks old and still small enough to hold in one hand. As soon as we saw her, we knew she was the one. She was solid gray and round, with a smiling face just like Iris, the cat we had shared our lives with for sixteen years.

On the other hand, I did not understand Diesel, my brother John's Bull Mastiff who would be arriving any minute. John, his wife Cheryl, and Diesel had been handed an emergency evacuation notice just two days earlier when one of the furious fires in California jumped a fire line and raced toward their house. The three of them would be staying with us until they got the "all clear" to return home.

The serious issues swirling around us were numbing. In addition to worrying about the immediate fire threat, Covid-19 and maintaining safe social distancing with houseguests, I was on edge about how Violet and Diesel would get along. Until a month earlier, she was technically still a kitten and she hadn't spent time with a dog before.

My concern only got worse when everyone arrived and I opened the door. Diesel had become a 120-pound small grizzly bear with the facial expression of Alfred Hitchcock. As we unloaded the car, Diesel wandered around the house making loud noises I'd only heard at farms until then. He did not seem to be in distress, but I was starting to be. I had no idea what all those sounds meant and it made me edgy. I was used to an occasional polite feline squeak. If Violet makes the slightest noise, I know exactly what's on her mind.

I looked up Bull Mastiff on my laptop for some help. Apparently snorting, snuffling, wheezing, grunting, loud snoring and flatulence are normal. I thought about the sounds coming from the kitchen and identified them as snorting, wheezing and grunting. I figured flatulence could come at any moment. Wikipedia added helpfully that I should follow Diesel around with a large drool towel.

That afternoon, John and Cheryl left to do some errands, so I took Diesel for a walk to let him sniff around the neighborhood. When we got back home, I played Frisbee with him in the yard to give Violet a chance to watch him through the window. Then I had to leave the house for an hour, so I put Diesel in his double-wide crate in the laundry room. The dog is so big that my brother made him a giant crate by splicing two large ones together. Diesel didn't seem to mind getting in and before long his nasal snuffle turned into a loud snore.

When I returned home, the house was quiet, to my great relief. The whole time I was away, I had visions of one of them injuring the other one so badly it would require a rush to the emergency vet. I peeked in the laundry room and there was Violet, sitting on top of the washing machine, with her paws folded neatly underneath her. She was calmly staring across the room at our sleeping visitor.

While I was gone, Violet had dragged one of her placemats from the dining room table through the kitchen and into the laundry room where she left it for Diesel, right in front of his crate — a welcome gift to her canine guest.

Violet is a very good hostess.

— Suzanne Cushman —

43

Oh, Henry!

If cats could talk, they wouldn't.
~Nan Porter

hortly after settling into our new Florida home, my husband Dave and I unexpectedly became foster parents to a couple of feral cats living in our subdivision. We didn't set out to become their primary caregivers. It transpired as they repeatedly showed up at our front door for a bite to eat. We didn't know if the previous owners had fed them or if someone else living in the community had moved and the cats were searching for another place to get some food. Anyway, we fed them, and, in time we named them Tiger and Midnight.

As they became comfortable around us, Dave and I trapped them and brought them to get spayed and neutered. To keep down the feral-cat population, the Humane Society provides these services for free. Although they remained outdoor cats, Tiger and Midnight became part of our family. We didn't mind tending to their needs: providing food, water, and shelter outside. After all, it wasn't their fault they were homeless with no one to care for them.

A few years later, another cat showed up at our door. We didn't know where he came from. We never saw him roaming the neighborhood. I felt sad for him. He looked tired and hungry with his big, puffy-looking face and scrawny body. We fed him with the other two. And soon they became a pack of three. We named him Henry.

Unlike Tiger and Midnight, whom we could catch and bring

in to get fixed, Henry apparently knew better. I suppose his age and familiarity kept him from biting the bait. Another thing that was different about Henry was that he roamed the neighborhood, and he would stay away for days on end. Tiger and Midnight stayed within the boundaries of our property.

One morning, upon opening my front door, I spotted Henry. Immediately, I blurted out, "Oh, Henry! What happened to you?" I thought, *Boys will be boys, and feral cats will be feral cats.* By the looks of him, he must have gotten into a ruckus with another cat. He had an open wound on his neck. The best I could do was to give him some food while feeding the other two. As I placed his dish in front of him, I said, "Henry, if you stop prowling around at night and stay around here, you won't get hurt."

Two days later, Henry showed up for a bite to eat. I was shocked when I saw him. The open wound had miraculously healed. I couldn't believe my eyes! I shouted to Dave, who was inside the house, "Honey, you've got to get out here and see Henry. You won't believe this! He's all better."

After inspecting Henry, Dave said, "Wow! He heals quickly." Being naïve, I assumed the same. We fed him, along with the other two, and left it at that. For several days, Henry stayed around our house and remained injury-free.

However, after being AWOL for a while again, I spotted Henry limping toward my front door. Immediately, I said, "Oh, Henry! What happened to you now?" I thought, *Maybe he fell from a tree or sprained his leg trying to get away from another cat.* I felt bad for him because he could not put any weight on the injured leg. Since we couldn't catch him to bring him to the Humane Society to get checked out, we did the best we could by feeding him some good, high-quality food.

A few days later, Henry showed up at our house, but he was not limping. I thought, *Wow! This cat heals quickly.* I asked Dave, "How can he be better that quickly?"

Dave responded, "I don't know. Maybe the chicken we fed him two nights ago helped him."

"I don't know about that," I replied. "But, anyway, I'm glad he's better."

For months, this happened over and over — injuries followed by miraculously quick healing. Dave and I were dumfounded by what was taking place. We knew there was no way that Henry could heal from his injuries that quickly. Yet, he did!

It wasn't until one morning, after Dave came in the back door and I came in the front, that we figured out how Henry was healing so quickly. Dave commented, "Henry's in the back yard waiting for food."

Surprised, I responded, "No, he's not. I just left him at the front of the house."

Pointing out the back window, Dave said, "Look, he's sitting right there." As I peered outside, realizing Henry was there, I thought to myself, *Then, who's in the front?* Quickly, we headed to the front to see if the Henry I saw was still there. To our surprise, he was. Turning to Dave, I exclaimed, "There are two Henrys!"

Those two cats were identical. It was odd because few cats look like them, with their big puffy faces and scrawny bodies.

As both cats began coming around at the same time to eat, I could distinguish one from the other. Henry #1 has eyes that are open wider than Henry #2, who looks like he's squinting. To this day, Dave still struggles with figuring out which is Henry #1 and which is Henry #2.

And, yes, when one of our Henrys shows up with a bruise, I still say, "Oh, Henry! What happened to you?"

— Barbara Alpert —

44

Ninja Cat

Nothing inspires forgiveness quite like revenge.
~Scott Adams

Sammie was a stinker. Our middle-aged orange tabby loved to play his own brand of feline practical jokes on us whenever the opportunity arose. And the opportunity seemed to be arising more and more every day.

Whether Sammie was leaping from atop the stairs onto my head, grabbing my foot from underneath the sofa, or jumping on my back when I bent down, he never failed to shock me. The most terrifying move of all, though, was what my husband Bill called "The Ninja." In this maneuver, Sammie would wait patiently around a corner or behind a piece of furniture until one of us passed by. Then, he would literally fly through the air and land on a thigh, securing all four sets of claws into it. It was unnerving.

One day, I heard strange growling emanating from our basement. Never imagining that it could be coming from our usually silent tabby, I crept down the stairs to find him sitting on a window ledge, eye-to-eye with a neighborhood cat on the other side of the glass. The growling increased as the other cat taunted Sammie with his presence, moving this way and that. Yet, when Sammie hissed and smacked the window with his paw, the other cat ran for his life.

Ninja Cat, proud of his brave efforts, refused to leave his stronghold. He pressed against the window, craning his neck to the left and the right, searching for any sign of the other cat's return. Even an hour later, Sammie still held guard at the basement window. Promise of dinner and the shaking of the treats bag could not entice him back to the first floor. I climbed halfway down the stairs and beckoned him to come back up. He never flinched. Then, I got an idea.

In my bedroom, I have one of the famous FAO Schwarz toy lions that sat regally in their display near the entrance of the Manhattan store. Sammie may have had the courage to face off with a neighborhood cat, but a lion several times his size? I didn't think so. From there, I formulated a plan for Sammie to receive his comeuppance for all the ninja attacks we had endured through the years.

I interrupted Bill as he watched the evening news and held up the stuffed lion. "I'm going to play a trick on Sammie with this, and I need you to help me."

With the memory of Sammie's most recent hijinks still fresh in his mind, Bill responded eagerly, "Count me in. What do you need me to do?"

"I'm going to sneak outside and move the lion around in front to the basement window. I need you to grab your cellphone and go downstairs and record Sammie's reaction on video. That," I said, "I've got to see."

With that, Bill proceeded to his spot in the basement as I crawled outside, next to the window, with the lion in my arms. Then, with all the stealth of a Nighthawk attack, I shook the lion in front of Sammie's face. Ha ha! I'd done it! I'd finally given Sammie a dose of his own medicine. I ran into the house and straight into Bill.

"Show me the video! Show me the video!" I exclaimed.

"You're going to be disappointed," Bill replied. "I couldn't get very much."

"I want to see it! I want to see it!" I cried with all the enthusiasm of a five-year-old being handed a gift-wrapped box at Christmas.

So, Bill played the video.

He was right. There wasn't much to see.

"Play it again," I instructed. I looked closer. All I could see was a two-second video of a giant, puffed-up tabby tail trailing behind a rocket-ship blast of orange cat running for cover. The video may have been short, but it was enough. I had beaten Sammie at his own game, and I even had proof. Ahhh, sweet victory was mine! Finally.

—Monica A. Andermann—

45

The Shy Girl

*Somewhere along the way, we must learn that there is
nothing greater than to do something for others.*
~Martin Luther King, Jr.

To say that I was shy when I was ten is an understatement — I was basically afraid of people. Kids, adults, pretty much everyone made me nervous. I was also what most teachers and parents would call a "good kid." I followed the rules, got good grades in school and rarely questioned authority. But then one day, one single ride on a school bus changed all that.

The school bus that day was crowded, hot, humid and smelly. The windows were all rolled up — bus driver's orders — it was simply raining too hard to have them down. Only a few of my classmates were looking through the windows at the torrents of water filling the street, overflowing the curbs and drains; most of the other kids were engaged in animated conversations, arguments and games. I sat alone as usual, speaking to no one.

I thought that the road outside looked like a flooded stream. I could make out tree limbs, bags, even an umbrella washing down the boulevard. People raced here and there, gripping umbrellas or covering their heads with bunched-up jackets and papers. Over and over, I carefully wiped a small circle through the cloud on my window so that I could see the rushing water outside.

The bus stopped, waiting for an accident to clear. The driver was particularly tense that day and had snapped at several kids who had been messing around, standing up in their seats, yelling, making faces at drivers in passing cars and even one kid who had been licking the window.

As I sat quietly, waiting and watching, I saw a kitty across the street on the other side of the road. Poor cat, I thought. He was all wet and didn't seem to know where to go to get out of the rain. I wanted to go get the kitty, but I knew that the bus driver, Mrs. Foster, would never allow me off the bus. It was against the rules to even stand up, so I knew that I would get in big trouble for trying to rescue a cat across a busy, rainy street. I also thought that if I pointed out the miserable cat, the other kids would probably think that I was weird, even weirder than they already thought I was. I was sure that some of the kids would laugh at the soaked, dripping animal; they would see his misery as their entertainment. I couldn't bear that; I didn't want things to get any worse than they already were.

My window was hazy again, and when I wiped the window clear, I could see that the kitty was now struggling in what seemed to be a surging, grimy river. He was up to his neck in cold water, grasping at the slippery metal bars covering the storm drain in the street. Twigs and other debris rushed past him and down into the black hole. His body had already been sucked into the dark opening of the storm drain, but his little front paws were clinging to the bars. I could see him shaking. He swallowed water and gasped for air as he fought the current with all of his strength. His movements revealed a level of fear that I had never witnessed before. I saw absolute terror in his dark, round eyes.

My heart was racing. Tears were rolling down my cheeks. I felt like I was drowning along with the little kitty. I wanted to rush off the bus without asking permission, and pull the stray cat from the drain, and wrap it up in my warm jacket, safe in my arms. But I also pictured getting into trouble before the cat could be saved, the other kids staring and laughing, and my parents' disappointment in my behavior.

I sat motionless, unable to act. Helpless. The bus began to move forward, the accident traffic finally in motion.

The cat's eyes locked on to mine. He was begging for help. Although the bus was noisy with the clamor of active children, I was sure that

I heard his terrified meow. I could see that he was panicking and needed help right away. I glanced around, but no one else seemed to have noticed.

When Mrs. Foster yelled for me to sit down, I was startled. I hadn't even realized that I was standing up. I immediately sat back down. I did not break rules. I cried as the bus lumbered into motion. I prayed that someone else would notice and rescue my courageous friend. As our bus slowly turned the corner away from the flailing cat, I saw a car drive by the storm drain causing a wave to rise up and over the kitty's head. He appeared again coughing and sneezing but this time with some blood trickling from his mouth and nose. One ear was completely folded back, like it was flipped inside out. The weight of hopelessness blanketed down around me. None of the people on the street seemed to notice the tiny orange feline.

Somehow I managed to stand up again, directly disobeying the bus driver.

"Mrs. Foster!" I cried.

Every single person on the bus stopped talking and looked at me. Waiting.

"A cat. There's a cat in the drain," I stammered. "If we don't help him, he'll drown." I held out a shaking hand and pointed.

The bus driver, to my amazement, did not yell at me. Nor did the other kids laugh at me. Instead, Mrs. Foster pulled the bus to the side of the busy road.

"Children," she said sternly. "No one is to leave this bus."

Then the woman rushed out into the traffic and rain. She sloshed across the street to the drain as we all watched in silence. Even the boys looked concerned. No one was laughing. I noticed that I wasn't the only one crying.

With one quick movement, Mrs. Foster grabbed the cat and pulled him into the safety of her arms. She cradled the terrified, clawing creature, removed her own coat to wrap him in it, and then she raced back to the bus. We all cheered until she motioned for us to be quiet.

"We'll have to look for his owners to see if he has a family already," Mrs. Foster said, as she handed me the sopping bundle.

"I know," I stammered.

"I'll help you," the girl sitting in the front seat whispered to me.

"Me too," came another voice, then another and another.

The other kids did help; we put flyers up all over town, one girl's dad put an advertisement in the paper, and we contacted the local animal shelters, veterinarians and pet stores. That means I was forced to talk to a lot of people, both kids and adults. There was no room for shyness and fear. To my surprise, I slowly gained more confidence in myself and made friends with some of the kids who had helped me. We never did find anyone to claim that cat, so he became a cherished member of my family.

Sure, I was still a pretty good kid after that day, but I learned to speak up, to overcome my shyness. I also learned to say a little prayer and then go for it when something really matters.

— Laura Andrade —

46

The Ugliest Cat in the World

Beauty is not in the face; beauty is a light in the heart.
~Kahlil Gibran

The first time I ever saw Smoky, she was on fire! My three children and I had arrived at the dump outside our Arizona desert town to burn the weekly trash. As we approached the smoldering pit, we heard the most mournful cries of a cat entombed in the smoking rubble.

Suddenly a large cardboard box, which had been wired shut, burst into flames and exploded. With a long, piercing meow, the animal imprisoned within shot into the air like a flaming rocket and dropped into the ash-filled crater.

"Oh, Mama, do something!" three-year-old Jaymee cried as she and Becky, age six, leaned over the smoking hole.

"It can't possibly still be alive," said Scott, fourteen. But the ashes moved, and a tiny kitten, charred almost beyond recognition, miraculously struggled to the surface and crawled toward us in agony.

"I'll get her!" Scott yelled. As my son stood knee-deep in ashes and wrapped the kitten in my bandanna, I wondered why it didn't cry from the added pain. Later we learned we had heard its last meow only moments before.

Back at our ranch, we were doctoring the kitten when my husband, Bill, came in, weary from a long day of fence-mending.

"Daddy! We found a burned-up kitty," Jaymee announced.

When he saw our patient, that familiar "Oh, no, not again!" look crossed his face. This wasn't the first time we had greeted him with an injured animal. Though Bill always grumbled, he couldn't bear to see any living creature suffer. So he helped by building cages, perches, pens and splints for the skunks, rabbits and birds we brought home. This was different, however. This was a cat. And Bill, very definitely, did not like cats.

What's more, this was no ordinary cat. Where fur had been, blisters and a sticky black gum remained. Her ears were gone. Her tail was cooked to the bone. Gone were the claws that would have snatched some unsuspecting mouse. Gone were the little paw pads that would have left telltale tracks on the hoods of our dusty cars and trucks. Nothing that resembled a cat was left — except for two huge cobalt-blue eyes begging for help.

What could we do?

Suddenly I remembered our aloe vera plant and its supposed healing power on burns. So we peeled the leaves, swathed the kitten in slimy aloe strips and gauze bandages, and placed her in Jaymee's Easter basket. All we could see was her tiny face, like a butterfly waiting to emerge from its silk cocoon.

Her tongue was severely burned, and the inside of her mouth was so blistered that she couldn't lap, so we fed her milk and water with an eyedropper. After a while, she began eating by herself.

We named the kitten Smoky.

Three weeks later, the aloe plant was bare. Now we coated Smoky with a salve that turned her body a curious shade of green. Her tail dropped off. Not a hair remained — but the children and I adored her.

Bill didn't. And Smoky despised him. The reason? He was a pipe smoker armed with matches and butane lighters that flashed and burned. Every time he lit up, Smoky panicked, knocking over his coffee cup and lamps before fleeing into the open air duct in the spare bedroom.

"Can't I have any peace around here?" he'd groan.

In time, Smoky became more tolerant of the pipe and its owner. She'd lie on the sofa and glare at Bill as he puffed away. One day he looked at me and chuckled, "Damn cat makes me feel guilty."

By the end of her first year, Smoky resembled a well-used welding glove. Scott was famous among his friends for owning the ugliest pet in the country — probably, the world.

Slowly, oddly, Bill became the one Smoky cared for the most. And before long, I noticed a change in him. He rarely smoked in the house now, and one winter night, to my astonishment, I found him sitting in his chair with the leathery little cat curled up on his lap. Before I could comment, he mumbled a curt, "She's probably cold — no fur, you know."

But Smoky, I reminded myself, liked the touch of cold. Didn't she sleep in front of air ducts and on the cold Mexican-tile floor?

Perhaps Bill was starting to like this strange-looking animal just a bit.

Not everyone shared our feelings for Smoky, especially those who had never seen her. Rumors reached a group of self-appointed animal protectors, and one day one of them arrived at our door.

"I've had numerous calls and letters from so many people," the woman said. "They are concerned about a poor little burned-up cat you have in your house. They say," her voice dropped an octave, "she's suffering. Perhaps it should be put out of its misery?"

I was furious. Bill was even more so. "Burned she was," he said, "but suffering? Look for yourself!"

"Here, kitty," I called. No Smoky. "She's probably hiding," I said, but our guest didn't answer. When I turned and looked at her, the woman's skin was gray, her mouth hung open and two fingers pointed.

Magnified tenfold in all her naked splendor, Smoky glowered at our visitor from her hiding place behind our 150-gallon aquarium. Instead of the "poor little burned-up suffering creature" the woman expected to see, tyrannosaurus Smoky leered at her through the green aquatic haze. Her open jaws exposed saber-like fangs that glinted menacingly in the neon light. Moments later the woman hurried out the door — smiling now, a little embarrassed and greatly relieved.

During Smoky's second year, a miraculous thing happened. She began growing fur. Tiny white hairs, softer and finer than the down on a chick, gradually grew over three inches long, transforming our ugly little cat into a wispy puff of smoke.

Bill continued to enjoy her company, though the two made an incongruous pair — the big weather-worn rancher driving around with an unlit pipe clenched between his teeth, accompanied by the tiny white ball of fluff. When he got out of the truck to check the cattle, he left the air conditioner on maximum-cold for her comfort. Her blue eyes watered, the pink nose ran, but she sat there, unblinking, in ecstasy. Other times, he picked her up, and holding her close against his denim jacket, took her along.

Smoky was three years old on the day she went with Bill to look for a missing calf. Searching for hours, he left the truck door open whenever he got out to look. The pastures were parched and crisp with dried grasses and tumbleweed. A storm loomed on the horizon, and still no calf. Discouraged, without thinking, Bill reached into his pocket for his lighter and spun the wheel. A spark shot to the ground and, in seconds, the field was on fire.

Frantic, Bill didn't think about the cat. Only after the fire was under control, and the calf found, did he return home and remember.

"Smoky!" he cried. "She must have jumped out of the truck! Did she come home?"

No. And we knew she'd never find her way home from two miles away. To make matters worse, it had started to rain — so hard we couldn't go out to look for her.

Bill was distraught, blaming himself. We spent the next day searching, wishing she could meow for help, and knowing she'd be helpless against predators. It was no use.

Two weeks later, Smoky still wasn't home. We were afraid she was dead by now, for the rainy season had begun, and the hawks, wolves and coyotes had families to feed.

Then came the biggest rainstorm our region had experienced in fifty years. By morning, flood waters stretched for miles, marooning wildlife and cattle on scattered islands of higher ground. Frightened rabbits, raccoons, squirrels and desert rats waited for the water to subside, while Bill and Scott waded knee-deep, carrying bawling calves back to their mamas and safety.

The girls and I were watching intently when suddenly Jaymee

shouted, "Daddy! There's a poor little rabbit over there. Can you get it?"

Bill waded to the spot where the animal lay, but when he reached out to help the tiny creature, it seemed to shrink back in fear. "I don't believe it," Bill cried. "It's Smoky!" His voice broke. "Little Smoky!"

My eyes ached with tears when that pathetic little cat crawled into the outstretched hands of the man she had grown to love. He pressed her shivering body to his chest, talked to her softly, and gently wiped the mud from her face. All the while her blue eyes fastened on his with unspoken understanding. He was forgiven.

Smoky came home again. The patience she showed as we shampooed her astounded us. We fed her scrambled eggs and ice cream, and to our joy she seemed to get well.

But Smoky had never really been strong. One morning when she was barely four years old, we found her limp in Bill's chair. Her heart had simply stopped.

As I wrapped her tiny body in one of Bill's red neckerchiefs and placed her in a child's shoe box, I thought about the many things our precious Smoky had taught us — things about trust, affection and struggling against the odds when everything says you can't win. She reminded us that it's not what's outside that counts — it's what's inside, deep in our hearts.

— Penny Porter —

Wild Turkeys and Cat Calls

Motivation is what gets you started.
Habit is what keeps you going.
~Jim Rohn

After studying wildlife in the hot, harsh African bush for twenty-three years, my husband Mark and I were sun-weary and snow-starved. We decided that it was finally time to trade our tattered desert tent for something more substantial and less sandy. So we relocated to a small, wild valley in northern Idaho.

Surrounded by mountains and forests, dotted with glacial lakes and lined with rocky streams, this land was the opposite of our African home, but we welcomed the change. Rather than observe lions, elephants and giraffes, we watched moose, white-tailed deer and black bears crisscross our meadows. But of all these animals, we became especially attached to the wild turkeys.

Several years before we arrived, the Idaho Fish and Game Department introduced wild turkeys to the area. These charismatic birds are not indigenous this far north and cannot survive without handouts during the long, frigid winters. We inherited a flock of about forty birds on our land, and we gladly participated in the Department's program of providing food for them in the winter. I took this job very seriously, and clad in my new wardrobe of fleece, wool and down, I waded into the deep snow every morning and evening to feed the turkeys.

About the same time that I adopted the turkeys, Mark surprised me with two kittens for our anniversary. He knew that after watching lions and leopards for so many years in the bush, I longed for a cat of my own that I could cuddle. However, due to the high density of coyotes and the occasional cougar, the cats weren't safe outside at night. Every evening when I fed the turkeys, I would call, "kitty, kitty, kitty," and they would scramble into the warm security of our cabin.

The turkeys soon learned that shortly after I called the cats, I spread the corn onto the snow. All the toms and hens would come running from the woods whenever they heard me. And they were not the only ones. The white-tailed deer and the crows also thought that "Kitty, kitty, kitty" meant, "Soup's on!" So whenever I called the cats, we would have forty turkeys, fifteen deer and numerous crows munching in the yard.

Perhaps I was a bit overenthusiastic in my feedings. In a few years we had more than eighty turkeys glaring at us through our windows if I was late with their food. These "wild" birds would prance around the picnic table and perch on the porch, flapping their wings until I emerged with the bucket of corn.

During mating season, the toms, wanting to impress the females, became very vocal. "GOBBLE GOBBLE GOBBLE" echoed through the forests and meadows for most of the day. The slightest noise would set them off, and to our amazement, whenever I called, "kitty, kitty, kitty," they would respond, "GOBBLE GOBBLE GOBBLE."

One day a local sportsman drove down our road and stopped his rifle-racked pickup at our cabin. He had noticed our large flock of turkeys and wanted a closer look.

"You can call 'em, you know. I'm pretty good at it," he said. "Old trick I learned from years in the woods. Ya wanna see?"

Before we could answer, he pumped up his chest, twisted his fingers into some kind of complicated knot, puckered his lips and produced a loud "GOBBLE GOBBLE GOBBLE." Sure enough, the turkeys answered rather weakly from the woods: "Gobble Gobble Gobble."

"Oh, yeah?" I replied. "Watch this."

In my sweetest voice, I called, "Kitty, kitty, kitty."

And from the woods came a resounding thunder:

"GOBBLE GOBBLE GOBBLE." Then, more than eighty birds came

running toward us as fast as their scrawny legs could carry them.

Later, I told Mark that I hoped I hadn't offended the old guy.

"I wouldn't worry about it. Just wait until his friends catch him in the woods during turkey season, calling, 'Kitty, kitty, kitty!'"

—Delia Owens—

48

Under His Spell

Dogs have owners, cats have staff.
~Author Unknown

I can feel him watching me
Through golden eyes, unblinking,
And I can't help but wonder
Just what it is he's thinking.

I know his habits, I know his ways
But his moods are hard to tell
The only thing I know for sure is
He knows I'm under his spell.

For eating he's claimed my nicest dish
To nap, my favorite chair
And anytime I want to sit,
He's comfortably resting there.

For play, he's got expensive toys
To chase and romp and caper
But still he's only happy with
A balled-up piece of paper!

He's always begging for attention
To be scratched beneath his chin
And when my writing takes me away from him
He steals my writing pen!

Despite our unique relationship
People ask, "Just who owns who?"
It's really nice to have someone
To look forward to come home to.

And so, I stay enchanted with
This crazy pet of mine
For nothing keeps you spellbound
Like a furry, finicky feline!

—Tami Sandlin—

We Are Family

49

Just Right

*Christmas magic is silent. You don't hear it —
you feel it. You know it. You believe it.*
~Kevin Alan Milne

wrote out the letter in my best handwriting before walking to the
post office with my mother to mail it.

Dear Santa,

> *Thank you once again for the Giant Book of Fairytales last
> year. It was smashing. I choose a different bedtime story every night.*
> *We moved houses this summer, but Mummy says you'll know
> where to find us. Our new house doesn't have a chimney. I hope
> this isn't a problem.*
> *This year I'd like a cat, please, but I don't know how you
> will deliver one. I am responsible and will feed and brush the cat
> every day. I promise.*
> *I hope you and the workshop elves are all well.*
> *Please give the reindeer a pat for me. I'll leave out carrots
> on Christmas Eve.*

Love from Sue

On Christmas morning, I found an enormous, gaily wrapped box
with my name on the label. I started to tear off the festive paper but

remembered I'd told Santa I was a responsible girl, so I gently peeled away the wrapping, careful not to scare the cat inside.

When I lifted the flaps and peeked in, I found cat litter and a tray, along with boxes of dried and canned cat food. There was a food bowl and a water dish, both decorated with paw patterns, and a sparkly cat collar with a jingle bell. A stocking was filled with cat toys: things that rolled and clicked, and catnip-infused, neon-coloured feathers on elastic. There was even a grooming kit of a brush and claw clippers so I could be true to my word and brush the cat every day. Squished at the bottom lay a plush cat bed.

But there was no cat.

I started to cry. "Santa thought I wanted presents for a cat."

"Santa doesn't make mistakes," said Mommy. "Look. What's that envelope?"

The red envelope bearing my name lay hidden under wrapping paper.

Dear Sue,

I couldn't put your cat in my sack. He'd get scared and claw his way out.

He is waiting for you at the shelter.

You will recognise him.

I am glad you are still enjoying your book.

The elves and the reindeer say hello.

Merry Christmas,
Santa Claus

I spent the day arranging and rearranging the bed and toys. My mother helped me clear a shelf in the larder for the cat food.

The next day, we visited the shelter. I thought that Santa must have been very busy with cat requests because there were lots of other children there, too.

Then I saw it. There were kittens galore, but an older striped cat cowered at the back of the enclosure, hissing at whoever approached. That cat looked like he might be the one I was supposed to recognise. I sat cross-legged in front of the open cage and waited patiently. He eventually limped out and climbed into my lap. He curled up, closed his orange eyes, and rumbled like a train.

"Thank you, Santa," I said over my new cat's purring head. "He's absolutely perfect."

—Sue Mitchell—

50

The Catmas Tree

There is, incidentally, no way of talking about cats that
enables one to come off as a sane person.
~Dan Greenberg

When we first got a housecat, our concern was that he would chew on the cords of the Christmas tree lights. We need not have worried about that particular issue, as the aptly named Stinker had other ways of aggravating the bipeds. He had no interest in the electrical cords circling the tree.

He wanted to eat the tree itself. And climb it.

December became the month when small piles of regurgitated pine needles would appear around the house. When we acquired a second housecat, Mr. Z, he also showed no interest in the electrical cords, but the quantity of regurgitated needles increased.

Verbal admonishments have no effect on cats, so we needed a different approach to deter them from nibbling on the conifer. When winter rolled around, our very creative Mom would carefully brush hot habanero sauce onto the needles of the Christmas tree, at least on the lower branches. She also cut small habanero chilies into thin slices and hung the small rings of orange and red pepper around the lower branches of the tree like tiny ornaments. The idea was that a tree that rated 100,000 to 350,000 on the Scoville heat scale would be unappetizing to our fuzzy housemates. It seemed to work to some extent — there were fewer piles of barfed up needles scattered around the house. However, perhaps in retaliation, the felines began chewing on the edges of any gifts placed beneath the tree, and trying to eat the wrapping paper. In response, Mom dusted the Christmas presents with a fine layer of powdered cayenne pepper.

The spicy odor that emanated from the Christmas tree seemed to keep the cats away but also made the area somewhat unpleasant for people. An alternative solution that had occurred to several of us was to replace the real tree with a fake one, in the (vain) belief that the cats would find synthetic needles unappealing. It took a while to convince Dad that this was the course to take, as he is a man of habit who prefers dragging a dead tree into the house every December.

At first there was joy in the house that the tree-shaped decoration would not have to be drenched in capsaicin juice. The joy subsided when a small pile of regurgitated silk needles was found near the front door.

These days, we have a kind of truce during the Christmas season. The housecats haven't completely given up on chewing the tree, but they do seem to find synthetic needles less appetizing. As for us humans? Well, at least the presents don't make us sneeze anymore.

— E. Sutton —

51

Wild Kingdom

Heav'n has no Rage, like Love to Hatred turn'd,
Nor Hell a Fury, like a Squirrel scorn'd.
~"Chippy" Congreve

I was eight years old and I would remember that Christmas forever. It all started when my father made the announcement at dinner that we were not going to do our typical "tree night." We always did the same thing. We would go out to dinner, drive around a bit to enjoy the holiday lights, and then wind up at the same tree lot. We made a big deal out of choosing just the right tree, and then drove home with our prize tied on top of our car. We would spend the rest of the evening setting it up and decorating it. I would get to stay up as late as I wanted, but typically wound up asleep on the couch, leaving my parents to finish the decorating.

Mom and I had already made dozens of cookies with red and green ribbons through them that we would hang on the tree. As the boxes were slowly unpacked there was a bowl of popcorn to munch on while listening to Mom telling the same, familiar stories of Christmases past that were attached to each ornament.

But this year, my father said we were going to cut down our own tree. I wasn't too happy about this. Dad was definitely not the outdoor type. But, he said, business friends of both my parents had recently bought some land that had a lot of Douglas fir trees on it and they offered to let us choose one for Christmas. We could drive out to their ranch early in the morning, enjoy a nice visit and brunch with them, cut our own tree and be home by late afternoon to set it up. It would be fun.

It took some cajoling to get me to go along with it. I didn't like change. I preferred the comfort of our rituals. However, when Dad told me they had horses, I changed my mind. Like a lot of kids, I was horse crazy.

So it was all set. The day came and the trip was long, but the ranch was beautiful and there were a lot of fir trees. They had to drag me away from the horses to actually help choose one, but finally it was done and Dad and his friend cut it down and tied it to the top of the car.

I had to admit that it was a beautiful tree. It was much deeper green and very thick. It was much prettier than the trees on the lots. The ritual at home went as it always had. Dad set up the tree in the stand and attached the lights. Mom told stories as she unwrapped the ornaments. We munched popcorn and hung the ornaments, cookies and tinsel, while the music of familiar carols filled the air.

I don't know what time I fell asleep on the couch, but I do remember it was 3 a.m. according to the clock by my bed when I woke up to hear my parents yelling, a cat screeching, a dog barking and what sounded like a train rumbling and bumping from the living room and down the hall between our bedrooms.

The bumping and banging was the Christmas tree. Our dog Lassie was completely entangled like she had on a harness in the light strings and was now charging up the hall back toward the living room hauling the tree behind her. A terrified squirrel was about two feet ahead of the raging dog, only to be met by Mom's cat, Mr. Mitty, who dove off of the top of the drapes at the terrified animal.

Mom pushed me back into my room and dashed after Dad to help. Of course, I came out and watched from the hall. Dad managed to grab Lassie but she was so tangled in the light strings the best he could do was carry her back into the hall where he and Mom pushed her into the bathroom, tree and all, and shut the door. Lassie, however, was not going to go silently and a volley of barking came from behind the door.

Mitty had the terrified squirrel cornered on the mantel, which was now devoid of all holiday decorations. The squirrel was ready to fight. Dad tried to move between the cat and the little beast, just as Mitty took a leap. He missed the squirrel but landed on Dad's back with all four paws — claws out. Dad screamed, fell over a chair and the cat took off for parts unknown. Now it was just Mom, Dad and one very upset gray squirrel. Evidently, that tree had been his or her home and the branches were so thick that the little creature simply hid away in them until the decorating was done and the lights went out. Then it ventured out, only to be met by a Collie and a Tomcat. It probably jumped back into the tree for safety, but both the other animals had already seen it and jumped into the tree too.

Dad motioned to Mom to open the back door. She slipped past him, opened the door and then she hurried back. Dad picked up a magazine and swung it at the squirrel and started yelling. Mom picked up a throw pillow and did the same. Not to be left out, I ran into the living room yelling and waving my arms. We went through the house like hunters beating the bushes for game until the squirrel took the best path of retreat and dashed out the back door and up a tall elm tree to safety.

It was now around 3:30 in the morning and we all stood looking at a house in total ruin. Instead of getting mad, Dad started laughing, Mom joined in and we all went into the kitchen. Mom made some hot cocoa and we sat at the kitchen table reliving the event and laughing even harder — until Lassie started to howl.

Dad got up to go take care of the poor dog and see if anything at all could be salvaged from the ruins. Mom hustled me off to bed.

Mom and Dad spent the wee hours of Christmas morning putting everything back into place the best they could, and when I got up, although short a few ornaments, and all of the cookies (Lassie ate them), the tree looked perfect to me. The presents were there and all was right with the world — except Mom and Dad were not quite as chipper as they were on other Christmas mornings.

It was our first and last venture into cutting down our own tree. However, it did create a memory that lasted through generations.

— Joyce Laird —

52

Bake Bubba Happy

Grandmas never run out of hugs or cookies.
~Author Unknown

M y husband was racing down the highway, trying to make it through the border before it closed completely due to the COVID-19 crisis. He had just picked up his mother, who lived alone in France, a short twenty-five-mile journey from the German border. He was bringing her back to our house near the NATO base in Ramstein, Germany.

He had taken much more time than he had planned to load her things into the van because she had insisted on taking her whole pantry of food supplies along with her. I rolled my eyes when he told me about it over the phone. She is strong-willed and not always the easiest person to get along with, so there was no sense in arguing with her about it. We would have to grin and bear it over the next few months that we planned to live together.

My mother-in-law is a pack rat who has always kept a vast supply of non-perishable food items in her house, along with vegetables that would last for a long time. A cellar full of potatoes had saved her family from starvation in France during the Second World War, a lesson she never forgot. The COVID-19 epidemic brought back the desperation of the war years, so she doesn't take food storage lightly. When my husband went to pick her up, she insisted on taking all the goods with her. Now it was questionable whether they'd make it through the border before the total lockdown.

Biting my nails, I finally received a text from my husband saying they had made it through just as the guards were shutting down the border. I was relieved that they would be able to make it back to our house and had managed to load up all of Denise's stuff. We kept a reasonably well-stocked pantry at home, but it paled in comparison to hers. All the extra foodstuffs would come in handy during a long isolation period.

Our black Labrador, Bubba, would be thrilled when Denise arrived. He considered her his grandma and was always spoiled with treats and snuggles during her stays with us. He had been less than pleased with us lately since we were already rationing the treats for ourselves and all our pets during the lockdown. He could also sense our high level of anxiety.

As soon as Grandma Denise arrived, Bubba ran to greet her and jumped for joy, almost knocking her to the ground with his enthusiasm. His tail was wagging so hard that half his body jerked back and forth. She was his person. She hugged his scruffy neck and tossed him a couple of snacks, which he scarfed in the air before they hit the ground. Then they walked inside together like two old buddies, while my husband and I stood there watching before lugging in box after box of groceries.

The next morning, we awoke to a wonderful aroma wafting from the kitchen. Pancakes! Throwing on our robes, we made haste to the kitchen to get them while they were hot off the griddle. We needn't have hurried. Bubba was already there in the kitchen, leaning his head on Grandma's leg as she flipped his special doggie gluten-free buckwheat pancakes. She had even made him a tasty peanut-butter sauce as a topping. Bubba's tail was beating the kitchen cupboards like a drum. In this new age of social distancing, it was delightful to see them snuggling. We would just have to wait for our favorite pancakes to be made afterwards, but it would be worth it. We had to admit that Denise was an excellent cook, certainly better than we were. Bubba was bringing out the best in her.

As many people learned during the coronavirus shutdown, it's tempting to eat extra snacks when hanging around the house more than usual. While working from home wearing gym clothes, it's easy to miss any weight gain. Putting on the Coronavirus Fifteen had already become a thing, so we had made a point of not stocking up on many extra snacks. We had already been regretting that decision, so the sweet aroma of cookies coming from the kitchen later that day had us moaning in anticipation and soon scooting in that direction. We arrived in time to see Denise sitting with Bubba's head in her lap, with our other rescue dogs lying at her feet, all patiently waiting for her homemade doggie biscuits to bake. It looked like she was baking enough to last through the whole pandemic. Happily, a couple of trays of cookies for humans were on the kitchen counter, waiting for their turn in the oven. We were beginning to see who had priority here, though we were happy to wait for our share.

We always had a ragtag mix of stray cats around that called our place home. Bubba was a friendly giant who loved all other creatures and tried to befriend them. But the cats were generally wary of our dogs and stayed aloof. Now, however, they were curious about the wonderful aromas from the kitchen and the special relationship Bubba had with Grandma, the source of all the delicious goodies. Soon, they were circling around her legs as well as Bubba's as she continued to bake goodies for everyone in our place while he stuck to her like glue.

Bubba couldn't have been happier. His humans were all in one place and always home now, including his favorite person on the planet. The other dogs looked up to him because he had such a special relationship with the person who baked the treats. And he was now finally befriended by the elusive cats for the same reason. His exuberant disposition had managed to unite us all.

We were happy again, too. The lockdown gave us a break from our hectic lives, while working from home allowed us to become reacquainted with each other. Our relationship with my mother-in-law was improving quickly as well because we had finally slowed down enough to appreciate her again. We also saw the wisdom of her planning and forethought when it came to keeping supplies, not to mention the enjoyment we derived from the fantastic meals she put together. Not only had she baked Bubba happy, but she had melted all our hearts in a kitchen filled with love.

—Donna L. Roberts—

53

Guilty Steps

Every day I will find something to laugh about.
~*Richard Simmons*, The Book of Hope

In my on and off battle against the bulge, the bulge was winning to the tune of 20 pounds. Okay, 25 pounds. That didn't mean I was waving the white flag and giving up. No, I simply retreated to the couch with my honor guard, a six-pack of donuts, to decide on my next step.

Step? Of course, that was it. I'd walk myself thin. I would become, pardon the pun, a foot soldier in the battle against fat. And I would start immediately. Well, immediately after I finished eating my faithful troops. After all, I was going to need the energy for my walking.

To put my program on a scientific footing, I went out and bought an electronic pedometer, a device that counts every step you take. Now, as long as the batteries held up, I would have a daily record of my progress.

I even bought a calendar and a bright red pen to write down the number of steps I took each day. I put the calendar on the fridge where I would see it every time I opened the fridge. That way the calendar and I would be seeing a lot of each other.

Then I opened the package and took out my nifty pedometer. I felt healthier just holding it. Although the instructions were obviously written by someone whose first language wasn't English, I finally figured out which little red buttons to push to make the thing work.

I held my breath, sucked in my stomach, stretched out the

waistband of my pants, and popped the gizmo on. I slowly released the waistband, hoping nothing would explode. But my pants and the gizmo looked fine.

So, I got off the couch and started walking around the house. Then I remembered to turn it on and started walking again.

Ten steps from the couch to the fridge, 12 steps from the couch to the bathroom, 25 steps from the couch to my bedroom. The fact that I kept using the couch as my reference point told me I hadn't bought the gadget a minute too soon. But as I watched those little numbers add up, I felt a surge of optimism.

This was going to be easier than I thought.

That night I put the pedometer next to my bed so I would remember to put it on as soon as I got up. The next morning I rolled out of bed, popped the gizmo on my pj's and started walking. Let's see, go to the bathroom, feed two cats, go upstairs, give third cat medicine, go back downstairs, walk to the closet and get clothes, get dressed, go back upstairs. Oops, run back downstairs, take gizmo off pj's and put it on pants.

By the end of the day I had logged 954 steps. By the end of the week my calendar was filled with little red numbers, each day showing a bigger total. I admit some of the increase was when I discovered I could have my cake and eat it too. Instead of sitting down to eat, I ate while walking around the house. By the way, don't try it with soup.

The more I ate, the higher my little red numbers went. I figured the steps canceled out the calories. The scale, however, took a different view.

Unfortunately, in the middle of the third week the cats found the pedometer on the night table. It took me two days and a lot of crawling around on my hands and knees before I finally found it under the couch hidden behind old candy wrappers, elastic bands and enough cat hair to knit another cat.

Based on the tiny teeth marks I found on it, I think the cats hoped it was food, then decided it was a toy. Or maybe they also tried the eat-and-walk program.

Although I felt I had gotten a lot of exercise crawling around, technically it wasn't walking. I wrote those two days off which meant two blank days on the calendar. I promised myself I would get right back on the bandwagon the next day and I did. And the day after that.

Then came the fateful day. I had every intention of walking, really I did, but it was raining outside and the couch looked so inviting and I was reading a good book and the cats all decided to sit on me.

One thing led to another, or in this case didn't lead anywhere. By the end of the day the number on the pedometer was so dismal that I didn't have the heart to write it on my calendar — I just left the square blank.

That was the beginning of the end. Every time I walked into the kitchen to look at the calendar and saw those blank squares, I felt a little pang of guilt which led to chocolate cake guilt, ice cream guilt and potato chip guilt. The guilt just got bigger and bigger and so did I. I finally realized I had to do something about the guilt or I would end up the size of my refrigerator.

I ripped the calendar off the fridge and went back to my couch.

All was not lost. I gave the pedometer to the cats who have been running and batting it all over the house and the numbers just keep growing and growing. I'm pretty sure two of them have lost a little weight.

You know something else? Now that I don't feel guilty, I've lost five pounds.

— Harriet Cooper —

54

Sweet Metamorphosis

Find what makes your heart sing
and create your own music.
~Mac Anderson

y dog Foxy has turned into a cat. He refuses to eat dog food
of any kind, canned or kibble, he sleeps with a fifteen-year-
old tomcat draped across his back, and he has taught himself
how to meow. His backstory is complicated and strange, but
considering the dog, it's not totally surprising.

In 2007 I rescued my best friend, a Pug/Jack Russell Terrier mix
who was about three years old. I found him the week of the Fourth
of July and named him Sparky. I scoured the neighborhood to see
if anyone lost him, and ran a "found ad" in the local paper with no
response. Some kids at my local park told me they'd seen a driver pull
up and toss him out, then drive away.

That did it for me. I updated all his shots and got him a new
collar and license.

He was an amazing friend. He loved cats and was very protective
of me, his rescued cat family and our house, but still a total love-bucket
to people he met on our walks and friends who came to visit.

In 2010, Sparky rescued a sidekick — a matted, rag-tag pup who
had been severely abused, neglected and finally abandoned behind
the locked gate of an abandoned house when his family was evicted.
Sparky adopted him, and I named him Foxy because he looks like a
black, furry fox.

Unfortunately, Foxy was brain damaged from the abuse he suffered as a pup with the rough kids in that family. It was not anything that would kill him or require special treatment, but he basically never grew up. He has remained "puppy-like" all of his life.

Sparky was always Foxy's guard, guide and mentor. Whatever Sparky did, Foxy did. Foxy developed Sparky's great love for cats and kittens and even went one step further. While Sparky was tolerant of all the cats, his heart belonged to the litter he had found in the bushes of our front driveway. Foxy loved them too, but also loves all cats, allowing them to snuggle into his long, thick fur on cold days.

One big difference between the two dogs was that Sparky loved to jump onto the couch and curl up with his rescue cat Ringo. Sparky and Ringo also slept on my bed with me every night. Foxy was and still is, terrified of furniture, probably from brutal experiences with his former owners. Nothing can cajole him to jump onto furniture or even jump up to be petted. If I try to entice him with treats, he falls over on his side and whimpers. I rub his furry belly and give him a goodie and then he runs around in circles in puppy heaven. The issue was solved with dog beds that Foxy loved but Sparky totally ignored, preferring my furniture and his cat.

In mid 2019, I noticed a small lump on Sparky's chest and took him to the vet. It was cancer. Sparky died in his sleep in the spring of 2020. As hard as this was for me, it was devastating for Foxy. His big brother, hero and mentor was suddenly gone. For Ringo the cat, his father was gone. Sparky had raised him from the day his little cat eyes opened. Both animals were devastated. The other eleven cats felt their pain and rallied around them for comfort. It was a very hard time for Foxy. He kept close to me for comfort for a long time and searched for his best friend for days.

Slowly, strange things started to happen. First it was the food. Foxy would not touch any dry dog food, but ate only cat kibble. I wound up putting the dog kibble outside for the raccoons so it would not go to waste. The canned dog food was not wasted because cats are not as picky and happily gobbled it all up along with their food. Foxy would, and still will, only eat canned cat food.

Then strange sounds started coming from the back yard. At first the neighbors and I thought a bobcat or some other wild creature had drifted down into our area because of the many recent forest fires. It was a very loud "Meow-r-oo-oow" — a huskier sound than any normal cat could make. We all kept an eye out for the beast and hoped for the best.

Then I caught him. I heard the yowl and rushed to the back door to see if I could spot the wild thing before it disappeared again. I peeked through the curtain, hoping not to scare it away by opening the door. But it wasn't some strange wild animal; it was Foxy. He was sitting on top of the doghouse with old Ringo lying next to him, practicing his best canine version of a meow. I think Ringo was tutoring him. Now all the neighbors know what the sound is and Foxy is proud to show off his "new language" to anyone on cue.

Every creature on earth has a way of coping with loss and heartbreak. With Sparky gone, my little thirteen-year-old Foxy has decided to become a giant cat and take over as leader of our feline tribe. He and Ringo are curled up next to my chair as I type this, and looking down at them snuggled together makes me smile.

— Joyce Laird —

55

The $100,000 Stray Cat

Most cats, when they are Out want to be In,
and vice versa, and often simultaneously.
~Louis J. Camuti

O ne orphan kitty with golden eyes — it's hard to believe all he has inspired.

I've always loved cats. But until nine years ago, my pet cats suffered a high mortality rate. I decided that my next cat was going to live indoors only. Besides, I love wild birds, and this way I could be sure my cat wouldn't hunt birds or little woodland creatures.

But then came Oliver. My sister works at a veterinarian's office. One day she called up and pleaded with me to come see a six-month-old kitten that had been abandoned there. They were having trouble finding him a home. The other staff found him ordinary. They only kept him because he was a willing blood donor. It broke my sister's heart to see the little kitten offer his paw for the needle and then purr while his blood was being withdrawn.

I went to the office and within thirty seconds had fallen in love. The kitten had short but soft black fur with a white undercoat, a round, pudgy face and luminous golden eyes. He was dignified but affectionate. I instantly thought of the name Oliver, after the Charles Dickens orphan. Home we went — together.

But Oliver didn't want to be an indoors-only cat. He cried at the door, paced around the house, and tried to run outside whenever we opened a door. After much family discussion, we decided to build an outdoor cat run, an enclosed area where Oliver could safely spend time during the day. With the help of my dad, a retired carpenter, we built a thirty-by-fifteen-foot structure that had chicken-wire fencing on its sides and top.

Inside the cat run was a long strip of grass, food, water, litter pan, toys, scratching posts, a planter with catnip, and plenty of perches and high shelves. Oliver adored it. He loved lying in the grass, basking in the sun, chasing bugs and watching birds fly by.

But that wasn't the end of it. Oh, no. The cat run overlooked our vacant, one-acre lot. Wouldn't it be wonderful, I decided, if we could grow a wildlife garden there to attract more creatures for Oliver to watch? So I read books and magazines, visited nurseries and went on garden tours to educate myself. I was a little nervous about tackling such an ambitious project — I'm rather shy, really — but, I reasoned, no one would ever see the garden but us.

I recruited my dad to help. He quickly became so enthusiastic that he began adding his own ideas. His contagious spirit spread to my other family members, and before I knew it, we were all out there clearing the field, preparing the soil, marking out paths and starting to plant. We put in trees, shrubs, perennials, annuals, bulbs — thousands of plants over a two-year period. Dad built arbors, trellises, pergolas, benches, a pond with waterfalls and a bridge. We started collecting all sorts of garden décor — statues, stepping stones, fountains, planters, wind chimes, flags, birdhouses and wind vanes — all with cat designs. A friend even made me wooden signs saying "Meow Meadows," "Cat Country" and "Kitty Grazing Area." Everything was purr-fect!

And even that wasn't the end of it. A friend recommended our garden for Spokane's big annual garden tour. So on a hot August Sunday afternoon, I had five thousand people tour our garden. People went nuts over it! They didn't respond as much to the planting scheme as to the heartfelt emotion that went into it all. For weeks afterward, I was in the newspaper and being interviewed on TV. People called constantly.

Since that day, the Meyer Cat Garden is no longer our "little family secret." Over 10,000 people have visited it — everyone from nursing home residents to a tour group from a national garden convention.

During my now well-practiced speech, I emphasize the importance of caring for your pets properly so they don't harm wildlife.

And wildlife we've got. As the garden has grown, it's attracted birds, frogs, squirrels, chipmunks, even raccoons, skunks and deer. I've grown, too. I'm now a master gardener and president of our local garden club, and I'm comfortable with both writing and public speaking. And our whole family has grown: Working on such a tremendous project has drawn us all closer together.

And what about Oliver? He watches it all contentedly through his cat run—his window to the world. Our family joke is that if we added up the cost of all the thousands of plants, cat decorations and hours of labor that went into the Meyer Cat Garden, we have easily spent over $100,000.

That's why we call Oliver our $100,000 stray cat.

But you know what? He was a bargain.

— ViAnn Meyer —

56

Vavoom's Lesson in Love

You can't stay in your corner of the forest waiting
for others to come to you. You have to go
to them sometimes.
~Winnie the Pooh

The Bible says that "perfect love casts out fear." I had never seen that demonstrated until I met Vavoom, a tiny calico feral cat.

Vavoom blew in with a blizzard one winter, and spent her days with two male companions in the relative warmth and safety of my crawlspace. Despite the temperatures dropping well below zero several times that January, Vavoom never showed any inclination to come into my house; I could *feed* her, but she insisted that I keep my distance, thank you very much! Like many feral cats, Vavoom and her friends viewed me as the enemy, a necessary evil in their environment who provided food and shelter, but who could never fully he trusted.

Spring came, and Vavoom became pregnant. She remained in the crawlspace of the house, popping out twice daily to meow at the back door for her dinner. She felt comfortable enough to ask for food, but still would flinch and run if I attempted to pet her.

Then the rain came. Lots of it. Enough in one morning to turn my back yard into a small pond, which began to drain into the crawlspace.

The power of the rainfall and wind had knocked over some potted plants I kept outside. I went out into the torrent to upright them and noticed, running toward me, a very skinny Vavoom with something small and pink in her mouth.

She had a look of urgency in her eyes and came straight toward me. She dropped her parcel on my shoe, and meowed.

It was a newborn kitten.

The kitten was hairless, premature, and turning blue from wet and exposure. I immediately picked it up and put it in the pouch of my sweat top to warm it. I picked up Vavoom without a struggle, and took the family into my utility room, where I had a cardboard box. I filled the box with soft rags, and placed the kitten into the box. Mother Vavoom jumped happily into her nest. I brought her a dish of food and some milk, sat down next to the box, and started to pet her. Instead of ducking, Vavoom thrust her head back into my hand and purred.

The next day, I found her other three kittens; they had drowned during the flooding. Apparently, Vavoom knew she could only save one, and believed I was her kitten's only hope of survival. Her desire to save her kitten's life was more important than her own fears and mistrust.

Vavoom and her kitten, George, are still part of my family. As a matter of fact, George is my brat cat — as friendly and companionable as his mother was shy and aloof. George has known only love during his life, beginning with the perfect, mother's love that saved him.

— Jean Fritz —

57

Barney

Kindness is the greatest wisdom.
~Author Unknown

Mary Guy figured that becoming a national celebrity was probably about as much as a squirrel could hope to achieve in one lifetime. But Barney is not your average squirrel.

Mary has a bottled water business in Garden City, Kansas. She is also a known animal lover. One day in August of 1994, one of her customers showed her an orphaned baby fox squirrel that he had found. When he asked if she could care for it, she felt she had to at least give it a try.

It so happened that a week earlier, Mary's cat, Corky, had had four kittens. Mary's husband, Charlie, suggested they try adding the squirrel to the litter of kittens — and it worked! Barney (named by a grandson after a particular purple dinosaur) was not only adopted by Corky, he was accepted as a sibling by all four kittens. He became especially close with one feline sister, Celeste.

Some of the Guys' guests thought this cat/squirrel family was so adorable that they contacted the local newspaper about it. The paper ran a story with a photo of the mother cat nursing her four kittens and Barney under the headline: "One of these kittens seems sort of squirrelly."

The unusual story was picked up by the Associated Press and sent to newspapers all over the country. As a result, Mary received calls and letters from all over the country, and even Canada, by people who were impressed with the story and picture. Barney was a celebrity!

Unfortunately, there was a downside to Barney's fame.

The article was seen by employees of the Kansas Department of Wildlife and Parks. A state official contacted the Guys and told them that it is illegal to keep a squirrel as a pet in the state of Kansas. They would have to return Barney to the wild.

Mary was thunderstruck. Not only had she become attached to her unusual pet, she feared for his life if he were turned loose. He had no fear of cats—he'd been raised by one! But squirrels are rodents and cats are natural enemies of rodents. If Barney were turned loose, he'd be lunch for the first stray cat he met. She explained this to the authorities, but to no avail. The law's the law.

"Well, ma'am," suggested one officer, "if you buy a hunting license, you can legally keep him until the end of squirrel season. It runs until December 31."

It was a temporary solution, but Mary hurried out to pay the thirteen dollars for a hunting license.

Mary grieved as the end of the year approached. She had come to truly love the mischievous little guy and was certain that turning him loose was tantamount to a death sentence.

Also, by this time, all of the kittens had been adopted except Celeste; and she and Barney were now best friends. They played together, slept together and chased each other all over the house. If Mary separated them, Celeste wailed miserably. And Barney showed not the slightest interest in life in the great outdoors.

Mary again approached the newspapers. Perhaps the same notoriety that had landed Barney in this mess could lead to a solution.

The story of Barney's plight went out over the Associated Press wires. By early December, Mary was deluged with calls and letters from all over the country offering their prayers and moral support. Some callers who lived in states with differing laws even offered to take in both Barney and Celeste.

The Wildlife and Parks Department also received calls and mail from around the country. Not wanting to look heartless, they suggested that Barney might be released at the Garden City Zoo's park.

The Kansas Attorney General called Mary and suggested that she give Barney to a "rehabilitator" who would teach him to survive in the wild before releasing him.

Still, Mary feared for the safety of her beloved pet — and knew he didn't want to leave his happy life any more than she wanted to lose him.

As New Year's Eve approached, the Guys saw one slim chance. The new year would bring a new administration into the Kansas statehouse. Mary arranged for friends who were invited to the new governor's inaugural celebration to take information about Barney with them.

One of the first acts of the Kansas governor's office in 1995 was to issue the Guys a special permit to keep their squirrel.

And so Barney became the first squirrel in history to not only become a national celebrity, but to receive a pardon from the governor.

No, not your average squirrel at all.

— Gregg Bassett —

58

Tiny and the Oak Tree

Tears are the safety valve of the heart
when too much pressure is laid on it.
~Albert Smith

He was scary-looking. Standing about six-foot, six-inches tall, he had shoulders the width of my dining room table. His hair hung to his shoulders, a full beard obscured half of his face; his massive arms and chest were covered with tattoos. He was wearing greasy blue jeans and a jean jacket with the sleeves cut out. Chains clanked on his motorcycle boots and on the key ring hanging from his wide leather belt. He held out a hand the size of a pie plate, in which lay a tiny, misshapen kitten.

"What's wrong with Tiny, Doc?" he asked in a gruff voice.

My exam revealed a birth defect. Tiny's spine had never grown together, and he was paralyzed in his back legs. No amount of surgery, medicine or prayer was going to fix him. I felt helpless.

The only thing I could tell this big, hairy giant was that his little friend was going to die. I was ashamed of my prejudice but I felt a little nervous anticipating the biker's reaction. Being the bearer of bad news is never pleasant, but with a rough-looking character like the man in front of me, I didn't know what to expect.

I tried to be as tactful as possible, explaining Tiny's problem and what we could expect, which was a slow, lingering death. I braced myself for his response.

But the big fella only looked at me with eyes that I could barely see through the hair on his face and said sadly, "I guess we gotta do him, huh, Doc?"

I agreed that, yes, the best way to help Tiny was to give him the injection that would end his poor, pain-filled life. So with his owner holding Tiny, we ended the little kitten's pain.

When it was over, I was surprised to see this macho guy the size of an oak tree just standing there holding Tiny, with tears running down his beard. He never apologized for crying, but he managed a choked "Thanks, Doc," as he carried his little friend's body home to bury him.

Although ending a patient's life is never pleasant, my staff and I all agreed that we were glad we could stop the sick kitten's pain. Weeks passed, and the incident faded.

Then one day the oak-sized biker appeared in the clinic again. It looked ominously like we were about to repeat the earlier scenario. The huge man was wearing the same clothes and carrying another kitten in his pie-plate hand. But I was enormously relieved upon examining "Tiny Two" to find he was absolutely, perfectly, wonderfully normal and healthy.

I started Tiny Two's vaccinations, tested him for worms and discussed his care, diet and future needs with his deceptively tough-looking owner. By now, it was obvious that Mr. Oak Tree had a heart that matched his size.

I wonder now how many other Hell's Angel types are really closet marshmallows. In fact, whenever I see a pack of scary-looking bikers roaring past me on the road, I crane my neck to see if I can catch a glimpse of some tiny little kitten poking its head up out of a sleek chrome side-car — or maybe even peeking out from inside the front of a black leather jacket.

— Dennis K. McIntosh, D.V.M. —

59

Bedroom Secrets of Pets Revealed

Most beds sleep up to six cats.
Ten cats without the owner.
~Stephen Baker

A long, long time ago, people slept in the house; dogs slept in a doghouse in the backyard; and cats, well, they "catted around" and slept in the barn or alley. That was before our pets migrated from the backyard to the bedroom to sleep, and from the kennel to the kitchen to eat. Now, the average doghouse has three bedrooms, two baths, a spa, an entertainment center and a two-car garage. Yes, the doghouse is our house.

Consider this: Before the arrival of our four-legged bed-partners, human bed-partners decided which side of the bed they would sleep on; we carved out property lines on the mattress. But then we decided to welcome pets into our homes, hearts and bedrooms. That was the last day any of us got a decent night's sleep.

I was reminded of this recently when, after a hectic trip, I headed home from New York to Almost Heaven Ranch in northern Idaho. Between airplane breakdowns and storms, it was a nightmare trip that took two sleepless days of travel instead of the usual one.

Fighting extreme fatigue, I finally made it home, stumbled into our log house, and headed directly to my bed, ready to slip between the flannel sheets and nestle under the goosedown comforter next to my beloved wife, Teresa. Now at long last I would be able to sleep. It sounded great in theory, but I was dreaming!

Three formidable barriers to my sleep were sprawled across the king-size bed. Scooter, our wired wirehaired fox terrier, was lying perpendicular across the bed, while Turbo and Tango, our two Himalayan-cross cats, were asleep on each pillow. I shoehorned myself next to Teresa and collapsed into deep sleep. I was sawing the timber and dreaming sweet dreams when suddenly, I was shot in the ribs with a deer rifle! At least that's what it felt like.

It was actually Teresa's elbow that had poked into my side as a last resort to stop my snoring. Sleepily, I looked across at her. She was crowded onto the tiniest sliver of mattress at the edge of the bed. The cats were wrapped around her neck and face, and our twenty-pound, flabby, fur-covered, thorn-in-the-side, Scooter, was dreamily snoring away, her feet pushing against Teresa's head. But would Teresa shove an elbow into Scooter, or disturb Tango or Turbo? Are you kidding?

Now, if I snore, Teresa's sure to find a way of letting me know it, and if I cross over to her side of the bed, she waits only a nanosecond before shoving me back onto my side or onto the floor. But there she lay, unwilling to move a muscle or twitch an eye, because she didn't want to interrupt the fur-queen's sleep!

I turned over, pulling instinctively on the down comforter to make sure that Teresa let me have my fair share of it. Yet through this sleepy tug-of-war, I was careful not to disturb my "Scooter Girl," who slept lying across me, looking warm, toasty and content.

And who needs an alarm clock when you have pets? I had managed to doze off again, but Scooter woke me up before the crack of dawn to be let outside. Again, I looked across at Teresa. Turbo and Tango were kneading her hair and licking her face to show they were ready for breakfast — now!

It was clear that Scooter, Turbo and Tango had had another great night's sleep, while Teresa and I were battling for shuteye scraps. I knew the pets would fly out of bed fully charged, while my wife and I, chronically sleep-deprived, would crawl out from under the blankets to start another day on the hamster wheel of activity we call life.

And yet... that's not quite the whole story. I knew full well that our four-legged bed partners had as usual gotten the best end of the sleeping arrangements, but I regarded it as just a small payback for the great gift of unconditional love that they give us, twenty-four hours a day, seven days a week.

So as I got out of bed, I paused to kiss Teresa's cheek, pat Scooter's furry head and stroke the cats' tails. Our bed was in purr-fect order and I had had a grrr-eat night's sleep after all.

— Marty Becker, D.V.M. —

Natural Therapists

The Perfect Companion

A cat has absolute emotional honesty: Human beings,
for one reason or another, may hide their feelings,
but a cat does not.
~Ernest Hemingway

My grandma was an amazing lady. She was still driving and gardening well into her eighties. As she got older, she started using a cane for her daily walks around the farm where she lived with us, and she allowed my older sister to drive her to church.

Then one spring, things really started to change. Grandma's daily walks around the farm stopped. She spent more and more time sitting in her rocking chair, staring out the window. She was too tired to read to my younger brothers, check on her flowerbeds, or bake a loaf of bread. She began to lose weight. Even though I was a busy teenager, I knew we were losing her.

One day, on my way into the house, I noticed a half-grown stray cat standing by the door as if he belonged there. He was sleek and black with bright green eyes. We had several cats around the farm, but they dared not brave the yard full of dogs. This cat, however, showed no fear. I thought about picking him up and taking him out to the barn, safely away from the dogs. Then I heard Mom calling me.

Mom needed help with Grandma. I forgot all about the stray cat as Mom and I helped Grandma out of bed and then to the bathroom. We helped her change and settled her into her rocking chair by the front window. She seemed so frail to me, not the spunky woman who had been such a big part of my life. I went to make her a cup of tea. When I came back, the black cat was sitting calmly on Grandma's lap, his big green eyes blinking as Grandma stroked his back. For the first time in months, Grandma was smiling.

Mom loved animals, but she did not believe they belonged in the house. In that moment, Mom made an exception — not because I begged, but because my dying Grandma was smiling. From that day forward, the cat spent all his time curled up in Grandma's lap. Where he came from was a mystery. We asked all the neighbors, but no one was missing a half-grown green-eyed black cat. Dad's hounds roamed the farm, and they didn't like cats, so how the stray survived was unknown.

The cat was attached to Grandma. In a house full of kids of all ages, he treated all of us with disdain. He spent all his days curled up on Grandma's lap. He spent his nights beside her in bed. I tried in vain to make friends with him. I was the biggest animal lover in the house. I was the one who had wanted a pet in the house for as long as I could remember. None of that mattered; he was devoted to Grandma.

Grandma began to fade, but the stray persisted. Grandma spent more and more time lying in her bed. There beside her, always within arm's reach, was the black cat. He curled up on one side of the double bed as Grandma slept. When Grandma was awake, he would stroll closer to purr and rub against Grandma's hand until she smiled. Some days, it was hard to coax either of them to eat.

One morning, we heard a thump and a feeble cry for help. We found Grandma lying in a pool of blood on the floor. We called the ambulance, and they took my now unconscious Grandma to the hospital. Through it all, the black cat stood on a tall dresser, its gaze knowing and unwavering.

Grandma died a week later. She had never returned to our house. Through all the busyness of neighbors, friends and family dropping by with condolences and food, the black cat stayed in Grandma's room. He sat on Grandma's bed and seemed so sad. I tried to comfort him, but he just stared at me with his big green eyes.

The day of Grandma's funeral was hectic. Besides the inherent sadness and grief of the day, there were practical matters at hand. Farm chores still needed to be done. Everyone needed clothes ironed for the funeral. We had our individual parts to practice for the mass. We rushed through our chores that morning, anxious not to be late. I remember taking care of Grandma's cat that morning, scratching him behind the ears as I left her room.

It was a long day and we were all exhausted by the time we got home. The first thing I did was to go check on Grandma's cat. I expected to see him curled up on a quilt at the foot of the bed. The cat wasn't there. We searched the whole room and then our whole property.

The cat had disappeared from our lives as suddenly as he had appeared. We never found out what happened to him. Some of the family came up with practical reasons for his disappearance. Mom and I knew the truth: He was sent to Grandma to help her make it through her last little bit of time on earth. He was an angel in a little cat's body.

— Theresa Brandt —

61

The Assignment

Who hath a better friend than a cat?
~William Hardwin

We all know someone who loves angels. You know, the kind of person who has every nook and cranny of her home filled to capacity with those endearing porcelain, china or dollar store nickknacks?

I have always pictured an angel as a soft, feminine form with cascading luminescent tendrils of hair, porcelain skin and eyes the colour of the Caribbean Sea. That was until... I actually met one.

Not the feminine form I'd imagined, but feline. Not cascading tendrils or porcelain skin, but soft, silky, taupe fur. Beautiful turquoise, soulful eyes, albeit somewhat crossed. Yes, my angel was a Siamese cat!

My daughter Jessica was nine years old at the time. She had fallen off the monkey bars in the playground. A compression fracture wrapped in a cast was her souvenir after spending eight hours in the emergency room. Nice gift to get the week before summer vacation! At our one-week checkup with the orthopedic surgeon, X-rays were taken, an exam made, and we received disappointing news.

Although things looked okay on the outside, the bones weren't in perfect alignment. The surgeon recommended a return visit to the operating room the next day to remove the cast and re-set the bone. My daughter was terrified, especially when she learned that her dad and I weren't allowed to be with her during the procedure.

The ride home was very quiet. You could see the worry in her watery eyes and in her body language. There was no consoling her. After encouraging her to have some lunch I suggested she go outside to get some fresh air.

At her age, most kids were pining for the latest video game or electronic gadget, but she was pleading for a cat. Being an only child was lonely and I had always felt guilty about not providing her with any siblings. I was trying to come up with an activity to distract her, when all of a sudden I said, "Look!"

A beautiful Siamese cat was walking atop the fence in our yard. Strutting her form like an Olympic gymnast, she was showing off her beautiful lines and languid curves.

Where did this exquisite cat come from? We'd lived in this neighborhood for fifteen years and had never seen this cat before. I couldn't believe it. The one thing that would truly make my daughter happy had just appeared out of thin air! The cat dismounted with gymnastic perfection and crossed the yard to softly rest at my daughter's feet.

She let out a meow as if to say, "All is well; I'm here for you." That Siamese angel was hugged, rubbed, petted and loved all afternoon. She followed my daughter everywhere and was a faithful companion and confidante. I kept peeking outside in utter disbelief.

Dinnertime rolled around and I regretfully called my daughter inside. Her trusty companion kept vigil outside the patio door for a few minutes, making sure she was in good hands. Then as quickly and quietly as she had come into our little world, she vanished, her assignment here on earth completed.

We never saw that cat again, but we have a photo that we truly treasure. I was so moved by the encounter that I wrote this story and originally titled it "Angels Among Us." I was thrilled to be able to submit it to this book with the same title.

— Catherine Rossi —

62

Paisley

There are few things in life more heartwarming
than to be welcomed by a cat.
~Isabel Abdai

During the chaos of family and funeral plans, my bedroom became an oasis for the two of us. A place where we could be alone with our thoughts. A place to escape, to be together, to remember, to cry and, hopefully, to feel.

About two weeks post-funeral, my daughter and I were enjoying the comforts of our refuge. We were snuggling together on the bed amid tears and tissues, reminiscing and embracing the art of distraction known as the Internet.

At the time, Craigslist was a place to buy and sell things you thought you once needed but, for many reasons, discovered you could live without. While scrolling through the farm category, my daughter paused, glanced at me, and said, "Mom, I've always wanted a house cat, but Dad always insisted he was allergic even though he wasn't. Do you think I can have one now?"

What do you do for an eleven-year-old girl who just lost her father? Say "yes" to any remotely good idea that pops into her head. I became overwhelmed by the parental instinct to coddle and care for my little one, to bring her some sense of happiness in a time of great sorrow. I wrapped my arm around her shoulders, pulled her close, and replied, "Why, yes! Of course, we'll get you a cat."

I clicked on the pet category. "Let's look and see what kitties are up for rehoming."

We scrolled through the postings, formulating our list of must-haves for this new family member. Being that we already owned two small dogs, a dog-friendly cat was a must. For consistency, we decided to stick with the same gender: female. I retained some sense of sanity, convincing her that a mature cat versus a kitten would be a better fit as she would most likely be spayed and, more importantly, her personality and tendencies were known.

Thankfully, she agreed. Perfect.

We began to scan the posts for a female, dog-friendly adult cat. We were no more than a handful of posts in when our girl, ticking all the required boxes, came into view. A classy jet-black cat with charming bright yellow eyes jumped off the screen straight into our hearts.

Two days later, we heard from her current owner. She was still available and located just a few miles down the road from our home. We planned a visit for the following evening.

When we pulled up to the house, the front door was open, and a small dog romped in the yard. The foyer was filled with boxes. "Must be rehoming due to a move," I said to my daughter and her best friend as they bounded toward the door.

After crossing the threshold, we met Pat, a lovely woman who appeared to be happily preparing the home for change. After the customary introductions between humans, we met our girl, Paisley. Initially, she'd been a barn cat living on a farm. When circumstances changed, she became a mostly indoor cat.

The girls quickly began to interact with Paisley, and she graciously tolerated their attention. I followed Pat into the kitchen.

Once we reached the kitchen island, well out of earshot of the girls, Pat turned to face me. She gazed straight into my eyes and said, "My husband died in a car accident seven years ago."

I struggled to breathe.

She went on to tell me about a series of life events that had led her to this moment. She'd reconnected with a high school friend back home and was moving to South Dakota to begin a life with him. While I tried not to show it, I was completely blown away. How did a simple exchange become a crystal-clear view into the looking glass of my life?

In understanding the reason for Paisley's rehoming, I had a decision in front of me. I could keep this interaction as light as possible or embrace the fateful moment that life had afforded me. I chose the latter.

"I didn't think I would be telling you this," I uttered in complete amazement. "My husband died in a motorcycle accident three weeks ago."

It felt as if a veil lifted and we were instantly connected. Pat and I began to share the details of our experiences. We talked for over an hour. She enlightened me on the paths yet to come and spoke of a support group that was helpful to her and her daughter. I made note of it.

Regarding Paisley, Pat was explicit. She'd been a great comfort to her during a time of tragedy, and now it appeared her role must continue.

"Paisley belongs with your family now," Pat declared. "Your daughter will need her. They will need each other."

My heart knew this as well. I looked over at the girls, giving them a thumbs-up glance. They quickly tucked our new kitty into the pet carrier and headed for the car. It was time to escort Paisley home.

— Beth Bullard —

63

Mental Health Hijacking

Animals are such agreeable friends — they ask no questions, they pass no criticisms.
~George Eliot

Twenty minutes into André's session, a small girl appeared behind him, holding a betta fish by its tail. "FISH!" I yelled, which, in retrospect, was not the best reaction from a mental-health therapist. I should have said, "Excuse me, André. I'm sorry for interrupting you, but your daughter has taken the fish out of its tank." Instead, I panicked.

André swung around and, with impressive agility, picked up his six-year-old daughter, dipped her over the fish tank as if they were dancing, and calmly said, "Let Slippers go." She dropped Slippers into the tank. He gently placed her on the ground and said, "Pappi is in his meeting, and when he's in meetings, you have to stay upstairs. Remember?" She laughed and ran out of the camera's view.

"I'm sorry," André said as he sat in front of his laptop. "She just wanted to show you her fish."

"Slippers is a beautiful fish," I said. "And you never told me about your Olympian Dad Moves."

"That's what my wife says," he laughed.

When the pandemic hit, mental-health clinicians like me were forced to learn how to provide therapy over computer screens. We created makeshift offices in our homes as we sat in our bedrooms, living rooms, basements, and any place we could find that was private. I loved it. Telehealth allowed me to see my clients in their natural environments, and the flexibility made it possible for more people to participate in therapy. A bonus was the many pets who made guest appearances.

I gazed upon a bearded dragon named Ferguson, who sat on my client's shoulder during every session and rarely moved. He'd angle his head to the side as if to say, "Look at me. I'm handsome." I made friends with a turtle named Daisy, who would walk across the keyboard and occasionally press a button that abruptly ended the telehealth connection. Her human would call back, stating, "She did it again." Yet, nothing compared to the time when I was utterly outwitted.

Jada, my sixteen-year-old client, closed her eyes and became absorbed in a virtualization exercise.

"Notice the sounds around you," I said softly. "Some sounds are obvious while others are in the background. Try to notice the background sounds."

The tip of a white tail appeared in the corner of the screen.

"Listen to those sounds," I whispered as I watched the tail grow slowly into a massive fluff that ascended higher and higher behind Jada's left shoulder. It was as long as Jada's head and neck and perfectly still.

"Notice what you see," I continued, as I am a professional and not easily distracted by fluffy tails. Slowly, a pair of erect ears appeared directly in front of Jada and her camera.

"Notice these details," I said as a giant, white head appeared, and two dark eyes stared directly at the camera. This dog, which looked like a mixed German Shepherd and Samoyed, was not looking at my image on the screen as humans do but slightly upward at the camera. I looked directly into my camera to meet the beast's gaze. That was my mistake. I shouldn't have made eye contact. Its ancestors, wolves, considered eye contact threatening and just plain rude. The challenge was officially accepted.

A mouth came in my direction, and there was a flashing of images of teeth and a tongue.

"Boris, no!" Jada screamed as I watched the ceiling in sporadic bursts of movement. "Bring me back my therapist!"

I realized Boris had taken her iPad into his mouth and was running through the house. I was hijacked by the family dog.

"Amanda, are you still there?" she yelled.

"Yes, still here!" I said as I listened to the sounds of a wild chase. "Save me!"

"I'll rescue you!" Jada laughed, out of breath. Then, there was darkness.

"Boris, you are so bad," she said as she picked up the iPad, and her face came into view. "Sorry, that's Boris. He likes to steal things."

"Thank you for saving me. I thought I was a goner."

Jada laughed, and we agreed that Boris could join all therapy sessions in the future if he agreed not to steal the therapist.

It wasn't only my clients' pets who engaged in hijinks. My small black cat, Mr. Bojangles, habitually showed his butt to my clients. Cat owners began calling this phenomenon Accidental Cat Butt. This occurs when a cat moves into the camera's view to get its human's attention. When they circle to face the human, their tail raises to signal that they are either interested or simply enjoying the affection provided. As the tail raises, the butt in all its glory is exposed to the camera and whoever is watching.

"I get so angry at her. I just can't…" Accidental Cat Butt.

"Wow, there it is," observed Alejandro.

"I don't want to quit, but I can't work all these hours for much longer. I tried to…" Accidental Cat Butt. "Aww, look at him. He's so cute. Can I see his face this time?" asked Dorothy.

"It's been stressful. My parents want me to visit, and I want…" Accidental Cat Butt. "Hey, nice butt, Bo!" complimented Ruth.

It's been three years since the pandemic broke out, and Mr. Bojangles and the many pets of my clients still either attend teletherapy or make guest appearances. These animals have always been a vital part of the fabric of mental health and therapeutic healing. Telehealth has given them a platform to connect with healthcare providers, and I hope we can continue to be open to these connections. And if you should ever find yourself in a telehealth session with me, please excuse the Accidental Cat Butt.

— Amanda Ann Gregory —

64

Father Meets Cat

A little drowsing cat is an image of perfect beatitude.
~Jules Champfleury

My father hated cats. Or so he told us when my sister and I begged for one when we were kids. If we persisted, he catalogued all their bad traits. Cats were lazy. Cats ripped furniture. Cats required too much care. The list went on and on.

After I graduated from the university, I moved to another city. As soon as I unpacked, I headed to the local humane society and adopted a black and brown striped tabby named Tiger. My father harrumphed at the news and predicted a dire end for all my furniture. Tiger must have overheard the conversation because she set out to prove him right.

My father harrumphed even louder the first time he encountered Tiger. The meeting did not go well. As I pointed out to him while I bandaged his hand, drumming one's fingers on the edge of a chair could be seen as a game if you're a cat.

"Only if you're an attack cat," he muttered under his breath. He glared at Tiger who turned her back on him and proceeded to wash her paws.

From that day on, my father and Tiger gave each other a wide berth. My mother, on the other hand, sent Tiger birthday cards and posted pictures of her on their fridge, much to my father's disgust.

I replaced my sofa and got a second cat. A lovely gray and salmon color, she came complete with parasites. Although I officially named her Salmonella, I called her Sammy for short. I waited a month before breaking the news to my father. This time, he snorted in addition to harrumphing.

On his next visit, when he thought I was downstairs, I overheard him talking to Sammy outside my bedroom. "Aren't you a pretty cat. What nice soft fur you have." From the sounds of her purring, I'm fairly sure their encounter involved some serious tummy-rubbing, too.

Over dinner, I asked him what he thought of the newest addition to the family. "She's okay," he said, "for a cat." Then he quickly changed the subject.

A week later, my mother told me my father, whose name was Sam, proudly informed all his friends and relatives I named the "good" cat after him. I didn't have the heart to tell him differently.

During his visits over the next couple of years, Sam and Sammy forged a bond.

Once I thought he was sufficiently softened up, I began a campaign to get my parents their own cat. I mentioned how nice it felt to come home to a warm, furry body that licked your hand in appreciation. I also quoted studies that proved having an animal provided health benefits.

No matter what I said, my father countered with a reason not to get a cat. When my mother weighed in on my side, he gave her a choice: get a cat or continue to travel. With both her daughters and granddaughters living out of town, she conceded defeat. She would have to get her dose of cat-cuddling during her visits to me.

Although my father thought he'd won the war, I knew the battle had just begun.

Five years later, my father was diagnosed with kidney disease and began dialysis. I decided that would be the perfect time to get my parents a cat so they would have something to focus on besides his illness. Since their traveling days were over, he couldn't use that argument anymore. As far as I was concerned, it was a win-win situation. I would win the war, and they would win — a cat.

I visited on Mother's Day and informed them that my mother's gift would be a cat. My mother beamed. My father snorted. I pointed out that the cat was for her, not him, and he could ignore the animal all he wanted. He snorted a second time and marched out of the room.

Two hours and one hundred and ninety dollars later, Puss Puss came home, accompanied by a red nylon carrying case, a litter box, forty pounds of kitty litter, a brush, four different kinds of cat food, three toys and a scratching post. My mother and I set up the litter box, showed Puss Puss where it was, and watched as she explored the basement.

Loud footsteps announced my father's arrival. He stared at the cat for a minute and proclaimed, "The first time she scratches the couch or me, she's out the door." Satisfied he had made his point, he glared at me, turned around and went back upstairs.

Puss Puss, unaware of how tenuous her welcome was, purred her approval of her new home. After playing with her for a while, my mother and I decided to let her investigate by herself, and we went upstairs for coffee. Half an hour later, I headed down to check on her. No cat.

I called her name. I got on my hands and knees and peered under furniture. I rattled a box of food. Still no cat.

I raced upstairs, thinking she might have sneaked up unnoticed. I checked the living room and dining room. Nothing. I went to the second floor and checked my old bedroom and my sister's. Empty.

That only left one room. As I neared my parents' bedroom, I saw my father stretched out in his La-Z-Boy chair — with the cat curled up in his lap. He was so engrossed in petting her that he didn't hear me. I tiptoed away and told my mother that everything was all right. In fact, it was perfect.

For the next three years, Puss Puss was my father's constant companion. Every time I visited, he told me the same thing: "That cat is great company — for your mother."

Like I said, a win-win situation.

— Harriet Cooper —

65

Mama-Cat

A meow massages the heart.
~Stuart McMillan

When I was nearly four years old I was just a mere bit of a girl. Curly hair framed my happy little freckled face, and my lively blue eyes looked at everything in curious anticipation of delights yet to be. One beautiful September day, my mother stretched out on the sofa and called to me. She asked me to bring her a cool, wet cloth for her forehead. She said she had a headache. I was happy to do such a grown-up thing and felt very important as I brought her the cloth. With that done, I skipped outside to play in my yard.

I never saw her again. My mother died of polio three days later — just one week before I turned four years old. The loss was total, irreversible and devastating. And I could not change it. No matter how I cried. No matter how good I promised to be. No matter how many threats I issued. No matter how desperately I wanted her back. My mother was gone — never to return to me. Never again to hug me close, or brush my hair, or tuck me in bed, or sing softly to me as I drifted off to sleep in perfect peace. Nor would she ever again gaze at me with love. And tragically, all too soon after she died, she began to fade from my memory. It was difficult to remember what her face looked like — or remember the tender gaze that always transmitted how much she loved me.

I was tormented by the idea that perhaps my mother left me

because I was bad. I couldn't remember what I had done, but I must have done something to cause her to leave. That burden weighed heavily on my heart. There was no peace for me. Only dreadful longing and unutterable guilt.

Soon after her death, while trees were still dressed in scarlet and gold — before the leaves had floated to the ground and left limbs bare, I overheard the mailman speak to a neighbor of mine. He called out as he passed her home, "Those are sure cute kittens." Although I had been withdrawn and listless, the idea of seeing kittens drew me to the neighbor's home. I avoided being seen by anyone as I entered the backyard. There in a wooden tool shed was a box that held a beautiful white cat who had recently given birth to kittens. She was tucked away in the corner of the neat, dry shed. It was a cozy place. The mother cat snuggled close to her babies. It reminded me of the times I had snuggled close to my own mother. The grief that had engulfed my heart began to ease a little at the sight of the mother cat. I wanted my mother, but I could not have her anymore. After a few minutes, my four-year-old mind came up with a simple plan. I would become a kitten.

And this beautiful mother cat would be my second mama. And since she was a mother herself, I reasoned, I could talk to her about my own mother. I knew she would understand. The eyes of the mama cat seemed to transmit the sweetest love to her kittens, and it reminded me of the special loving look my own mother used to gaze at me with. For the first time since my mother died, I smiled.

Each day I would visit Mama-cat. She liked being gently stroked by my little hands. Her fur was silky and soft and somehow comforting to me. Mama-cat purred loudly and talked to her babies in soft meows. She began to include me in her circle of love, too. She would gaze at me and purr loudly whenever I was near. I knew what she was saying — a four-year-old just knows these things — she was saying, "I love you, my babies," and I knew she included me in that, too.

I talked to her about my mother and how much I missed her. Mama-cat always seemed to understand. I could not speak to anyone else about the confusing jumbled-up pain that was in my heart, but I could talk to Mama-cat. She always listened patiently, and she seemed to be very wise.

My heart began to heal during the days that followed as Mama-cat showed me how much she loved all of us. I was absolutely certain that when I was with my Mama-cat I was a kitten. I believed if someone were to glance into the tool shed he or she would not see a child — they would see me as a kitten, so strong was my imagination as a four-year-old.

As time passed, and the kittens grew bigger, they no longer listened to the mother cat as well as they should have. They would ignore her worried meows to behave and stay close. They would race in and out of the tool shed and even climb way up a tree. I could always tell when Mama-cat was worried. My own mother used to get the same worried look when I would climb too high on my swing set after being told not to. She would rush over, lift me down and chide me for not listening to her. Then she would kiss me, smile and extract a promise that I would be more careful, though the following day I would be back up on the top of the swing set again.

In watching how much Mama-cat loved her misbehaving kittens, I came to understand the profound truth that my mother didn't leave me because I was bad, nor had she stopped loving me when I disobeyed her. Knowing that eased the ache in my heart.

For one very special season, I took refuge in the innocent land of make-believe. Within my young mind, I was one of the kittens this mother cat loved. That Mama-cat loved me was certain. That she eased a profound loss was also true. And her tender acceptance of me helped me fix the memory of my mother in my mind forever. When Mama-cat snuggled against me and comforted me, it was always a reminder of when I had snuggled in my mother's arms. Mama-cat was always glad to see me, just as my real mother had been. She would gaze at me with love — as my real mother had done.

No one else looked at me that way anymore. No one else was glad to see me. No one else worried about me, yet Mama-cat did, I was sure of it — just as my real mother had done. Mama-cat helped me keep the sweetest memories of my real mother from fading.

Many years later I became a mother. When my son was an infant I would hold him in my arms and gaze at him with tenderness. As he grew older, each year brought more delight, and my heart would fill with love. And sometimes, my heart would wander back to the tender memory of my own mother's love — and to a Mama-cat that helped a lonely, motherless little waif of a girl come to terms with loss. In my mind, even now, I can still see the face of my own mother and her tender loving gaze. And I can still see the sweet loving acceptance in the eyes of Mama-cat.

— Lynn Seely —

A French Cat

It is impossible for a lover of cats to banish these alert,
gentle, and discriminating little friends, who give us
just enough of their regard and complaisance
to make us hunger for more.
~Agnes Repplier

Recently, my husband Gene and I traveled throughout Europe. We rented a car as we always do and drove along the back roads, staying in quaint, out-of-the-way inns. The only thing that distracted me from the wonder of the trip was the terrible longing I felt for our cat Perry. I always miss him when we travel, but this time, because we were gone for more than three weeks, my need to touch his soft fur and to hold him close became more and more intense. With every cat we saw, the feeling deepened.

We were high in the mountains of France one morning, packing the car before resuming our trip, when an elderly couple walked up to the car parked next to ours. The woman was holding a large Siamese cat and speaking to him in French.

I stood watching them, unable to turn away. My yearning for Perry must have been written all over my face. The woman glanced at me, turned to speak to her husband and then spoke to her cat. Suddenly she walked right over to me and, without one word, held out her cat.

I immediately opened my arms to him. Cautious about the stranger holding him, he extended his claws, but only for a few seconds. Then he retracted them, settled into my embrace and began to purr. I buried my face in his soft fur while rocking him gently. Then, still wordless, I returned him to the woman.

I smiled at them in thanks, and tears filled my eyes. The woman had sensed my need to hold her cat, the cat had sensed that he could trust me, and both, in one of the greatest gifts of kindness I have ever received, had acted upon their feelings.

It's comforting to know the language of cat lovers — and cats — is the same the world over.

— Jean Brody —

67

Kitty Magic

Friendship is a sheltering tree.
~Samuel Taylor Coleridge

After a meeting one night, I felt very tired. Eager to get home and get to sleep, I was approaching my car when I heard mew, mew, mew, mew... Looking under my car, I saw a teeny little kitten, shaking and crying, huddled close to the tire.

I have never had a fondness for cats. I'm a dog person, thank you very much. I grew up with dogs all my young life and cats always bugged me. Kind of creeped me out. I especially hated going into houses that had cat boxes. I wondered if the residents just ignored the awful smell. Plus, cats always seemed to be all over everything — not to mention their hair. And I was semiallergic to them. Suffice it to say, I had never in my life gone out of my way for a cat.

But when I knelt down and saw this scared little red tabby mewing like crazy, something inside urged me to reach out to pick her up. She ran away immediately. I thought, Okay, well, I tried, but as I went to get into my car, I heard the kitten mewing again. That pitiful mewing really pulled at my heart, and I found myself crossing the street to try to find her. I found her and she ran. I found her again and she ran again. This went on and on. Yet I just couldn't leave her. Finally, I was able to grab her. When I held her in my arms, she seemed so little and skinny and very sweet. And she stopped mewing!

It was totally out of character, but I took her into my car with me. The kitty freaked out, screeching and running at lightning speed all over the car, until she settled herself right in my lap, of course. I didn't know what I was going to do with her, and yet I felt compelled to bring her home. I drove home, worrying the whole way, because I knew my roommate was deathly allergic to cats.

I got home very late, put the kitten in the front yard and left some milk for her. I was half hoping she would run away by the time morning came. But in the morning she was still there, so I brought her to work with me. Luckily, I have a very sympathetic boss. Especially when it comes to animals. Once we had a hurt sparrow in the office for weeks that he had found and nursed back to health. All day at work, I tried to find someone who would take the kitten, but all the cat lovers were full up.

I still didn't know what to do with the kitty, so I took her on some errands with me when I left work. Again she freaked in the car and this time wedged herself under the seat. My last stop that afternoon was at my parents' house.

Recently my father had been diagnosed with prostate cancer. He had undergone hormone treatment and the doctors now felt they had arrested the cancer. At least for the present. I liked to go there as often as I could.

That afternoon, parked in front of my parents' house, I was trying to coax the kitten out from under the seat when she zoomed out of the car and into the neighbors' bushes. There are a lot of bushes in that neighborhood, and I realized after looking for a while that it was a lost cause. I felt a bit sad but consoled myself that this area had many families with kids. Surely someone would find her and give her a good home, I told myself.

To be honest, I felt somewhat relieved because I didn't know what I would have done with her. I visited with my parents, and as I was leaving, I told them to call me if the kitty came around their place and I would come pick her up. I kidded my father, saying, "Of course, you could keep her if you wanted," to which he replied, "Not on your life!" I supposed that Dad wasn't that interested in having pets, particularly cats.

That night there was a call on my answering machine from my

father. The kitty had actually shown up on their front doorstep! He said he had her in the house and she was okay, but could I come pick her up the next day? My heart sank. What am I going to do with this cat? I thought. I didn't have the heart to take her to the pound, and I was sure that my roommate wasn't feeling up for a hospital trip to treat a cat-induced asthma attack. I couldn't see a solution.

I called my father the next day and told him I would come over and pick up the kitty. To my great surprise, he said not to rush. He had gone out and bought a cat box (oh, no!), cat food and a little dish. I was amazed and thanked him for his generosity. He proceeded to tell me what a character the kitten was and how late the previous night she had been zooming back and forth across the floor. I listened, open-mouthed. The topper came when he said that "Kitty" came up and lay on his chest when he was lying down. I asked, "You let her do that?"

"Oh yes. I pet her and I can feel her motor running," he replied lovingly. "So take your time, dear, finding a home for her. I can keep her until you do."

I was floored. My dad, Seymour, Mister "Keep-Those-Dogs-Outside," had a kitty purring on his chest. In his bed, no less!

As the weeks went on, Dad got weaker. His cancer had reappeared. Yet whenever I called Dad, I heard more and more about how cute Kitty was, how she zoomed around, how loud her motor was, how she followed him everywhere. When I was at the house, my father would call for her, have her come up on his lap, pet her, talk to her and say how much he loved her.

"Dad, aren't you allergic to cats?" I asked once, as he was putting his handkerchief away after one of his infamous loud honks. He just shrugged his shoulders and smiled sheepishly.

As he got sicker, and could barely move without terrible pain, one of his few joys was to have Kitty lay on his chest. He would pet her and say, "Listen, her motor is running. That's a good Kitty, good Kitty." We all watched in awe at Dad's unabashed affection for this little feline.

Kitty worked her magic on both Dad and me. Charming a reluctant pet owner, the little cat became one of my father's single greatest comforts in his final days. And me? Kitty opened my eyes to the wonder and mystery of how life unfolds. She taught me to listen to my heart, even when my head is saying no. I didn't realize on that unusual night that I was simply a messenger. An unknowing courier delivering a most beautiful and needed friend.

—Lynn A. Kerman—

68

Simon

The mind of God may be glimpsed in the eyes of a cat.
~Celtic Saying

Only fifty-three animals in the world have ever received the Dickin Medal, an award presented to animals connected with the British armed forces or civil defense who have displayed "conspicuous gallantry or devotion to duty." The medals, named for the founder of the People's Dispensary for Sick Animals (PDSA), Maria Dickin, were given to the animals for their heroism during World War II or in conflicts directly following the war. The recipients were eighteen dogs, three horses, thirty-one pigeons and one cat. That one cat was Simon, of His Majesty's Ship Amethyst.

In the early morning of April 20, 1949, the British warship Amethyst was anchored in China's Yangtze River. The crew included a small black-and-white cat named Simon.

All seafaring ships need cats. Mice and rats love to live on ships, creeping in on hawser cables, jumping aboard from docks, coming in along with freight shipments. Mice and rats damage ships, raiding the food storage areas and chewing fabrics to make nests for their young. They also carry viruses, which can be passed on to crew and passengers by mosquitoes or fleas that bite infected rodents and in turn bite a person. Having Simon on board was better than 100 rat traps.

That April morning, the captain was waiting for daylight to continue his voyage up the dangerous river. The Chinese Nationalists, in control of the river, had forbidden all night traffic. Civil war was ready to explode at any moment, and the captain of H.M.S. Amethyst had been ordered to sail upriver to Nanking to protect the British embassy there.

Shortly after dawn, before the Amethyst could escape, the Yangtze river became a war zone. Explosions shook the air. Shells screeched over the ship, and one rocket and then another crashed into the ship. When the shelling stopped a short time later, many British sailors lay dead on the Amethyst's deck. A large number of crew members were wounded, including Simon. The disabled Amethyst was trapped right where she was, and it looked as if the British ship would be stranded for political reasons for quite some time. When the captain checked their stores of food, water and fuel, he found supplies enough for about two months. Surely they would be able to escape before then, he thought.

Life on the Yangtze settled into a dull, hot, humid procession of boring days of sweat and ship repair. Simon recovered from his injuries sufficiently to continue his duties as chief rat-catcher.

One day during this time, the ship's doctor saw Simon limping past the sick bay on his way to the hold to look for rats.

"Why don't you come in here and visit these chaps?" the doctor asked, and held the door open. Simon walked inside, where row on row of cots each held an injured lad.

"I'm going to try something," the doctor told his attendant. He picked Simon up and carried him over to a bed in the corner, where Seaman Mark Allen lay with his eyes closed. The boy, who was only sixteen, had lost both legs below the knee in the shelling. For four days, since regaining consciousness, he had refused to talk or eat or even open his eyes.

The doctor set Simon on the boy's bed. Simon sat looking at him, but the boy's eyes remained closed. The doctor moved Simon onto the boy's chest and placed the limp hand on the cat's back.

"Somebody's here to see you, Mark," said the doctor.

Mark opened his eyes just a little. When he saw Simon's steady gaze, he opened them further. The corners of his mouth quirked ever so slightly.

"I have a cat at home," he said. "But I'll never see him again." He pushed Simon away and turned his face into his pillow.

The next day the doctor took Simon to see Mark again and left him sitting on Mark's bed. Simon crawled up on Mark's stomach and began kneading, as he often did before settling down. Mark opened his eyes. His thin hand reached out and stroked Simon's rough fur. The boy began to sob.

The doctor hurried over. "Cook's got some good vegetable soup in the galley. How would you like me to get you a bowl of it? Simon will stay here with you."

Mark nodded ever so slightly. He stroked Simon, who settled down by him and began purring.

From that day on, Mark began eating and gaining strength. Simon visited every day. By the time a month had passed, Mark was able to get around the ship in a wheelchair.

Day after day passed; the days turned into weeks. The thermometer rose to 110 degrees Fahrenheit every day below decks. Between the heat and the severely limited rations, life on the ship became almost intolerable.

The crew looked thin and pinched about their mouths as their energy deserted them in the sweltering heat. Only one sailor kept up his daily activities with spirit and good will: Able Seaman Simon. He patrolled the ship, visited the sick, killed mice and rats, and made life bearable for his fellow shipmates. He never complained about the heat or his health.

On July 19, the temperature reached 110 degrees on the decks and 118 degrees in the engine room. Even Simon walked the decks very slowly. They wouldn't be able to last much longer. Their stores were almost depleted and there was barely enough water to drink, a terrible hardship in the unrelenting heat. The ship was fixed now, but they were held hostage by the warring Chinese and could not sail without again risking serious damage to the ship and her crew.

By the start of August, they couldn't stay where they were any longer. They decided to make a run for it under cover of darkness. It was a serious gamble, but they had no other option.

A combination of weather conditions, some cleverly executed

deceptions and sheer good luck enabled the ship to escape. On August 3, the Amethyst, free at last, sailed down the China coast to Hong Kong. Hundreds of British citizens waited on the docks to cheer the ship as she steamed into the harbor.

Soon after, one of the ship's officers wrote to the PDSA in England to nominate Simon for the Dickin Medal. While they were docked in Hong Kong, a reply came — the awards committee unanimously conferred the Dickin Medal on Simon. The presentation ceremony would occur after the Amethyst returned to England. In the meantime, they sent a tricolor collar for Simon to wear and made an announcement to the world press: "Be it known that from April 22 to August 4, Simon of the H.M.S. Amethyst did rid the ship of pestilence and vermin with unrelenting faithfulness. Throughout the incident Simon's behavior was of the highest order and his presence was a decisive factor in maintaining the high level of morale in the ship's company."

Simon became an instant hero. The little black-and-white cat's photograph appeared in hundreds of newspapers and magazines. For weeks, Simon received more than 200 pieces of mail a day. Simon seemed unimpressed with the attention. He posed reluctantly for pictures and continued killing rats.

While en route to England, Simon picked up a virus. Weakened from the wounds he had suffered during the shelling, the cat died. The ceremony to honor Simon, scheduled for when they reached England, turned out to be his funeral.

The PDSA Pet Cemetery has an arched wrought iron gate with the words "They Also Serve" stretched over the entrance. On the day of Simon's funeral, a small casket covered by a Union Jack stood surrounded by baskets and sprays of flowers in the special cemetery.

As the ceremony was about to begin, a handsome young man in a navy uniform with H.M.S. AMETHYST on his cap walked slowly through the gate and joined the small crowd of people grouped around the open grave. He used crutches, but he stood tall and the shoes on his feet shone in the sun. It was Mark Allen, the sailor who perhaps more than anyone owed his life to Simon.

And as they buried the little hero of the Amethyst, it seemed fitting that it was Mark's strong, young voice that rang out in the morning air: "The Lord is my shepherd, I shall not want..."

— Rosamond M. Young —

Medicine Cat

Cats' eyes seem a bridge beyond the one we know.
~Lynn Hollyn

The doctors sent my mother home to die. A fifteen-year survivor of breast cancer, she had suffered two heart attacks when advanced cancer was found in her lung.

Mom had struggled to raise three daughters while holding a full-time job, yet worked hard to maintain a cozy home for her family. Growing up, I knew only two things about my mother: She had an iron will, and she loved nature. During her days of illness, she told me a third: "I've had a miserable life."

My dad was a difficult man to live with, but my mom did not complain, probably because she could not put words to her own need. But when it became clear that because of her progressive deterioration, my dad regarded her as a burden, she and I decided that she would move to my home.

I had three weeks to make a myriad of arrangements. I changed my work schedule, found transportation, an oncologist, cardiologist, hospice care, medical equipment, a caregiver and bather. My plan for Mom's final days was simple: She would live with love, and die with grace.

Upon her arrival, after an exhausting five-hour trip, Mom was examined by the home health-care nurse. The nurse took me aside and asked, "How long do you think your mother has?"

"Two, maybe three months," I said.

The nurse looked at me sadly. "Adjust your thinking," he said. "She has days, maybe a week. Her heart is weak and unstable."

My home, small and comfortable, was a haven to four cats and a golden retriever. The animals had the run of my house. During my parents' infrequent visits, they'd seen the cats prowl the kitchen counters, the dog snooze on the couch and knew the cats shared my bed. This made my father angry and my mother uncomfortable. I was worried my mother would be bothered by my pets.

We installed the electric hospital bed and oxygen machine, which frightened the cats from the bedroom. I'd moved their furniture, and they were peeved. The retriever, on the other hand, an immature dog with bad habits, was excited by all the changes in the house. She jumped up, barked and shed more profusely than usual.

One cat, however, seemed to adjust perfectly. Otto had been an ugly, smelly kitten adopted from the animal shelter, but he grew into a handsome cat. His short coat was white with black and tan tabby patches, accented by bold orange spots. The veterinarian decided he was a calico. "Unusual," she said, "because calicos tend to be female."

Otto was as smart as he was unusual. He had learned to retrieve paper balls, ran to the telephone when it rang and even gave useful hints about how to fix the toilet. Once when I was trying to repair the toilet, he kept reaching into the open tank, pushing on the float with his paw. Since I was not having any success with the repair, I decided he might be on to something. I went to the hardware store and bought a new float mechanism. It worked.

Otto was the one cat who was not afraid of the hospital bed, the oxygen machine or the medicinal smells. Nor was he afraid of the frail woman who had scolded him down from the kitchen counter. Otto jumped onto the foot of Mom's hospital bed, and stayed.

He was not startled by the nurses. He did not interfere when Mom was fed, nor when she was transferred from bed to commode and back. Whether the disturbance was from changing her bed or because of bathing, he simply waited to resume his post. With the exception of eating and using the litter box, Otto never left Mom's room.

Days passed, and Mom started to rally. "Not unusual," I was told, "a rally is often a sign of imminent death."

I grieved. But Otto would not give her up so easily. He used her improved condition to reposition himself from the foot of her bed to her side. Her thin fingers found his soft coat. He leaned into her body, as if clinging to the threads of her will to live. Though weak, she caressed the cat and would not allow me to take him.

Days turned into weeks and Mom continued to fight. Once, after the nurses had gone for the day, I heard the sound of Mom's voice coming from her room. I found her with the head of the bed raised. Otto was tucked into the crook of her elbow, listening adoringly as she read from the newspaper. I will forever cherish the memory of Mom's face with Otto's paw, claws retracted, caressing the side of her chin.

Being vigilant, I made sure juice, water and pain medications were always available. One evening I was surprised to find Mom unassisted in the bathroom, filling her empty medication dish with water. "Mom, what are you doing?" I asked.

Without looking up, she replied, "Getting a drink set up for Otto." I helped her back to bed. Mom sipped apple juice while Otto drank from the stainless steel dish. Getting that drink set up became her evening ritual.

Eventually, using a walker, Mom began to take walks through the house. She was trailed by oxygen tubing and Otto. Where she rested, Otto rested. Where she moved, Otto shadowed. It seems I had forgotten my mom was a mother. Somehow, Otto knew, and during those days he became her cat child, giving her life purpose. We had come a long way from the days when she used to chase him off the kitchen counter.

Exactly three years have passed since then. The hospital bed and oxygen machine are long gone. The medicines and nurses are gone, too. But Mom's still here. And so is Otto. And so is the bond that united them in days of sickness.

"You know, I swear that Otto knows my car when I drive up!" Mom says.

He does. Whenever Mom returns home from running an errand, he greets her car at the curb. She carries him up the driveway. They just pick up wherever they left off, with his front paws wrapped around her neck.

Happily, I prepare meals with Mom watching from a stool, and Otto next to her on the counter.

When we saw the oncologist a while ago, he patted himself on the back. "I can't believe it, Lula," he said. "I can't find your cancer and your heart is strong. When your daughter brought you to me, I thought you were a ship that had sailed."

We let the doctor think what he likes, but Mom gives the credit to Otto.

Thankfully, my mother has put off dying, and Otto continues to share his gift of love—a medicine more potent than any drug a doctor could prescribe.

—Joan M. Walker—

70

The Cat Doctor

Oh, my friend, it's not what they take away from you
that counts. It's what you do with what you have left.
~Hubert Humphrey

Dr. MacFarland, a veterinarian who goes by the name The Cat Doctor, has a practice in my hometown, where we bring our cat, Ragamuffin. At one point, we had to put Ragamuffin on a strict diet of prescription food, sold only at the vet's office. One time, when I went there to get a refill, I saw one of the saddest sights I have ever seen — a cat whose hind quarters were paralyzed and could get around only by dragging his back legs behind him.

I asked the receptionist about the cat. She told me his name was Slick, and that some people had found him by the side of the road a couple of years earlier and brought him in. The poor little guy had been shot and left for dead. The Cat Doctor treated him and when he recovered, they decided to keep Slick as the office mascot.

At first, it just broke my heart to see him pull himself around the office, using just his front legs. But Slick has such spirit, that each time I saw him, I seemed to notice his difficulties less and less.

Not too long ago, Ragamuffin became ill and I had to take him to the vet. The cat was scared to death to leave our house. Although he was in horrible pain from his illness, he put up a terrific fight. He fought his way out of the cat carrier three times before I could secure it.

I finally got Ragamuffin into the car and headed over to see The Cat Doctor. Ragamuffin howled and cried the whole way. Even as I carried the carrier into the office, my cat was putting up a fight. He was terrified of being in this strange place filled with new cat and people smells.

As I looked around, I noticed Slick sitting on a little cat bed across the room, oblivious to all the commotion I'd brought into his kingdom. He ignored us, continuing to groom himself.

Setting the carrier down on the floor, I tried not to listen to Ragamuffin's strident pleas for help as I filled out the proper paperwork.

Then suddenly it got quiet. Really quiet. No more screaming. No more howls. I cocked my head to listen as I continued to calculate Ragamuffin's weight in my head. Still, silence.

A sudden fear rushed over me as I realized that the front door to Dr. McFarland's office was still open. Omigosh, I thought, Ragamuffin must have gotten out of the carrier and run outside! I dropped my pen and turned to bolt out the door. I hadn't taken more than two steps when I stopped short — captivated by the scene before me.

Ragamuffin, still in his cage, had his pink nose pressed up against the bars. He was exchanging a calm little cat greeting with Slick, who had managed to crawl all the way across the room to comfort the agitated Rags. Slick, with his paralyzed hindquarters splayed behind him, pressed his nose to the bars as well. The two cats sat quietly, Slick continuing to soothe Ragamuffin's fears in a way only another cat would know how to do.

Smiling, I realized that there was more than one Cat Doctor around this place.

— Norma and Vincent Hans —

Canine Friends

71

A Collie Without a Herd

Women and cats will do as they please, and men and
dogs should relax and get used to the idea.
~Robert A. Heinlein

Spicy, a black-and-white Border Collie puppy, came to live with us at the age of six weeks and immediately began searching for a herd. Although we raise cattle on our Central Texas farm, we've streamlined our cattle handling facilities so a pickup truck and a few bales of hay or buckets of Range Cubes do the work once required of cowboys on horses and working cow dogs. Believe me, it's much easier to lure the thousand-pound beasts into pens with treats than it is to chase them over hundreds of acres of land, a practice which works best in old Western movies.

At first, Spicy dedicated herself to herding our four grandchildren, the youngest of whom, a clumsy two-year-old, tripped over her and squashed her flat under his diaper-swathed backside many times before Spicy accepted the fact that grandchildren do not possess a herd mentality. Her brief contacts with the weanling heifers in the pen below the house were just as frustrating. Full of high-protein feed and rambunctiousness, they chased her gleefully across the pen with their tails in the air.

Border Collies are born with the instinct to herd other animals. The good ones have an inborn trait called the "collie eye" — they fix the target animals with an unwavering stare that communicates their dominance, and then move them wherever the handler (or the dog) wants them to go, ducking and dodging with agile grace to keep the unruly creatures together. Anyone who has watched a sheepherding demonstration at the fair has witnessed the Border Collie's uncanny ability to know which way the sheep are going to turn before they do.

We worked with Spicy on basic obedience lessons and she learned amazingly fast, but her life wasn't complete without something to herd, and we have no sheep or goats, not even a flock of ducks, which are sometimes used to train Border Collies. Although she loved people, she wasn't interested in fetching balls or sticks or any of the other favorite puppy pastimes. Finally, in desperation, she focused her attention on Pepper, a tortoiseshell cat. Pepper was a rescue cat, eternally grateful to be free of the shelter cage that had been her home before our daughter adopted her. As long as she didn't have to go back to the shelter, Pepper was cool with anything.

When I first noticed Spicy crouching in front of Pepper and giving her the "collie eye," I laughed. But I was a bit concerned that Pepper might run, encouraging Spicy to chase her. Pepper sized up the situation, arched her back, and rubbed under Spicy's chin, purring. She was happy to have attention — even from a dog. From that day forward, Pepper rarely went anywhere without Spicy at her side, glaring at her with an intensity that Pepper totally ignored. Tail in the air, she continued to her planned destination as though the black-and-white blur dancing around her didn't exist. Spicy raced from one side of the strolling cat to the other, pretending that Pepper was headed exactly where Spicy wanted her to go. Obviously, she didn't understand that "herding cats" is impossible.

As Spicy outgrew the playful puppy stage, I thought she might see the pointlessness of trying to herd a cat, but at the age of eight, her fascination with this pastime is just as strong. Pepper has a few carefully selected perches where she can escape when she's fed up with playing the part of the sheep, but mostly it's a symbiotic relationship. Pepper seems to view Spicy as her own personal escort and protector, a large, black-and-white lady-in-waiting, perhaps proving the truth of the old saying: "Thousands of years ago, cats were worshipped as Gods. Cats have never forgotten this."

— Martha Deeringer —

72

Who's Your Daddy?

Call it a clan, call it a network, call it a tribe,
call it a family. Whatever you call it,
whoever you are, you need one.
~Jane Howard

Everyone has read articles, seen stories on television, or watched videos on social websites about mother animals adopting babies of another species: mother cats nursing puppies and visa versa, cat and dog mothers adopting and nursing squirrels, fox cubs, coyotes, rabbits and skunks—I once saw a story about a dog that nursed and raised an African lion cub. All are amazing. My Sparky adds a little twist to this nurturing instinct that appears to be very strong in all types of mothers... regardless of species.

From the time I rescued him, I knew my Pug-Beagle mix was a cat lover. That's why he fit right into my little family of three cats. Wherever he came from, he had obviously shared his life with cats. He wanted to be friendlier with them than they preferred, but the two old toms and one queen accepted the little dog with resigned dignity, hopping out of his reach if he got too affectionate.

I learned quickly that Sparky takes accepting cats farther than any other dog I have owned. He adores them. If it were up to him, he would take every cat he saw home with us when we go on our walks. He cries, he moans, he begs with sad eyes focused on them, then on me... for more cats. This makes him quite the dog in our neighborhood. Everyone jokes about him.

In his first year with me, one cat in particular became his best friend on our walks. She was just a simple gray-striped little tabby and she would run out to greet us from her yard as we passed by each day. She would rub against Sparky and he'd lick her, and they would tumble on her front lawn until I had to pull him away. He would follow me reluctantly.

One day, I saw the moving trucks in front of the cat's house and told Sparky, "It looks like your Miss Kitty is moving away."

Unfortunately, within a few days after the trucks left Miss Kitty appeared again. I don't know if she was abandoned or if she snuck back home after the move. The good news was that the people next door to the now vacant house said they would take her because she was so loveable.

The bad news was that they did not spay her. Within a few months, I could tell she was very, very pregnant. Sparky seemed to think the whole idea was wonderful because they still played together every time they met on our walks.

Miss Kitty had her kittens under a rosebush in a front yard driveway and was immediately disowned by her new hosts because a cat with kittens was simply too much to deal with. With her friendly attitude toward dogs, and with dogs that were definitely not like Sparky running loose in the neighborhood, I couldn't leave this little family under a rosebush two feet from the main sidewalk. I'd seen too often what happened to kittens when roving dogs found them or if they wandered into the street.

Once we had the mother and kittens safely settled in a spare bedroom, Sparky stepped in. Overwhelmed with delight, he became the surrogate father to the three kittens. He moved in with Miss Kitty and her babies, gently washing them, letting them snuggle up to him and allowing the little blind squeakers to crawl all over him. Miss Kitty could go rest by the window when she wasn't nursing her crew, safe in the knowledge that Sparky would take good care of them.

As the kittens grew, I wondered what they thought. Did they think that Sparky was some weird looking — and weird smelling — cat? Did they think that they were puppies? I couldn't imagine.

All I knew was that the little family grew up, rolling and playing together like puppies, not cats… and yet they still kept all their feline instincts and actions with the other cats in the household. I assume they thought, and still think, that they are some type of cross-species creatures.

That was three years ago and they are all still together, all safely spayed and neutered. The young tom, Ringo the Third, is taller than his daddy, Sparky. They still roll, play and chew on each other like dogs, with Ringo keeping his claws retracted. The two girls, Duchess and Friday (named Friday because she was born a day later than the other two), still sleep on top of their daddy, Sparky.

In the last three months, another throwaway rescue dog has come into our house and he seems to take it all in stride. Although he does look at Sparky with a questioning face when he sees the cats pile on top of him to sleep on the couch.

Sparky is a protective father even though the kittens are all grown. If one of the older cats picks on Miss Kitty or one of his "family," or if the new dog growls when Duchess or Friday try to jump on him, Sparky is at the ready with a bark, leap and a quick snap at the offending animal, as if to say, "Nobody messes with my kids!"

Talk about a mixed relationship. However strange, the one thing that is very clear is that they love each other. And I guess that says it all. In the end, it's always love that really counts, isn't it?

—Joyce A. Laird—

73

The Odd Couple

The purpose of a liberal arts education is to learn
that a person can like both cats and dogs!
~Author Unknown

Once I thought pet adoptions were only done by people. Never would I have dreamed that a pet might adopt another pet until our shaggy Collie-Shepherd, Chandu, chose a cat to be his very own.

Over summer, while walking Chandu the length of the alley that ran behind our block, we saw a large orange Persian cat in a back yard. She was exceptionally beautiful, that first time standing stiff-legged with fur fluffed up when she saw us. Chandu did not bark at her or strain at his leash. He merely muttered a soft sound of acknowledgment, and we continued walking. Later on when we walked down the alley, the cat hopped onto a gate to watch us and once followed us from a distance. It was most curious.

On an autumn afternoon when I came home from school, there sat the big orange cat on our front steps. Chandu was sprawled on the porch in his usual waiting-for-Marcia place. The cat jumped up and skittered away when she saw me approaching. Ears cocked, Chandu gave me a look that said, "Hey, I was just getting acquainted with her and you scared her off!"

A few days later my mother reported that she saw the cat drinking from Chandu's outdoor water bowl and that the feline appeared to have lost weight. That evening when Dad and I walked Chandu down the alley to the vacant lot where all the neighborhood dogs were walked, we saw that the grass had not been cut at the house where we thought the cat lived and the curtains were gone from the windows.

"I think that orange cat's people have moved away," I said. "The house looks empty."

Dad agreed and we saw no sign of the cat.

But the next day when I came home, Chandu was waiting on the porch to greet me and the big orange cat was sitting on the top step near him. This time she did not run away as I came up the steps. I noted that her thick coat was matted and she was definitely thinner. She meowed and I stooped to pet her. Chandu stood up proprietarily near the cat, his plumed tail wagging fast and friendly. When I opened the front door, he did not rush forward as usual but stood to one side watching the cat. He made a soft sound, as if urging the cat to go inside first. And she did, Chandu and I following. She warily circled the living room, one eye on us all the time.

Chandu proceeded to the kitchen, gave a small whuffle and nudged his food bowl. I opened a can of his dog food, filled his bowl, and expected him to rush forward and scarf down his food as he usually did. Instead, again he stood by as the cat, smelling food, came into the kitchen and attacked the dog food as if she had not eaten in days.

When she was full, Chandu advanced slowly and finished off what remained of his supper. The cat retreated to a corner under the table and washed her face, then walked to the front door to be let out. For a week we never knew where she spent her nights, but she appeared on our front porch each afternoon and the pattern was repeated.

Could such a beautiful cat have been abandoned? It would seem so, according to the neighbors we questioned. It was wartime and the huge army camp outside town had brought vast changes, including sudden moves by hundreds of people as troops were transferred. Wives and families followed, often with little notice. Others simply moved away from our small town to take high-paying defense factory jobs. It was not unknown for an occasional pet to be left behind.

There came an evening when both animals had filled their bellies, and after the meal the cat went close to Chandu and rubbed against his legs. The dog stood still, giving a sigh, obviously enamored with the attention. When he lay down on his regular evening spot on the living room rug, the cat came and curled up next to him.

From that moment Chandu had his pet and companion. The two became inseparable. Chandu frequently gave the cat, whom we named Fluffy, a bath with his long tongue. Fluffy tried to return the favor but her small cat tongue was no match for a big Collie-Shepherd with a thick coat of fur.

In those days in small towns like ours, most dogs and cats ran loose during the day. Chandu watched over Fluffy as one might a small child, flicking her gently across the face with his tail if she ventured too near the street or followed where he did not want her to go. He shared his favorite ball with her, the two of them bouncing and chasing it around the back yard. She accompanied us on the bedtime walks down the alley, often running ahead and then pouncing out from a bush in front of Chandu, who pretended great surprise. Although Fluffy now had her own food bowl, the two animals liked to have their meals side by side. In cold weather, when Chandu bedded down for the night beside my bed, Fluffy arranged herself in the warm middle of his curled body. When he chose to spend time in his doghouse in the back yard, Fluffy joined him. And in afternoons, she joined him on the porch to wait for me to come home from school, the two sitting side by side.

One Sunday afternoon when the two were playing in the back yard, two dogs strange to the neighborhood jumped over our fence and barked ferociously as they chased Fluffy. She leaped on top of Chandu's doghouse and Chandu rushed to attack. Hearing the racket, I ran outside screaming at the intruders. Terrified, I watched the fight — which was over quickly — as the dogs were no match for Chandu, who moved like lightning. The strays were routed and sent howling back over the fence. Chandu chased them a short distance, gave a few parting barks, and returned to leap gracefully over the fence. He strolled across the lawn with all the dignity and pride of a conquering knight. He stood on his hind legs at the doghouse to check on his friend, who rubbed her face against his as he smoothed her fur with a slobbery tongue. In turn, Fluffy purred the loudest purr I ever heard from a cat.

All was well once more with our beloved dog and his cherished feline pet and pal, the odd couple.

— Marcia E. Brown —

74

Peace and Quiet

I just want to live in peace and quiet.
~Agnetha Fältskog

When we moved to the mountains of West Virginia, we brought all our animals with us including our dog, Honus. While Honus didn't seem to enjoy the humidity, he did seem excited to be in the forest where he barked at squirrels, chipmunks, and birds. His constant barking was a little annoying, but there wasn't much we could do about it. So much for living in the peace and quiet of the forest!

Honus was sixteen years young and this was an adventure for him, but I worried about what might happen if he came in close contact with one of these creatures. Would his animal instincts kick in? Would something a little bigger be able to hurt Honus?

"Worrying about it isn't going to change anything," my husband said. "Honus has never been around other animals, but hopefully if he does get into a scuffle, it will be with something small and he won't get hurt. You know he really is a gentle soul; I don't think he'd hurt a flea!"

My husband was right. Still, I hoped there wouldn't be any trouble and that the forest creatures would stay away from Honus. After all, he was a dog.

Honus was pretty quiet in the morning, but each afternoon the barking and whining started up. On one beautiful fall afternoon, I'd just finished dusting the bedroom when I noticed how quiet it was. I suddenly felt sick as I realized something must be wrong with Honus—it was the time of day he usually barked and whined at his forest friends.

"Please let him be okay," I said out loud as I ran to the window that looked out to the yard. There I saw Honus, lying on his stomach with his head extended in front of him, a few inches away from his food bowl. His eyes were wide open and he was lying perfectly still while a feral cat and her five kittens ate the leftover food from his bowl.

Running into the other room, I hollered for my husband to come and see. "I told you he wouldn't hurt a flea," said my husband as he put his arm around me. "I don't think you need to worry about him anymore!"

We spent the next couple of months watching the mother and her babies feed from Honus's bowl each afternoon. Arriving at the same time each day, Honus would wag his tail when he'd see them coming, then lie down in his usual position and watch them eat. It was a beautiful sight and it came with an extra special bonus: For the first time since moving to the mountains, we finally enjoyed the peace and quiet — the way we'd imagined it would be!

— Jill Burns —

Matty, the Cat Chaser

The average dog is a nicer person
than the average person.
~Andy Rooney

M atty was a sweet, lovable, easygoing yellow mutt that I adopted from the pound when he was about a year old. Of course, none of the neighborhood cats would agree with the attributes I bestowed upon Matty. You see, Matty loved nothing better than to chase any cat that dared show up in our yard while he was outside. Indeed, Matty seemed to think this was a wonderful game and that the cats loved it as much as he did. The goal of the game, according to Matty, was to chase the cat up one of the many trees on my property. Then he would give his loudest, most vicious victory bark, declaring himself the winner, before retreating to let the terrified cat "escape." If a cat chose to flee instead of climbing a tree, Matty would chase it as far as the edge of our yard, and then stand watching the retreating cat with a look of deep disappointment on his face. He clearly thought the fleeing cat had not played by the rules. After all, he wasn't allowed to leave the yard, so he lost the game by default.

Matty clearly loved the macho feeling he got from frightening the cats and watching them run in terror, but his goal was never to actually catch one. If he came too close to overtaking a cat, he would back off a bit while continuing to growl and snarl so the chased cat would not guess what a softie he really was. As if he could read my thoughts, Matty sometimes ducked his head sheepishly when he saw me watching him from the porch as he walked back toward the house and allowed the latest treed cat to safely escape.

Once, to Matty's surprise and alarm, a large orange tabby stood his ground, hissing and slapping at the stunned dog. Too overwhelmed to retreat quickly enough, Matty got raked across the nose by the cat's claws. I ran toward the two animals, not sure what Matty would do next. But Matty, shocked, ran to me, whimpering, seeking comfort. It never occurred to him to hurt the cat, which, in Matty's mind, had cheated him out of a victory.

One afternoon I went outside with Matty to play ball. I watched the red rubber ball sail through the air and land in front of an evergreen bush on the far side of the yard. Matty yelped in glee and ran after the ball. Instead of bringing the ball back to me, his attention was caught by something in the bush. Guessing it was a cat, I figured our game was over for the time being. I heard Matty give one deep, loud growl, and then grow silent while peering beneath the bush. I walked closer and saw a slender gray cat hiding under the bush. The cat didn't make a move to run, but its eyes were wide with fright. Matty hunkered down and stared at the cat, woofing softly, as if to coax the cat into playing the game with him. Unlike the orange tabby, the gray cat showed no signs of aggression. It just lay still and watched Matty warily. Matty looked back at me, confused. This one wasn't going to run and it wasn't going to fight.

I reached the bush and squatted down to see if I recognized the cat. It was scraggly and thin, obviously a stray. The cat looked as if it had come out badly in a fight, with one ear torn and one eye swollen almost shut. "Let it alone," I said sternly to Matty. "This one is in no shape to run."

Reluctantly, Matty picked up the ball and dropped it in my hand. Although he chased the ball willingly, he frequently stopped by the bush, hunkered down, and gazed at the cat, woofing softly.

When it was time to go inside, Matty hesitated, looking back at the bush beneath which the injured cat lay. He looked up at me, his soft brown eyes almost pleading. He clearly thought I should do something. "He'll be fine," I told Matty. I made up my mind to call Animal Control if the cat was still here in the morning. With one last backward glance toward the bush, Matty lowered his head and obediently followed me inside the house.

I gave Matty his dinner in the kitchen and settled down in the living room to watch the evening news. I heard a whimper and looked up to see Matty standing at the door with his dish of food in his mouth. He had not eaten a single bite. Astonished, I could only stare in disbelief for several seconds. Matty's intentions were perfectly clear. I took the dish from Matty's mouth and we both went outside to the bush where the gray cat still lay. The cat raised his head and watched us approach, the apprehension in his eyes giving way to hope as he smelled the food in the dish. I placed the dish in front of the cat and stepped back so he wouldn't feel threatened. Watching Matty and me warily, he took a small bite. Then, unable to contain himself, he gave in to his great hunger and stuck his head in the dish and ate greedily.

Watching the cat as it ate almost in a frenzy, I suddenly felt ashamed. Matty had shown more concern for this poor, hungry, injured creature than I had shown. I thought of how I would feel if it were Matty, lying under a bush somewhere, at the mercy of strangers. I would certainly want someone to show compassion for him.

I bent down and hugged Matty, blinking back tears. If not for Matty, I would have called Animal Control in the morning, hoping that they would find a home for the unfortunate cat. I was humbled to realize that a dog had a kinder heart than me. I once thought that I had done a noble thing when I rescued Matty from the pound. My actions paled considerably when compared to Matty offering his dinner to a stray cat. And I was supposed to be the superior creature.

I retrieved a towel from the bathroom to wrap around the cat, in case he panicked when I picked him up. I carried him inside the house to tend to his wounds as best I could. In the morning I would take him to the vet for a checkup. After all, if I was going to allow Matty to have a cat, I had to make sure it was healthy.

When I asked Matty what he wanted to name his cat, he only said "woof" so I called him Wolf. The love this dog and this cat have for one another is remarkable. Remarkable is also a good word to describe how I came to learn kindness and compassion from a dog.

— Joe Atwater —

Ubu Saves the Day

The better I get to know men, the more
I find myself loving dogs.
~Charles de Gaulle

The year my daughter was born, I was struggling with many issues. My husband chose to leave our marriage to seek a more carefree lifestyle. I owned a home that was a money pit, and my funds were limited as I was working on a freelance basis so that I could parent my daughter. And, as all new parents are, I was horribly sleep-deprived and felt overwhelmed.

The one constant in my life was my dear dog, Ubu, who was quiet when the baby slept, gentle when she would crawl onto his back, and always near me making me feel loved.

Each day, I would take my baby for a stroll around the neighborhood with Ubu in tow. Ubu had been trained to walk with me without a leash and was very responsive to my commands, so I never worried about his behavior on our walks.

One day on our walk, my daughter started getting fussy, so I sped up and headed for home. While I told Ubu to come, he stood next to a house around the corner from me and just looked at me. Since my daughter was warming up to a full-blown crying fit, I told Ubu I was going home and that I couldn't wait for him.

I got home and found the source of my child's distress, took care of the problem, and sat on the front porch to await Ubu's arrival. Fifteen minutes passed and he was still not home, so I loaded up the stroller

Canine Friends | 243

and we set off to find him. The first place I looked was successful. Ubu was lying next to the front stairs of the house where we had left him.

As I approached Ubu, and inquired as to what was so important, I heard the noises of several crying kittens. I'm allergic to cats and did not want to get involved in whatever was going on under the stairs, but Ubu would not budge.

I knocked on the front door and the older woman explained that a stray cat had come onto her property and she suspected the cat had given birth. I asked her if she would like our help in retrieving the cats, but she was not a cat lover and told us that we could just leave them there.

Ubu did not agree, so I asked the woman if it was okay for my dog to go under her porch and try to retrieve the kittens. She scoffed and said, "Don't come crying to me when that cat claws your dog."

I told Ubu to stay put and that I would be right back. I went home and called Animal Control to ask them what we could do. The man said that he would send someone over, and I gave him the address. Then I changed into sweatpants in case I had to crawl under the porch, donned working gloves, and grabbed a laundry basket that I covered with sheets. I loaded everything into the stroller, and we headed back to the house.

When I arrived, Ubu was not there. I felt a bit of panic, thinking that the cat might have attacked him. But as I moved closer to the stairs, I saw he had crawled under the porch and was guarding the opening.

When the man from Animal Control showed up, he was surprised that Ubu was standing guard. He chuckled and said, "Is he waiting for a free meal?" I found no humor in that and suggested that we get on with saving the kittens. He said that he was not going to crawl under the porch to retrieve the kittens, so I pushed the stroller closer to the hole and kept up a lighthearted conversation with my daughter. The opening was only about twelve inches tall. I looked at the opening and attempted to fight off my claustrophobia and the idea that there could be spiders, rotting leaves, and who knew what else under the porch. But even as I tried to overcome my fears, there was no way I would be able to crawl through such a narrow opening.

I looked to the Animal Control man for guidance, but he just sneered and said, "Send the dog to get them."

I sat down next to Ubu and explained what had to happen. He needed to crawl under the porch and bring the kittens out. He needed to be very careful and gentle. While I was talking to Ubu, the Animal Control man started laughing and said, "Now, I've heard everything."

My frustration with the situation and this man's attitude grew. I said, "You have been of little help and absolutely no encouragement, so I'm going to make you a wager. If my dog retrieves the kittens, you are going to buy him a large bag of dog food, the premium kind."

The man's smirk turned to a grin. "You're on."

So I went back and sat down next to Ubu and explained again what I needed him to do. He belly-crawled to the back of the porch and one long minute later came out with a tiny kitten nestled gently in his mouth. When I asked him to give me the kitten, he hesitated. I found that perplexing so I told him again to give me the kitten; he did not. I don't know what made me think of it, but I turned, put on my work gloves, and brought the laundry basket over to Ubu. He not only gently placed the kitten in the basket but nudged the sheets over it as well.

Ubu "delivered" twelve kittens in the same manner. The shock on the Animal Control man's face was reward enough for me. I handed him the basket of kittens and headed for home.

Later that afternoon, he returned with a fifty-pound bag of dog food. "You told me that you were allergic to cats, and while your dog was rescuing those kittens, what really amazed me is that he wouldn't let you touch them. It was almost as if he knew you were allergic."

I smirked at him. "He did."

—Judith Fitzsimmons—

A Light in the Heart

Fun fact: Some animal shelters test how a dog behaves around cats so they can advise people on whether the dog they want to adopt is "cat-friendly."

"Has anyone seen Charge?" I murmured, only half-expecting a reply. The kids were running around the house, each doing their own thing, and my husband was watching the football game. So I made a quick check of the bedrooms and looked out in the back yard. Since she had only been out of sight for a few hours, I wasn't overly concerned. I assumed she must be under one of the kids' beds, hiding from all the chaos that was normal for a Sunday afternoon in our home.

Charge was a homely, mixed-breed canine, to put it kindly. It wasn't her fault; she was simply gifted with the worst appearance traits from each of the breeds in her background. She was about the size of a Cockapoo, with gray-and-black wiry hair, short legs, and a long straggly tail. She constantly cowered when strangers approached, which definitely did not help her appearance. But she had a heart of gold, and we loved her.

My husband had found Charge wandering along the freeway one day on his way home from work. She looked as though she hadn't eaten in weeks, so he stopped and coaxed her into the car with bits of his leftover lunch. Not knowing what to do, he brought her home with the hope of finding her owners or at least a loving family that would take her.

However, once she was in the house, the kids were bound and determined not to let her go. After a day or two of whining and begging, we reluctantly gave in and told them we could keep her — a decision I never regretted.

After observing her actions for a few days, it was obvious that she had been abused. She was extremely untrusting and afraid of everyone. In time, though, she came to love the kids and slept on their beds every night.

Charge was exceptionally nurturing with the children. I wondered if the fact that she had been mistreated had conditioned her to be protective of those who were hurting.

Every time the kids cried, Charge would run to them and tenderly offer her comforting paw. This worked wonders when they were injured, but it more or less defeated the purpose when they were whimpering during a time-out!

Unlike our mamma cat, who had recently given birth to a litter of five, Charge would have been an awesome mother. Sadly, she was never blessed with puppies. We sometimes joked that she was too homely to attract suitors.

When I was finally able to get everyone's attention at the dinner table, I asked again if anyone had seen Charge. After a unanimous "No," I thought it would be a good idea to take a look around the neighborhood.

"Who wants to go look for Charge with me?" I hollered as I opened the door of the hall closet and reached in to get my shoes.

"CHARGE!" I screamed, because there she was in the closet! She looked up at me from inside the kittens' box as if to say, "Shhh, I just got them to sleep!"

We usually kept the closet door open a bit so Mamma Cat could go in and feed her litter, but she always left as soon as they finished nursing. Apparently, Charge knew they needed more Mamma time and was more than willing to help out.

The kids giggled with glee upon seeing the dog in with the kittens. My husband shook his head and quipped, "Only you, Charge. Only you!"

Charge continued to mother the kittens until they were placed in their new homes. She may not have been an attractive dog, but as Kahlil Gibran said, "Beauty is not in the face; beauty is a light in the heart." Charge truly had that inner beauty.

—Connie Kaseweter Pullen—

A Brother from Another Mother

You can't buy happiness, but you can rescue it.
~Author Unknown

I t had hit over a hundred degrees here in Southern California, so I decided Mollie the Beagle and I needed to go to the air-conditioned pet store to cool off. She could use a new toy, and I could pick up some dog food.

We have been through a lot together — some illnesses, my husband's death — but happy times, too. Mollie is my pal, and even though her roots are getting gray just like mine, she has some good years left. An only child, she pretty much runs the house and lets me live there. Mollie has her side of the bed, and I have mine.

So, when I started considering a feline addition to the family, I wasn't sure if Mollie would agree. Outside, she chases cats off our property, no matter how much I object. She has become my protector and companion. Would she let another member into our pack?

"Hey Mollie, let's go look at the rescue-adoption cages. Wouldn't a cat be nice? You need some company."

Mollie followed on her leash, unaware where I was taking her. We got to the glassed-in wall of cats, and a strange thing happened. Mollie didn't bark, whine or get excited but went over to a cubby on the bottom row. A beautiful gray-and-white fur ball walked up and pushed its nose against the glass. Mollie put her nose against his with only the cold pane between them. She sat there mesmerized as if in a trance. Could this be? Was this love at first sight?

Canine Friends | 249

I went to the checkout counter and asked a few questions. The cat was a male and he was roughly eighteen months old. Perfect! He was found living on the streets and eating garbage, which accounted for his thin frame. I asked when Mollie and I could adopt him.

"Come back Saturday with these papers filled out," the cashier said, handing me a questionnaire. "We sponsor Helen Sanders CatPAWS rescue, but the woman who handles everything won't be here until then."

"Thanks. Well Mollie, looks like you're getting a brother from another mother," I said.

Mollie seemed pleased, and although I was skeptical, I couldn't wait. Would Mollie feel so smitten when she found out he was moving in and staying?

Saturday rolled around, and with more tidbits, food, litter and toys than I'd need for ten cats, I took our new addition home.

Brodie turned out to be a real pistol. His name had been Mr. Magoo before I changed it, and I could see why. He had a goofy personality.

I followed the instructions I found on Google for introducing new cats to the family. Everything went smoothly, but Brodie was a very active guy. He'd run up and down the hall at a hundred miles an hour and slam into the walls. He loved to play with silver pipe cleaners twisted in a loop, jumping over six feet to catch them. He didn't want to be petted except when he said so. To do otherwise would get you a bite on the hand. He attacked my ankles when I walked down the hall, and he loved to run up, nip me and take off. He was a real hit-and-run artist.

I worried about how Mollie was taking to this spastic cat running all over the furniture and commandeering her doggie bed. Life on the streets had made him wary of any affection. Although they were able to be in the same room together without incident, they stayed clear of interaction. Brodie seemed spooked when Mollie barked, and she gave him a wide berth.

I was worried. Brodie wasn't the lovable guy I had first anticipated. I think Mollie was skeptical that he would ever be a worthy pack member.

One morning about three months later, while I was having my coffee, Mollie tried to play with Brodie. With her butt in the air in the typical doggie-play stance, she approached him and started to gently nudge him and whine. Brodie seemed to like this and put this head down to rub her. Then, all of a sudden, she started getting rougher, which got her a clean swipe on the nose that made her yip and head for my bed.

I was sad. Wasn't my little family going to work out after all? Was this the start of the end? I couldn't give up Brodie now. Who would put up with his antics? They would definitely send him to the shelter or worse! I loved him, and this was his furever home.

Upset, I left at noon and went to do errands. I was afraid when I came home that I would find some fur or bloodshed, but I had to see if they could work it out. I didn't think Mollie would hurt Brodie, but he was a feisty guy.

I prayed, "Dear God, please let my kiddos get along. I can't abandon one of your creatures."

When I arrived home about an hour later, they were cuddled together, yawning on Mollie's doggie bed. Mollie looked up as if to say, "What's up, Mom?" I started to cry; my little family had reached a truce.

It's been six years now, and Mollie has accepted Brodie as a crazy pack member. They continue to find their own compromises and are working it out. Brodie has calmed down, but his exuberance shines through. He chatters and makes crazy noises as he does yoga every morning. He's become quite a hit on my Facebook page doing his downward dog, which puts Mollie to shame. Brodie sleeps cuddled between Mollie and me. Brodie has learned that no one is going to hurt him. He loves kisses and lets me pet him all I want. I caught Mollie and him nuzzling each other last week.

Mollie knew what she was doing the day she chose Brodie. We needed a little spice in our lives, and we got a red-hot pepper.

— Sallie A. Rodman —

Pedro the Fisherman

There is no faith which has never yet been broken,
except that of a truly faithful dog.
~Konrad Lorenz

The most touching dog story I've ever heard was told to me thirty years ago by a neighbor on her return from a Mediterranean cruise.

The setting of the story is a little cove on the east side of the Spanish island of Mallorca. It was there that an Englishman, a professional diver, lived on his yacht with his dog, a springer spaniel. He had tied his yacht to a pier where diving conditions were ideal. Each time the Englishman made a dive, the dog sat anxiously on the pier, awaiting his return. One day the dog became so concerned when the Englishman disappeared into the water that he dove in after him.

Underwater, the dog saw a school of fish swim past. He grabbed a fish and carried it back to the pier. The Englishman, surprised and pleased, praised him. After that, the dog followed the man on his dives. In the course of the shared diving, the dog developed excellent fishing skills, to the man's considerable amusement. The Englishman told the island's residents of his dog's accomplishments, and they came to the pier to watch. Delighted, they began calling the dog Pedro, after Peter, the fisherman.

One day the Englishman became ill, and shortly thereafter, he died. Townspeople tried to adopt Pedro, but the dog would never leave the beach for fear he would miss his master's return. He waited on the beach through hot sun and driving rain. People tried to feed him, but eventually they gave up. He wouldn't accept food from anyone other than his master. Finally, to feed himself, Pedro went back to fishing.

It happened that on this same island there were a number of stray cats. Ravenous, they would gather to watch Pedro dive into the schools of fish, select the fish he wanted and bring it back to eat on the shore. Then the cats would fight over what the dog had left uneaten. The dog must have observed this, for one morning when Pedro had eaten his fill, he dove into the water again and came back up with a large fish, which he placed on the sand before the group of cats. Then he backed off and watched. One black cat, with greater courage than the others, approached the fish, grabbed it and ran. After that, in addition to keeping vigil for his master, the dog also seemed to consider it his duty to feed those less fortunate. For every morning thereafter, Pedro the fisherman shared his catch with the hungry cats of Mallorca.

— Bob Toren —

Friends

A friend is one soul abiding in two bodies.
~Aristotle

Twenty-one years ago, my husband gave me Sam, an eight-week-old schnauzer, to help ease the loss of our daughter, who was stillborn. Sam and I developed a very special bond over the next fourteen years. It seemed nothing that happened could ever change that.

At one point, my husband and I decided to relocate from our New York apartment to a new home in New Jersey. After we were there awhile, our neighbor, whose cat had recently had kittens, asked us if we would like one. We were a little apprehensive about Sam's jealousy and how he would handle his turf being invaded, but we decided to risk it and agreed to take a kitten.

We picked a little, gray, playful ball of fur. It was like having a road runner in the house. She raced around chasing imaginary mice and squirrels and vaulted from table to chair in the blink of an eye, so we named her Lightning.

At first, Sam and Lightning were very cautious with each other and kept their distance. But slowly, as the days went on, Lightning started following Sam — up the stairs, down the stairs, into the kitchen to watch him eat, into the living room to watch him sleep. As time passed, they became inseparable. When they slept, it was always together; when they ate, it was always next to each other. When I played with one, the other joined in. If Sam barked at something, Lightning ran to see what it was. When I took either one out of the house, the other was always waiting by the door when we returned. That was the way it was for years.

Then, without any warning, Sam began suffering from convulsions and was diagnosed as having a weak heart. I had no other choice but to have him put down. The pain of making that decision, however, was nothing compared with what I experienced when I had to leave Sam at the vet and walk into our house alone. This time, there was no Sam for Lightning to greet and no way to explain why she would never see her friend again.

In the days that followed, Lightning seemed heartbroken. She could not tell me in words that she was suffering, but I could see the pain and disappointment in her eyes whenever anyone opened the front door, or the hope whenever she heard a dog bark.

The weeks wore on and the cat's sorrow seemed to be lifting. One day as I walked into our living room, I happened to glance down on the floor next to our sofa where we had a sculptured replica of Sam that we had bought a few years before. Lying next to the statue, one arm wrapped around the statue's neck, was Lightning, contentedly sleeping with her best friend.

— Karen Del Tufo —

A Gentle Goodbye

True friends are never apart, maybe
in distance but never in heart.
~Author Unknown

everal years after my mother was widowed, she decided a cat would be the perfect companion. Since I shared my home with two cats, I was considered the feline expert. When my veterinarian told me about a litter of six-week-old kittens that had been dropped off on his clinic steps, I helped my mother pick out the perfect kitten, whom she named Cameo. From that point on, the sun rose and set on this black and white cat, who, unlike my cats, could do no wrong. Cameo quickly became my mother's pride and joy.

For the next eight years, Cameo lived as an only cat. Since Mommala and I lived near each other, we frequently exchanged visits and cat-sitting chores. When I visited Mommala accompanied by my golden retriever guide dog Ivy, Cameo would go into hiding as soon as we entered the apartment. After being unharnessed and unleashed, Ivy would go looking for a playmate, but Cameo would retreat further under the bed.

During my frequent travels, my two cats stayed at Mommala's house, and the three cats established a comfortable relationship. However, when Mommala traveled and Cameo came to stay with us, her shyness caused her to spend much of the time behind the stove or on the closet shelf. Frequently, the only sign of her presence was the emptied food bowl I set out for her at night while keeping the other cats enclosed in my bedroom. Although Ivy was gentle with cats, Cameo never learned to be comfortable around her.

At Mommala's death, Cameo's world turned upside-down. I had told Mommala that if anything happened to her I would adopt her beloved cat. Because I had recently married and moved from New York to California, Cameo's first hurdle was a coast-to-coast flight. To my delight, she traveled with hardly a meow in the carrier I placed under the empty seat next to me. Ivy, like most guide dogs, occupied the space for carry-on luggage under the seat in front of me. Following our arrival in Fresno, Cameo had to adapt to a strange new world, including one new cat and my husband's guide dog, Kirby. It had been bad enough dealing with one golden retriever, but now there were two of these playful creatures to reckon with!

As anticipated, Cameo went undercover for three weeks. It was her passion for food that eventually drove this timid creature out of hiding and into family life.

As a blind cat lover in a multi-cat household, I identify each cat by a distinctive-sounding collar bell. For Cameo, I selected one with a tiny tinkle that seemed to go perfectly with her petite and cuddly persona. The day I heard the tinkle of her bell hitting the food bowl, I knew we were entering a new phase of togetherness.

Whenever I sat in my favorite lounge chair listening to a book on tape and knitting, I knew immediately when it was Cameo who chose to share my lap. After a while she would butt her head into my hand indicating it was time to stop these other activities and begin brushing her. Delighting in being groomed, Cameo rewarded me with purrs and kneading paws. Occasionally, I felt her body stiffen, and I'd know one of the dogs was approaching.

During the first few months Cameo was with us, when Ivy or Kirby approached, she jumped off my lap and leaped onto a table, counter or the refrigerator. Soon realizing that dogs, although large, could easily be dominated by a powerful hiss or smack, she no longer relinquished lap time and administered doggy discipline as needed.

Over the next few years, Cameo coexisted peacefully with her canine and feline siblings. When the alarm clock went off in the morning and the dogs were invited to join us, she learned to make room in the bed for the canine corps. As time passed, she thought nothing of jumping over a dog for a cuddle from a favorite human.

When progressive loss of vision forced Ivy's retirement from guide work, and my new guide-dog partner, Escort, entered the family, Cameo met this challenge with newly acquired feline aplomb.

Escort, a young, playful and energetic golden retriever, was put in his place by hisses, spitting and, if needed, a smack on the nose. Like Ivy and Kirby, he learned that this small creature could readily communicate her desire to be left alone, particularly when she occupied my lap.

Although Cameo and my beloved guide dog Ivy lived together for six years, they could not be called friends. They resembled siblings, who, for the good of other family members, had agreed to live together but basically ignore each other's foibles.

During the year of Ivy's retirement, her health continued to deteriorate. The day came when the quality of her life had worsened to the point where I knew our partnership had to end.

I made the dreaded call asking our veterinarian to come to the house to euthanize my friend, helper and companion of eleven years. When the doctor arrived, my husband, our friend Eve and I sat on the floor in a circle around Ivy to provide comfort in her last moments. At this time, Cameo was fast asleep in her favorite chair. What happened next showed me a totally new and unexpected side of her personality.

She awoke with a start, and the sound of her tinkling bell alerted me she was on the way. Jumping over Eve, she joined the circle. Purring loudly and rubbing up against her human companions, she provided the comfort we so desperately sought in this emotion-laden situation. She seemed to adopt the role of grief counselor. At one point she flung herself into my arms, sending me a clear message that she felt my pain and was there to comfort me. No more aloof feline reserve for her.

And as Cameo walked back and forth between us all, it was obvious that she was no longer indifferent to her long-term house partner. Several times she stopped and licked Ivy's face, something she had never done before. As I held Ivy in my arms and reached out to touch Cameo, I felt Cameo's tiny paw touching Ivy's large paw. Cameo seemed incredibly attuned to the importance of touching the old dog, who was now totally blind.

But Ivy could still hear, and it comforts me to realize that the last sounds my treasured teammate heard as she slipped quietly into a gentle death were my murmured endearments and Cameo's soothing purrs.

— Toni Eames —

Dixie's Kitten

*There is something about the presence of a cat... that
seems to take the bite out of being alone.*
~Louis J. Camuti

ixie was a pretty dog, an English setter dressed in a white coat
adorned with black and brown markings. In her younger days
she had spent many happy hours in the fields, running and
hunting quail. But now Dixie was so old that she spent most of
her time lying in the sun, basking in the soothing warmth of its rays.
She especially loved to lie in the yard. There was a full water bucket
and brimming food dish within easy reach, and her outdoor shelter
was lined with clean, fragrant hay. There were times when her old
bones ached and pained her, and she would groan as she stood up to
move to another patch of sunlight. But sometimes there were wonderful days when somebody brought by a young bird-dog pup, and a
spark would leap in her tired eyes. She adored puppies and would
forget her age for a little while as she romped with the younger dogs.

"It's been a long time since you were a puppy, old girl," I told
her one day, stopping to comb my fingers through her silky hair. She
wagged her tail and looked toward the pup being admired in the front
yard. Then with a soft whine, she eased her aching body into a more
comfortable position and dropped her chin to her paws. Her eyes were
fastened on the younger dog and she seemed lost in thought. Probably
dreaming about the days when she was running through the fields
teaching the younger dogs to sniff out quail, I decided. I gave her one

last pat on the head, and went into the house.

Lately Dixie had seemed lonely. I remembered the family of ducks that used to cross the road in front of our house every evening to share her dish of dog food. Not once had Dixie growled or snapped at the ducks, and sometimes she would even move aside so they could have better access to her food. Visiting cats were always welcome to join in the meals, and it wasn't unusual at all to find her with her nose in the same bowl with several ducks, cats and whatever stray dog may have wandered up. Dixie was a gentle, social soul and nowadays there just didn't seem to be as many guests dropping by to chat over dinner.

One day there was a knock at my door. I opened it to find my next-door neighbor standing there with a concerned look on his face. "Have you seen my kitten?" he asked. "He slipped out and is missing."

It was a cute, fluffy little thing, not much bigger than a minute, and I knew my neighbor was right to be concerned. A tiny lost kitty would be no match for the coyotes and wild cats that roamed our rural area.

I told him I hadn't but that if I spotted it, I would give him a call. He thanked me, sadness etched on his face. "He's so little," he said as he headed for the next house. "I'm afraid if I don't find him soon, something bad will happen to him."

Later that afternoon I carried dog food out to Dixie. She was in her house and I could hear her tail thumping a greeting as I poured the food into her bowl. I fetched the water hose and filled her bucket, then called her out to eat. Slowly she emerged and painfully, carefully, stretched. As I reached down to pat her head, a tiny gray kitten stepped out of the dark doghouse and twined itself around Dixie's legs.

"What have you got there, girl?" I exclaimed. Dixie glanced down at the kitten, then looked back up at me with a gleam in her eye. Her tail wagged harder. "Come here, kitty," I said and reached for it. Dixie gently pushed my hand aside with her nose and nudged the kitten back inside the doghouse. Sitting down in front of the door, she blocked the kitten's exit and I could hear it meowing inside. This had to be my neighbor's lost kitten. It must have wandered through the thicket of bushes between our places and straight into Dixie's doghouse.

"Crazy dog," I muttered. Dixie wagged her agreement, but didn't budge from in front of the door. She waited until I was a safe distance away before she stood up to begin nibbling at the pile of food. I went into the house and telephoned my neighbor.

"I think I've found your kitten," I told him. I could hear the relief in his voice, then the laughter as I told him that Dixie had been hiding it. Promising to come over to collect the runaway cat, he hung up after thanking me again.

He showed up, eager to look at the kitten. "Yep, that's my cat!" he said as the little gray fur ball stepped out of the doghouse. Dixie backed away from us and nosed the kitten toward the door. Gratefully, the man reached for the cat. In the same instant, Dixie snarled at him.

I was shocked. She'd never growled at anybody before! I scolded her, and my neighbor reached for the kitten again. This time Dixie bared her teeth.

"Let me try," I said. I reached for the kitten but Dixie shoved it inside the doghouse, then followed it in and flopped down, blocking the tiny cat from us with her body. Nobody was going to take her kitten!

We could hear the kitten purring loudly inside the house. Then it stepped up, bold as brass, and rubbed itself against Dixie's face. She licked its fur and glared out at us. It was plain that she had adopted the little cat and planned to keep it. "Huh," I said. At the moment, it seemed the only thing to say.

"Well, it looks like the kitten's happy," my poor neighbor said after a few minutes. The little gray cat had curled up between Dixie's front paws and was grooming itself intently. Every once in a while it stopped to lick Dixie's face. Kitten and dog seemed perfectly content. "I guess she can keep the kitten, if she wants it that bad."

So Dixie was allowed to help raise the kitten that she had claimed as her own. Thanks to the kindness and understanding of my neighbor, the tiny cat and the old dog spent many happy hours together. The kitten benefited from the arrangement and grew into a fine, healthy cat. And Dixie was happy to live out her days basking in the sun, dreaming of kittens and puppies and romping in the fields.

—Anne Culbreath Watkins—

Chapter
9

A Cat's Purpose

83

A Furry Little Secret

In this life we cannot always do great things.
But we can do small things with great love.
~Mother Teresa

I grabbed a potholder and pulled the tray of blackened star-shaped cookies from the oven. Well, that about matched my holiday mood. Dark and up in smoke! Money was tight, schedules were hectic, the house was a mess. And the shopping list! I wanted to do something special, but I had no idea what to get my mom for Christmas.

Recently Mom had remarried and moved to Canada. With work, family schedules and limited vacation time, I didn't get to visit her very often. So I did my best to keep in touch with her on the computer via chat.

"The holidays are too stressful," I typed that night.

"Oh, dear. Don't worry about all that," Mom typed back. "Think about the carols, and the pretty snow... just think about the positives."

Well if that wasn't a mom thing to say! Over the next few days, I ran around shopping, helping with the kids' school programs, volunteering at church and making sure everything got done. I didn't take time to stop and listen to the cheerful music piped into the stores or to appreciate the beautiful snowflakes that decked the evergreen outside my kitchen window.

Instead, I worried about my gift list. I'd already shopped for my husband and the kids, but I still needed to get something for Mom.

Mom lived in a townhouse with her new husband, Hans. The transition to a new home and a new marriage hadn't been easy for her. She had Darlene — a friend from church — and a few others, but she still missed her old friends and family. She especially missed having pets.

To be fair, Hans was a cat lover, and had a cat of his own — an old black-and-white longhaired feline named Susie. But Susie didn't like Mom. Not one bit. Apparently the cat didn't want to share her affection with anyone but Hans.

"Why don't you get a cat of your own?" I'd asked.

"Nah, that's okay," Mom had responded. "I have enough here to take care of." But I knew the real problem was that Mom wouldn't do something special for herself.

Hans didn't get out much and hadn't thought of getting another cat for Mom. But a cat of her own would make Mom so happy. I wondered — could I get Mom a cat for Christmas? It's not like I could order one from a catalog. The idea lurked in the back of my mind.

"What are your Christmas plans?" I typed one day.

"I'm going to a party with Darlene," Mom responded. She went on to tell me about the church Christmas party and something called Secret Sisters. They drew names, and would exchange secret gifts at the party.

I stopped typing. Secrets? Gifts? A smile spread across my lips. Could this be my way to get Mom a special surprise?

I hurriedly signed off the chat so that I could set to work on my new idea. I found Darlene's address and tapped out an e-mail. "Dear Darlene," I wrote, "I have kind of an unusual request..."

From that day on, Darlene and I began plotting in secret. I found myself smiling and humming Christmas carols. I paused while washing the dishes and noticed how delicately the new-fallen snow laced the windowpanes. I made it to both the kids' holiday concerts, and even managed to bring a plate of un-burnt cookies for the bake sale! And when I chatted with Mom, I fairly burst from keeping the secret.

"Things must be going better," Mom typed. "You don't sound as stressed."

"Yeah, I guess you're right!" I typed back. "Maybe I just took some good advice."

The day of the Secret Sister party arrived. That night I logged onto my computer, wondering how the party went and if the details of the surprise had all worked out. I didn't have to wonder for too long. The chat messenger pinged.

"Hi!!!" Mom wrote. The number of exclamation marks she used suggested that she was very happy. "I just got back from the party. Guess who is here helping me type?"

"I couldn't guess," I teased.

"It's a beautiful little gray kitten! She's sooooo cute! I named her Misty, short for Mistletoe."

"Glad you like your surprise!" I wrote.

"She stole my heart," Mom wrote back.

I beamed, imagining Mom at her computer far away, with her little gray kitten purring beside her. She told me about the party and how Darlene placed before her a box with holes in the sides. When she'd reached into the box and felt the soft ball of fur, she'd been so happy she couldn't stop the tears. She couldn't write for too long; she had to do some important work getting her little friend settled down and accustomed to her new home. "Now, how'd you arrange something like this?" she asked.

"It must have been some Christmas magic," I replied.

After we signed off, I addressed a few last-minute cards. Only a week until Christmas. Everything wasn't ready; everything wasn't perfect. But that was okay. When the holiday stress built up, I knew the cure. I had taken Mom's advice a step further. Don't just think about the positives, do something positive. Like a little secret act to make someone else happy. Even if it involves a lot of miles, a box with holes in it, a secret sister, and one perfect gray kitten.

— Peggy Frezon —

84

Ready or Not

I am always ready to learn although
I do not always like being taught.
~Winston Churchill

R ight before my twenty-eighth birthday, my mother announced she was leaving New York to move to a retirement community in Central Florida with her boyfriend. Mom and her partner decided to toss the majority of belongings accumulated from their separate lives, leaving most of it curbside.

A few days prior to their departure, I went to Mom's for a farewell/ birthday dinner.

"I know how much you love my cat," Mom began, cutting nonchalantly into her chicken cutlet.

I knew where the conversation was headed. I did love our family pet, stoic black Sheba with her verdant eyes, but I was reluctant to accept her as a "gift."

"Um-hmm," I said, shoveling a mound of mashed potatoes into my mouth.

I was upset that my mother — my best friend — would be moving away, so having something as a daily reminder of our bond would be fantastic, but I wasn't yet ready to nurture another life.

Mom persisted: "You know, Steve is allergic to cats, so I was thinking…"

My fork picked up speed, now nervously galloping from plate to mouth.

Mom stopped and placed a warm hand on my arm. "Honey, are

you okay?"

I dropped the utensil and swallowed hard.

"I could bring her to an animal shelter, but I didn't think you'd want that for her."

There it was. *The guilt.*

"Fine. I'll take her."

Mom pumped her fist in celebration of another item ticked off her "Things to Purge Before I Move" list.

Acquiring Sheba was no easy feat. The co-op I had just settled into didn't allow pets, which meant she would have to be smuggled in. This didn't hinder Mom's agenda. The woman I grew up with—a straight-laced role model who abided by every rule—was rolling up her shirtsleeves and concocting a scheme.

"We'll give her a mild sedative and sneak her in through the back entrance where the trash receptacles are," Mom said, pointing out of the window of my apartment. "And from there we'll bring her up in the freight elevator."

Still unsure, I glanced out of the glass casement, wondering if we'd really get away with it.

"Ready to do this?" Mom turned to me and smiled. I looked at her and gave a meek nod.

"Oh, and before I forget," Mom said, dipping into her purse. She pulled out a small envelope and handed it to me. "It's a gift card for Petco. I'll send you one every month. You know, to offset the costs of litter and food."

I studied the yellow card, my official golden ticket into cat-lady-hood, and shoved it into the back pocket of my jeans. "Come on, let's get this over with."

I held the door as MacGyver, I mean Mother, led the way out. In the back seat of our family sedan was Sheba, awake but tranquil, in the plastic carrier Mom had managed to secure her in. I stood back as my mother shimmied the case out of the car. When the cat let out a screeching howl, I jumped away, expecting Mom to do the same. Instead, she casually reached into the car and grabbed a blanket from the floor. I watched in wonderment as she draped it over the cage and hushed the animal back to a calm silence.

"Have you done this before? You're like the cat whisperer," I said, only half-joking.

"No, I'm a mom." She winked and then put a finger to her lips, signaling for quiet. I proceeded with caution.

As we approached the freight elevator, I jabbed a finger on the button and scanned the area for the nearest surveillance cameras. Luckily, they were aimed in the direction of the exit doors, out of view from where we stood.

"Geez, don't ever try to rob a bank," Mom said, and nudged me.

A loud, grinding noise followed by a thud of heavy metal echoed in the vestibule. Mom jerked open the door to the freight elevator and waved me inside. Slowly, the machine lifted us to the eighth floor. As we ascended, a black paw poked out from under the blanket and swatted at my leg. I swatted back. The cat did it again, but this time rested her paw on top of my hand.

"She's playing with you," Mom said with a grin.

"I know." I knelt down and rubbed the side of Sheba's head through the grate. She let out a vigorous purr, the vibrato of her throat tickling my fingers and, surprisingly, my heart.

The elevator jerked to a halt. The cat retracted into the carrier as Mom yanked at the door handle to free us. Mom eased down the hall and into my residence. Once we were inside, she set the holder on the carpet and let Sheba out. The cat's head darted in one direction and then the other. I was sure she was going to run and hide under furniture — either the sofa or the bed. I lowered myself and sat on the rug, cross-legged and curious, waiting to see which way she'd go. When she noticed me sitting there, she strutted over, stepped into the crook of my lap, arched her spine into a big stretch, and then nestled down into a big black ball of fuzz.

"You're a natural," Mom said.

I looked down at Sheba and petted her warm, velvety fur. We bonded, and I laughed at the realization that mothers really do know best once in a while.

— Dawn Turzio —

85

Foiled Again

Never try to out stubborn a cat.
~Robert A. Heinlein

arly December is always exciting. Christmas spirit fills every corner of our house in the form of cookies, music and, most importantly, decorations. In our family, we have certain traditions when we decorate, including fastening the Christmas tree to the wall. This strange family tradition came about due to our cats.

Biscuit, Muffin, and Angus love Christmas just as much as we do. Unfortunately, that involves climbing the branches of the Christmas tree. These are fat cats, and they do a lot of damage. So, after they knocked over one tree too many, we fought back.

We started with a rope that was tied to hooks on the wall, but the "three mouseketeers" took down the tree without a hitch. We needed to be more aggressive. We placed a spray bottle next to the tree so we could spray any cat that crossed enemy lines. But we couldn't stand guard 24/7, so that didn't work either.

The next year, we added a baby gate around the tree, but they found their way around that. The following year, we brought in the big guns (or so we thought): We bought mats that were specially designed with spikes to keep cats out of certain areas. They still found their way to the tree.

Last year, we added even more armament by purchasing mats that emit a high-pitched sound when stepped upon. We believed we had finally solved the problem, but that didn't work either. The mats were very effective, but instead of keeping out the cats, the mats kept *us* out. Almost every day, someone would walk over to admire the tree and step on the mats, forgetting they were there. The deafening noise sent whoever stepped on them racing across the room.

Although our protection mechanisms continue to get more elaborate, the cats still find a way to outsmart us every year. Our attempts to protect the tree from the cats have created my favorite Christmas memories. Our family tradition isn't coming up with barricades; it's sitting around with my family and laughing about yet another plan that failed.

—Alexis Sherwin—

Miss Feather's Lesson

Kindness is the language which the deaf
can hear and the blind can see.
~Mark Twain

After school one day, I saw some boys poking a stick into a thorn bush and laughing. My worst fears were realized when I heard a faint "meow" from inside the bush. I ran over and grabbed the stick away from them and peered into the bush. There I saw the most pitiful kitten I'd ever seen. Her color was questionable because of the dirt and blood matted into her coat. The thorns of the bush were pushing into her little body, and she was crying with pain. I had to get her out of there.

Crawling carefully into the bush, I freed her from the entangling thorn branches. My arms got totally covered in scratches — not just from the thorns, but from her claws as well, as the frightened kitten tried to hold on to me.

When I got home, I called out, "Mom! See what followed me home!" My mother was used to me bringing home stray animals. This kitten would be no different — she would have a home if she wanted to stay with us.

After carefully removing thorns, cleaning wounds and bathing this poor creature, I found that I had a beautiful, snow-white, long-haired kitten with sky-blue eyes. Because of her silky coat, I called her "Miss Feather."

The following week, a new family moved into our neighborhood.

They had a daughter named Judy Ann. Judy Ann talked "funny" — funny to the kids in our neighborhood, anyway — and they laughed at her. I felt sorry for Judy. I protected her from the kids who were mean to her, and we became friends. Judy Ann adored Miss Feather as much as I did and helped me to take care of her.

One morning at breakfast, Mother said, "Molly, why don't you give Miss Feather to Judy Ann? She has no cats of her own — and you have so many!"

"But, Mom, I found Miss Feather!"

"You just think about it."

That night I lay in bed and thought, and thought and thought. I decided that it would be a good idea to give Miss Feather to Judy Ann. She lived just two doors down, and I could still play with Miss Feather whenever I wanted. Once I had made my decision, I couldn't wait for morning to come so I could tell Judy Ann about it.

Judy Ann was thrilled to tears! We hugged and hugged as I passed the purring kitten to her.

Most pure white cats with blue eyes are deaf, and Miss Feather was no exception. Because little Miss Feather couldn't hear, she required constant and faithful care. Judy Ann was the perfect mistress for her — no one would ever understand Miss Feather's needs as completely as Judy Ann. Do you know why? Because Judy Ann was also deaf.

— Molly Lemmons —

87

The Cat Who Knew How To Live

If some people didn't tell you, you'd never know
they'd been away on a vacation.
~Kin Hubbard

Cookie was a working cat. He lived in a New York grocery store that he kept mouse-free. Cookie was no slouch, and there wasn't a self-respecting mouse that would dare cross his path.

After patrolling the nooks and crannies of the store at night, he had the run of the neighborhood where he would spend his days wandering. As evening approached, you could almost set your watch by his return to the store. He would arrive promptly five minutes before the store closed.

One cool October evening, Cookie disappeared.

The store's owners and their children searched for him in vain.

The kids were brokenhearted. As autumn turned to winter, the snow began to fall, covering the streets. Everyone worried about Cookie, alone in the freezing weather. "How will he survive?" the kids asked.

Miracle of miracles, the following spring, Cookie magically reappeared, looking healthy and clean. Everyone figured Cookie must have been sowing his wild oats in another neighborhood.

Everything went back to normal at the store. Cookie once more checked all the nooks and crannies of the store to make certain there had been no unwelcome visitors while he was away. He did his job perfectly until autumn, when Cookie once again disappeared!

Once more there was considerable consternation by his owners and their children. How would Cookie weather the winter snows and the freezing cold?

The next spring, just when the baby leaves started to form on the trees, Cookie returned again!

Cookie's owners began asking neighbors for any information as to where he might have been. The kids asked their friends if any of them knew where Cookie went during the freezing winter months.

No one seemed to know.

Finally, one of the children rang the bell of an older couple who lived in a private house near the grocery store.

"You say, a big black cat?" the woman asked. "With white little paws? Oh, yes. My husband and I hated to see him out in the cold. So I gave him a saucer of warm milk. After that he hung around our house almost every day. But we were going to Florida for the winter, as we do every year. I felt so bad about leaving that poor little creature here with no one to take care of him in the freezing weather. So we bought a cat carrier and we've been taking him to Florida with us every year for the past two years. He seems to like it down there. Has loads of friends. But, between you and me, I think he prefers New York in the summer. I think he has a girlfriend up here."

— Arnold Fine —

88

The Captain

An open door is a welcome that makes
a stranger into a friend.
~Author Unknown

In the middle of Iowa, on acreage just on the outskirts of a little town, sits an old farmhouse. Inside the house there are lots of couches and soft comfortable chairs, hand-built perches and scratching posts, kitty doors that lead to outside pens with grass and trees and lots of sunny spots to stretch out in. Every day volunteers come to groom and pet and feed freshly cooked food to the many cats who have this farmhouse all to themselves. There is also a small staff who keep the cats' house sparkling clean.

There are dogs there, too. Out back behind the house, near the garden and the orchard, are large dog kennels with insulated and heated doghouses in them. Volunteers come to walk and feed and "love up" the rescued dogs who are brought there when their time is up at the city pound.

As you can tell, the Noah's Ark Animal Foundation runs an unusual kind of no-kill sanctuary. Yet it is a state-licensed animal shelter, officially run as a non-profit charitable organization for over a decade.

For many years I dreamed of running a shelter for lost, stray and abandoned animals. But I wanted the shelter to be comfortable and home-like. Plus, I wanted to feed the animals healthy high-quality food and treat any ailments with natural remedies. Noah's Ark has been that dream-come-true for me. It has been wonderful to watch as the often malnourished animals who come to the shelter start blossoming with health. Their shining coats and bright eyes make all the hard work worthwhile.

Their personalities blossom, too. Some of the cats assume the role of official greeter, strolling out to inspect anyone who comes to visit.

Freddy, a large and beautiful gray Persian, was one of these greeters at Noah's Ark. In fact, I called Freddy "the Captain." He was not a cuddly cat, being far too macho for that, but he was a friendly sort and no one came to the shelter who was not subject to the Captain's inspection, and perhaps a rub or two against the leg. Freddy had been at the shelter six or seven years and had become a personal favorite of mine.

One Saturday morning, I received a frantic call from one of the volunteers who had gone to feed the cats that morning. Something terrible had happened — I had to come over right away.

Nothing could have prepared me for what I found when I arrived at the shelter. During the night, someone had broken into the locked shelter and gone on a killing spree, using blunt instruments to murder and maim over twenty-five cats.

The shock was devastating, and I was almost numb as I called the police and other volunteers to come and help me care for the injured, gather up the dead and attempt to put the shelter back into some semblance of order. As the word quickly spread, a local church sent a crew of ten men to help out, including two of the ministers. It was the compassionate and conscientious labor of all these volunteers that got me through the worst moments of that morning.

After about an hour, I had a panicked thought. What about the dogs? Running out to the kennels to check, I was immensely relieved to find them all unharmed. Two of the dogs in our care, Duke and Dolly, are Rhodesian ridgeback–mastiff mixes, enormous and powerful-looking dogs with the hearts of puppies — when it comes to people they know and love. For once I was glad they looked so formidable, even though it's probably why they haven't found homes yet, for I was sure that was why no stranger had been foolish enough to take them on.

When I returned to the house, volunteers were placing the cats that had died in a cart for burial. I felt the tears come to my eyes as I recognized so many of my little friends. Then I saw the gray body, partially covered by a towel.

"Not Freddy," I moaned. "Please don't let it be Freddy." But the Captain was nowhere to be found, and I had to face the fact that Freddy was gone.

I felt physically sick when I thought that it was probably his friendly, trusting nature that had killed him — walking right up to people who had evil intentions toward this sweet and innocent animal.

The outpouring of concern and sympathy from supporters in our community was amazing. And after the local paper reported the incident, the national news services picked up the story, and soon calls and letters flooded in from all over the country. People even drove from neighboring states to adopt the survivors of the attack.

It was a painful time for me. I felt the grief of losing so many beings I had come to love, and I was bewildered by the senselessness of the whole thing. Three young men from the local high school were convicted of the crime.

The incident caused a tremendous uproar in our little town. The violence that ravaged the shelter was the subject of intense debate. A small but vocal minority felt the victims were "just cats," so what was the big deal? But the majority of people, outraged animal lovers, demanded justice.

I felt dazed, trapped in a bad dream that wasn't going away. Nothing could bring back the cats that had died. As we went about the sad business of looking for the terrified cats who had escaped to hide, and of caring for the traumatized and injured cats who remained, I mourned my friends, especially Freddy.

A few days later, as I was stepping out of the house, I saw a large gray Persian coming slowly toward me. I scared us both by yelling "Freddy!" at the top of my lungs. It couldn't be — but it was. He was wobbly and shaken, no longer the suave and debonair greeter of old, but he was alive! I scooped him up into my arms and held him to my chest, my tears falling on his head as I hugged and stroked him. Freddy had come back.

In the chaos of that terrible morning, I had confused Freddy with another gray Persian, lying dead, half-hidden by a towel, on the burial cart. Freddy had been one of the lucky ones to make it outside and escape the others' appalling fate.

Miraculously, it took only a few weeks for Freddy to come around. Eventually, he even resumed his duties as official greeter.

In my grief after the incident, I had felt like giving up — I just hadn't had the heart to continue. It was the gray cat's courage and willingness to trust again that helped mend my own shattered spirit. Ultimately, my love for Freddy and others like him made me decide to continue Noah's Ark's life-saving rescue work in spite of what had happened.

Today, if you visit our shelter, you will be greeted by a large and confident gray cat walking proudly forward to meet you. His green eyes miss nothing as he inspects you from head to toe. If you pass muster, then you may feel his large bulk pressing affectionately against your shins. For the Captain, I am happy to report, it's business as usual.

— David E. Sykes —

The Cat and the Grizzly

*It's strange how we find the best of friends
in the most unexpected people.*
~Aly Hunter

"Another box of kittens dumped over the fence, Dave," one of our volunteers greeted me one summer morning. I groaned inside. As the founder of Wildlife Images Rehabilitation Center, I had more than enough to do to keep up with the wild animals in our care. But somehow, local people who didn't have the heart to take their unwanted kittens to the pound often dumped them over our fence. They knew we'd try to live-trap them, spay or neuter them, and place them through our network of approximately 100 volunteers.

That day's brood contained four kittens. We managed to trap three of them, but somehow one little rascal got away. In twenty-four acres of park, there wasn't much we could do once the kitten disappeared — and many other animals required our attention. It wasn't long before I forgot completely about the lost kitten as I went about my daily routine.

A week or so later, I was spending time with one of my favorite "guests" — a giant grizzly bear named Griz.

This grizzly bear had come to us as an orphaned cub six years ago, after being struck by a train in Montana. He'd been rescued by a Blackfoot Indian, had lain unconscious for six days in a Montana hospital's intensive care unit, and ended up with neurological damage and a blind right eye. As he recovered, it was clear he was too habituated to humans and too mentally impaired to go back to the wild, so he came to live with us as a permanent resident.

Grizzly bears are not generally social creatures. Except for when they mate or raise cubs, they're loners. But this grizzly liked people. I enjoyed spending time with Griz, giving him personal attention on a regular basis. Even this required care, since a 560-pound creature could do a lot of damage to a human unintentionally.

That July afternoon, I approached his cage for our daily visit. He'd just been served his normal meal—a mix of vegetables, fruit, dog kibble, fish and chicken. Griz was lying down with the bucket between his forepaws, eating, when I noticed a little spot of orange coming out of the blackberry brambles inside the grizzly's pen.

It was the missing kitten. Now probably six weeks old, it couldn't have weighed more than ten ounces at most. Normally, I would have been concerned that the poor little thing was going to starve to death. But this kitten had taken a serious wrong turn and might not even last that long.

What should I do? I was afraid that if I ran into the pen to try to rescue it, the kitten would panic and run straight for Griz. So I just stood back and watched, praying that it wouldn't get too close to the huge grizzly.

But it did. The tiny kitten approached the enormous bear and let out a purr and a mew. I winced. With any normal bear, that cat would be dessert.

Griz looked over at him. I cringed as I watched him raise his forepaw toward the cat and braced myself for the fatal blow.

But Griz stuck his paw into his food pail, where he grabbed a piece of chicken out of the bucket and threw it toward the starving kitten.

The little cat pounced on it and carried it quickly into the bushes to eat.

I breathed a sigh of relief. That cat was one lucky animal! He'd approached the one bear of the sixteen we housed that would tolerate him—and the one in a million who'd share lunch.

A couple of weeks later, I saw the cat feeding with Griz again.

This time, he rubbed and purred against the bear, and Griz reached down and picked him up by the scruff of his neck. After that, the friendship blossomed. We named the kitten Cat.

These days, Cat eats with Griz all the time. He rubs up against the bear, bats him on the nose, ambushes him, even sleeps with him. And although Griz is a gentle bear, a bear's gentleness is not all that gentle. Once Griz accidentally stepped on Cat. He looked horrified when he realized what he'd done. And sometimes when Griz tries to pick up Cat by the scruff of the cat's neck, he winds up grabbing Cat's whole head. But Cat doesn't seem to mind.

Their love for each other is so pure and simple; it goes beyond size and species. Both animals have managed to successfully survive their rough beginnings. But even more than that, they each seem so happy to have found a friend.

— Dave Siddon as told to Jane Martin —

90

Double Duty

*Our perfect companions never
have fewer than four feet.*
~Colette

As a member of a "dog family," I had long been conditioned to believe that cats simply didn't possess the ability or desire to be loving companions. This belief was so deeply ingrained that, while I didn't actually dislike cats, I found them, for the most part, uninteresting.

Arriving home from work one afternoon, I discovered a cat at my doorstep. I ignored him, but apparently he was not offended, because he was there again the following day.

"I'll pet you," I told him, "but there's no way you're coming in."

Then one night soon after, as the rain beat down and thunder clapped, I heard a faint meow. I couldn't take it anymore; I became a cat owner.

My new roommate, now named Shotzy, quickly became more than just a stray cat to feed. I liked the way his soft purring greeted me every morning and the way he nudged his head against my leg when I came home each day. His playful antics made me laugh, and soon Shotzy seemed more like a longtime friend than a pet I hadn't really wanted.

Although I suspected Shotzy had been an outdoor cat for a good portion of his life, he seemed perfectly content to stay inside, except for one remarkable exception. As if an alarm had gone off, at about six o'clock every night he'd cry to go out. Then, almost exactly one hour later, he'd be back. He did this for several months before I finally discovered what he had been up to.

One day a neighbor who knew about Shotzy showing up at my doorstep told me she thought the cat might belong to an elderly woman who lived down the street. Worried that I had mistakenly adopted someone's pet, I took Shotzy to the woman's house the next day.

When a white-haired woman opened the door, Shotzy bolted from my arms, ran into the house and made himself at home in a big recliner. The woman just threw her head back and laughed, saying, "Jimmy always did love his chair."

My heart sank — my Shotzy was obviously her Jimmy.

I explained I had taken him in and only discovered the day before that he may have already had a home. Again, the old woman chuckled. She invited me in and explained that the cat did not belong to her.

"But, I thought you called him Jimmy," I questioned.

The woman, who said her name was Mary, explained that Jimmy was her husband's name. He had died about a year before, just a few months after being diagnosed with cancer.

Before Jimmy died, he and Mary would eat dinner at five o'clock every night.

Afterward, they would retire to the living room, Jimmy to his favorite chair, to talk about the day's events. The couple had followed that routine every night for the sixty years they were married. After Jimmy's death, with no other family nearby, Mary said she just felt lost. And more than anything, she missed their nightly after-dinner talks.

Then one night a stray cat meowed demandingly at her screen door. When she cracked open the door to shoo him away, he ran straight to Jimmy's chair and made himself comfortable, as if he had lived there forever.

Mary, who had never had a pet in her life, found herself smiling at the animal. She gave him a little milk and then he cuddled on her lap. She talked to him about her life, but mostly about Jimmy. At about seven o'clock, at which time she normally turned on the TV and made herself some hot tea, the creature slipped off her lap and went to the door. At six o'clock the next evening, the cat was back. Soon, Shotzy and Mary had their own routine.

"Now, I believe in the Good Lord," Mary told me. "I don't know about all that reincarnation stuff, but sometimes it feels just like I'm talking to Jimmy when that little cat is here. I know that sounds strange, and I guess what's important is that the cat is a real comfort to me. But it's interesting to think on, all the same."

So Mary and I continued to share Shotzy. At my house, he revealed to me the many daily joys that come with living with a cat. At Mary's, his presence served to fill the six o'clock hour with happy companionship.

Our marvelous cat seemed to have an uncanny knack for always being in the right place at the right time.

— Lisa Hurt —

91

Jake and the Kittens

Kittens can happen to anyone.
~Paul Gallico

From the beginning, Jake made his feelings clear about the subject of cats: they were best served on a plate, with a side order of fries!

Jake was our resident dog, a large dominant male, part Border collie and part Labrador retriever, with a little German shepherd thrown in. Jake was about two years old when he adopted us from the local animal shelter. He came into our lives shortly after I lost my beloved dog Martha to an unexpected illness. One day we went to the shelter searching for a shaggy-haired female (like Martha) to bring into our home. Instead, we found Jake, a shorthaired male, sitting tall, proud and silent in the middle of all that barking. We told the shelter worker that we wanted Jake to come home with us because we could sense he had a lot of magic inside of him. "That's great," she said. "Just don't bring him back when he shows you that magic!"

Jake immediately became a cherished member of our family. He loved watching the birds we attracted to our yard with numerous feeders and birdbaths. He played with the puppy next door and other dogs in the park, but made it extremely clear that cats would never be allowed on his property, chasing any feline that came too close.

One day I found a litter of wild kittens in our woodpile. Although I had been a "dog person" all my life and had never had the privilege of sharing my life with a cat, my heart went out to these little furballs.

They were only about four weeks old, and had beautiful gray-striped bodies and large, frightened eyes. Their mother was nowhere in sight. I put them into a box and brought them inside. Jake heard the meowing and immediately began to salivate. And drool. And pant. Every attempt to introduce him to the kitties ended in near disaster. It was clear we couldn't keep the kittens in the house, even long enough to help find them homes. Our veterinarian told us, "Some dogs just won't accept cats under any condition."

A year after the kitty experience, I looked outside onto our deck and saw Jake with his ears up and his head cocked sideways, staring at the ground. There at his feet was a tiny kitten, sitting very still. Using soothing words to try and keep Jake calm, I moved in closer, hoping to prevent the ugly attack I felt sure was coming. The kitten had badly infected eyes, and it probably couldn't see where it was or what was looming over it. But Jake just looked at the little creature, then looked up at me, and then back at the kitten. I heard some meowing, and discovered another kitten under the deck. So I scooped them both up and brought them into the house, depositing them into a box that would be their temporary home. I put the box in the garage and started making calls to all the animal people I knew, telling each the same story — my dog would never allow these cats into our home, and I needed to relocate them right away.

I bought baby bottles and kitten milk, and as I fed my two little bundles of fur, I told them how much I would have loved to welcome them into our family. But it could never be.

The next morning, we found three more kittens lying in a pile outside the door, huddled together for warmth and protection. So I took them in and added them to the box.

My heart was very heavy. Now we had five little kittens, all with infected eyes, who would be sent out into a world already crowded with unwanted little creatures. I spent the day making phone calls, only to be told over and over that no one had room for more critters. I knew I'd run out of options, so with tears in my eyes, I picked up the phone to make the call to the vet that would take the kittens out of my life forever. At that same moment, my eyes fell on Jake, calmly observing everything going on around him. There was no drooling, no panting. He didn't seem upset or anxious. He was definitely interested, but not in a calculating, just-wait-until-I-get-them-on-my-plate kind of way. I felt something was different. Slow down, I thought. Don't react. Just sit for a minute. Be still.

So I became still and I sat. And I heard a voice in my heart telling me what to do. I called our veterinarian and made an appointment to bring the kittens in and get their eyes checked. On the way home from the doctor, I went to a pet store and bought my first litter box. I came home and brought the box of kittens back into the house. Jake was waiting. The time had come, so I carefully put the babies on the floor of the kitchen and held my breath, ready to come to the rescue if necessary.

Jake walked over and sniffed each of the kittens. Then he sat down in the middle of them and looked up at me with a sweet, sappy grin on his face. The kittens swarmed over him, happy to find a big, warm body of fur to curl up next to. That's when Jake opened his heart to the five little kitties and adopted them as his own. I wondered if he remembered a time when he, too, had needed a home. I knelt down to thank him for his love and compassion and tell him how grateful I was he'd come into my life. But it would have to wait until later — Jake and his kittens were fast asleep.

— Christine Davis —

92

Me and My Mewse

Cats do care. For example they know instinctively
what time we have to be at work in the morning
and they wake us up twenty minutes
before the alarm goes off.
~Michael Nelson

According to my dictionary, a "muse" is any of the nine Greek goddesses who preside over the arts. This means that, as a writer, I not only get to work in my pajamas, I can also claim my own goddess who will answer my prayers in times of literary distress.

Luckily, there's no need, since I have Necco, a peach-colored tortoiseshell cat to serve as my own personal "mewse."

The cat discovered us at the local animal shelter. We were looking for a quiet, neat pet to complement our boisterous dog, Emma. We found Necco instead.

As soon as we entered the shelter, she called to us in a noisy chirp that made it clear she required immediate attention. The yellow tag on her cage — the symbol showing that this was her last day — backed up her urgent request. When the cage door swung open, she stepped into my arms and settled back with a look that clearly said, "What took you so long?"

Six months old and barely three pounds, Necco wasted no time establishing herself as the one in charge of our lives. The leather chair was her scratching post. The Christmas tree was her playground. And the mantel, neatly decorated with a collection of brass candlesticks of all shapes and sizes, was where she discovered the Feline Law of Gravity: Cats go up; candlesticks come down. The first dainty swipe of a paw resulted in a satisfying crash. So did the second, third and fourth. By the fifth crash, Necco's face bore the cat equivalent of a grin. She had discovered her purpose in life.

It happened that Necco's skills reached their peak just as my life reached a low point. My twenty-year marriage had shuddered to a stop, leaving me with a ten-year-old daughter, Katie, and a large home to support on an advertising copywriter's salary. Although I worked full-time, the pay was modest and I often found myself with more bills than paycheck. I soon realized I would have to work as a freelance writer just to meet expenses.

That meant getting up at 4:00 A.M., writing for two hours, and then getting ready for work. Eight hours later, I would return home, fix dinner, help Katie with homework, clean the house and get ready for another day's work. I fell into bed exhausted at 11:00 P.M. only to crawl out of bed when the alarm sounded at 4:00 A.M. the next day.

The routine lasted exactly two weeks. Despite gallons of coffee, I couldn't seem to produce anything. I was cranky, frustrated, lonely and ready to admit defeat. Writing was hard. Paying bills was even harder. The only answer was to sell the house and get an inexpensive apartment. Unfortunately, that would mean more losses for Katie and me. Especially since no apartment in town allowed pets.

I hated the thought of finding another home for us all, and I especially hated the thought of telling Katie about the changes in store. Depressed, I slept right through the 4:00 A.M. alarm the next day. And the next and the next. Finally, I quit setting it.

That's when Necco did a curious thing. Knowing that a sudden crash would make a human jump, she decided that the perfect time to make that crash was at 4:00 A.M. Her bedroom bombing raid was timed with military precision. First she set off a small round of artillery in the form of two pencils and my eyeglasses. I rolled over and covered my head with the blanket. Then she moved on to an arsenal of notebooks and the alarm clock. Each crash forced me deeper under the covers. Finally, she brought out the big guns. A half-filled glass of water splashed to the ground. A hardbound book crashed beside me. How could I sleep with the world literally crashing down around my ears? My mewse said it was time to get to work.

Wearily, I made my way to the computer. Necco hopped up on the desk, seeming to feel her job wasn't done yet. Sitting on a pile of unfinished story ideas, she watched with apparent satisfaction as I began to type. Whenever the words seemed slow in coming, she helped me along. Gliding across my keyboard with the grace of a goddess, she produced sentences like: "awesdtrfgyhubjikpl[;' dtrfgbhujni guhnj!" My translation? "I woke you up for a reason. Now, write!" I wrote. And wrote some more.

From then on, every day Necco got me up at 4:00 A.M. sharp, when the ideas were freshest and the world slept around us. With her watching over me as I wrote, I didn't feel so alone. My goals didn't seem so impossible. Slowly, over months of early mornings, stories were born, and polished, and sold.

Today the old house still surrounds us. Katie and I are both doing fine. And although both pets are treated like the cherished family members they are, whenever another story is sold, I give thanks to my muse — a little cat with a mischievous grin, who kept me company in my "darkest hours."

— Cindy Podurgal Chambers —

Over the Rainbow

93

Ghost Cat

All God's angels come to us disguised.
~James Russell Lowell

I was telling a friend about some of my psychic experiences when he interrupted me, saying, "Sorry, but I don't believe in that stuff." I said I didn't blame him. If you have never experienced any psychic stuff why would you believe?

So I changed the conversation to something we had more in common — cats.

Partway into that conversation he said, sheepishly, "I have a ghost cat."

"What?" I replied.

"It's true. Twice now couples have stayed in my guest room overnight and in the morning have reported a cat walked across the bed during the night. The door was closed and no cat was present in the room.

Then I had to tell him about our own cat, Molly, who we adopted as a newborn kitten and had for almost seventeen years. When my wife Sandy and I finally had to take her to the vet for her final visit, we were devastated. And I couldn't shake my guilt for tricking her into taking a sedative that last day. She never liked trips to the vet, and I thought she would be more comfortable and less stressed with the pills. I hoped she would forgive me.

About two months after Molly's passing I was lying in bed, face down, early on a Sunday, when I felt Molly walk up my back as she used to and sniff the back of my head. I thought for a moment how nice it was that Molly had come for a visit. Then, suddenly, I became fully awake and remembered she was no longer with us. I woke Sandy up and told her what had happened and we both had a good cry. Sandy was disappointed she hadn't experienced Molly's visit.

A couple of months later I was laying in bed and I could feel Molly jump on the bed, then come over and knead the mattress beside me as she used to do. This time I wasn't startled and I talked to her. I could feel the vibration of her purr and a sense of complete satisfaction. It lasted several minutes. Again I awoke Sandy and told her of the visit and again she was disappointed to miss it.

Later that summer we had friends visit us and stay in our guest room. The first morning, as we were all sitting around the breakfast table, they looked at each other sheepishly and had a short argument over who should tell us something.

"Tell us what?"

Getting up the nerve, she replied, "A cat walked across our bed last night." Her husband nodded in agreement.

Both Sandy and I burst out laughing.

"We're serious," they both said.

"Oh, we believe you," I replied. "Both of us have had visits from Molly this past year."

Needless to say, they were relieved to hear that, and we told them of other visits from Molly. By the time of Molly's last visit, Sandy had experienced Molly's spirit climb on top of her in bed and lie on her chest, too.

— N. Newell —

94

Little Bit

*The only real mistake is the one from
which we learn nothing.*
~John Powell

"Meow, meow, meow," is what I heard as I walked through the alley. I approached the noise, and I noticed a tail sticking out from under a piece of wood. Under the wood was a tiny black and white kitten. I picked him up and realized he must be freezing to death. I hurried home with the kitten wrapped in my jacket.

My new best friend, who soon became known as Little Bit, received his name because he was nearly weightless when I held him in my hands. He stood about five inches tall and his paws were the size of dimes. Little Bit's small size had a great advantage — he fit perfectly in the pocket of my jacket, which made taking him everywhere very easy. He would ride with me on my bike, play in the dirt with me, and catch frogs.

Little Bit was the best friend I had ever had. Any time I was home, he wouldn't leave my side. He was always eager to play with me. Anytime I ate cereal he would sit there patiently until I gave him my leftover milk. When I fell asleep at night, he would always curl up around my head to ensure that I was warm.

Unfortunately, I grew up. My teenage life weakened my relationship with Little Bit. I lived at such a fast pace that I stopped making time for him. My free time was spent with my friends instead. I would come in the house on my phone and not acknowledge him at all. His meows became an annoyance to me, but it wasn't his fault that he wanted his best friend back.

Time had taken a toll on Little Bit. His body began shutting down and by the time I realized something was wrong with him, he had already lost his balance. He lay there and looked at me, and to this day I still remember the sorrowful look in his bright green eyes. I took him to the vet, but there was nothing he could do. The last time I held him he wasn't the same tiny kitten I had found ten years before. He filled my arms now. Little Bit was put to sleep that day.

Little Bit's death made me realize how much he meant to me. I regret being so caught up in my own life that I never gave him the attention that he deserved. If I had been by his side all along, maybe I would have seen his symptoms and prevented them from getting worse. I'll always regret not being there for him. He was always there for me when I needed him.

I don't know why they always say that a dog is man's best friend — Little Bit was the best friend I ever had. I couldn't have asked for more from him. I regret our last years together, but I will always cherish the special memories we made.

— Steven D. Farmer —

95

Better to Have Loved

'Tis better to have loved and lost than
to have not loved at all.
~Alfred Lord Tennyson

Unita, my cat, had diabetes, but we found out too late. We had taken her to the vet for a sideways tooth. After the tooth was pulled, the vet asked if there was anything else bothering her, and my mom brought up the fact that Unita was always thirsty and we had to refill the water bowls every day to keep her happy. The vet had a feeling it was diabetes and did a quick test to see if it was. It came back positive. A blood test would make it definite, so blood was drawn. That was positive as well. Unita had diabetes. I got Unita to go back into the carrier, and it nearly fell off the table with her weight. My mom and stepdad, Mike, were going to be gone for a week and I was staying with my grandma while they were gone, so we decided not to treat her until they got back.

I was home after school feeding the cats during the week, but I didn't notice any difference until we were all home again that Friday and I saw that she was lethargic. We all knew that there was another trip to the vet coming up.

On Saturday, when my mom and Mike got back from the vet, I was cleaning the litter boxes. The mood in the apartment had darkened drastically. My parents said they would tell me what was going to happen to Unita when I was finished cleaning, but I still wouldn't let them say anything until Unita was beside me. As I stroked her fur, my mom told me that Unita was very sick and that we would have to put her to sleep. It was going to happen the next day, so I would have one last night with her.

"No," I cried. "Isn't there anything we can do?" My pleas were met with a solid no. I was lying on the couch crying into Unita's fur, like I had so many other times before, when my mom came over and asked me to bring Unita to my room. I figured she just wanted to get rid of me. I was wrong.

"This isn't her space; your room is," my mom explained, and I agreed. My mom picked up Unita, carried her into my room, and set her down on my bed beside me. "Lie down and say goodbye."

Later, my mom told me that she could tell by the way Unita's head was lolling that she had gotten worse and would probably slip into a coma before morning. The appointment we had made for the next day was moved up a few hours. It was nearly time to let her go.

The next morning, I picked up Unita and held her to my chest. We figured it would be less painful for us if we carried her in than if we brought home an empty carrier. We went down to the car and piled in. With a few final sniffles, we were off. Once we got to the animal hospital we were told to go into the first room on our right. I didn't want to let Unita go, but I had to. I set her down on the blanket that was on the table and gave her more affection. Then, the vet told us what would happen. All it was going to be was an anesthetic overdose, quick and painless. The drugs were to be administrated through Unita's rear leg, so we had to turn her around and put her facing away from us.

Unita was sitting with her back end on its side and her front paws resting flat with her head up. Once the vet put the needle into her leg Unita shifted so that she was lying on her side with her eyes closed. It was like she knew she was going to die. We were told that we could leave if we needed to. I nodded but I knew I'd stay until the end. When we were as ready as we could be, the vet injected the drugs. In a matter of moments, she stopped moving.

"She's gone," my mom said, and the dam broke. Looking back, I think I cried more that day than in all of fourth, fifth, sixth, and seventh grades combined. "She loved you most of all," my mom told me as she held me. The dam was completely smashed at this point. I couldn't — wouldn't — believe she was gone, but one look at her still body and I just knew.

Mike left and it was just me and my mom in the room. Once I had calmed down, my mom suggested we leave. Tears threatened to fall once more, and with willpower and the knowledge that she would always be with me no matter what, I held them back until I was sure they wouldn't fall. The drive home was sadder than the drive there by many degrees. Leaving Unita there was one of the hardest things I've ever had to do, and I hope my other two cats' lives end on a better note. Questions like "Would she still be here if we had started treatment earlier?" and, "Why didn't we go to the vet sooner?" have made the wounds deeper and even more painful.

Even though Unita's with me every day, I still miss her and love her with all of my heart. No matter what, Unita has shown me how to love without fear or questions, and she taught me that it is better to know how love feels than to have never experienced it before.

— Sara Drimmie —

96

All Cats Go to Heaven

*If angels rarely appear, it's because we all too often
mistake the medium for the Message.*
~Eileen Elias Freeman,
The Angels' Little Instruction Book

Losing a loved one is always hard, but being in my twenties and having to say goodbye to my best friend of eighteen years was unfathomable. She had always been there. She was there when I moved from my toddler bed to my day bed. She was there for my sixth-grade graduation, high-school graduation, college graduation, and wedding day. She was there throughout my awkward teenage years when I had no other friends. She was there for every breakup and heartache, volunteering her services as the world's cuddliest Kleenex. She was there after every major surgery.

She was a part of me.

And a part of me was actually convinced that she was invincible. She had, after all, survived the Neighborhood Cat-Poisoning Massacre of 2005, as well as the Great Tree Rescue of 2007, when my dad had to stand on top of a ladder on top of a bucket on top of a tractor just to get her down. She had won every fight she entered in 2009, no matter if her challenger was the German Shepherd next door or the alligator in the pond. She was fearless.

I tried to choke back my fear as I approached her for the last time. Her face lit up when she saw me. She tried to meow but no sound came out, so she silently laid her head in my lap instead. I stroked her matted fur, coated from the mud of the rain puddle she had walked through earlier in her delirium. "It's okay now. Mommy's here," I whispered as I petted her body, now so small and frail beneath my hands.

I kissed her stubborn forehead and whispered that it was okay to let go. I would still love her and be with her again. I prayed that she would not suffer and would go peacefully in her sleep, and she did. I was grateful for that, and that I got the chance to say goodbye.

During the drive home from the vet, I had a crisis of faith. I have always believed wholeheartedly in a heaven and an afterlife for human souls. But I was suddenly panic-stricken. Where did animals go? Their souls go to heaven too, right? I needed to know, and I needed proof.

I prayed desperately, *Dear Lord, please, if my cat is safe with you, just give me a sign that my Sugar is okay. That song I used to sing to her all the time — "Suga Suga" by Baby Bash — just let me hear it once, and I'll know....*

As soon as I had the thought, I dismissed it. How stupid could I be? I was expecting to hear a fifteen-year-old song on the radio — a song that everyone else had forgotten. To make matters worse, if I even had a chance at all of hearing it, it would have to be on a Flashback Friday when some of the radio stations play oldies. But it was Sunday. I gave up on the idea as quickly as I had it. I didn't want to set myself up for disappointment and more heartache.

After getting home and crying in my lunch, I logged onto Facebook to browse through some photos of her. Suddenly, I came across a post that one of my friends had sent me. It was a funny video compilation with various songs playing in the background for comedic effect. In that two-minute video, a certain song started playing at 0:36 seconds. That's right: "Suga, Suga." I was elated. But still, being the cynical human that I was, I chalked it up to mere coincidence.

Then, that same week, Walmart released a new commercial — one that featured the song "Suga, Suga." That commercial played every time I turned on my TV. Why would Walmart choose a fifteen-year-old song to promote their products? I'll never know, but I wish I could shake the marketer's hand and thank him or her for renewing my faith — and for reassuring me that all cats do, indeed, go to heaven.

— Kaitlin Hodnett —

97

The Day Basil Died

There is a comfort in rituals, and rituals
provide a framework for stability
when you are trying to find answers.
~Deborah Norville

The day Basil died, he and I were alone. My husband was away. Basil was a cat, a resplendent Abyssinian with russet fur, and a bladder and temper that were chronically inflamed. His twelve years were punctuated by episodes of aggression, mysterious fevers, and ever-changing regimens of diet and pills. Finally, the cells inside his bladder knotted into a tumor that could not be removed, and for which there were no drugs.

In spite of — perhaps even *because* of — all this, oh, how we loved each other. He napped draped across my shoulders as I sat at my desk. He would stand on the kitchen counter, wrap his arms around my neck, and press his face to mine with a purr that could be heard across the room.

The day Basil died, he could not urinate. Black blood dripped onto the floor as he walked. When I felt his belly, he cried out. I texted my husband: *B in trouble. Going to vet now.*

Weather can be eerie and violent in the Kansas prairie. I drove into a summer squall, into a bank of cloud or fog or both, with a screaming wind driving milk-white sheets of rain across the hood. It would have scared me if I wasn't already so distraught.

It's not that I hadn't done this part before: coming to the moment, knowing it was time and what had to happen. The tears, the farewell, murmuring my shattered love into his unhearing ear as he melted away from me. Before this, living then in a city house, we had to turn over "disposing of the remains" to others. They waited in the vet's freezer for the weekly pet-cemetery pickup, to be laid in a trench or incinerated with others, or we would go back a few days later to pick up a plain white box. A couple of times, we carried them there ourselves and waited in a hushed room while a gentle man in blue jeans fired up the furnace to cremate them then and there, and we went home an hour later with a still-warm urn.

This time, there was no pet-cemetery service. I was alone. It was raining. But we had seven acres of grass, trees and birdsong, and a corner by the front porch where Basil liked to lurk in the greenery and ambush grasshoppers.

I brought the crate and its motionless burden home. I went upstairs to my office and found a sturdy, lidded cardboard box that a laptop had come in. I placed the box on the dining room table and folded a soft green towel into it. I laid Basil's body in the box, arranging his paws and tail comfortably as though in sleep, although his eyes were still slightly open. I lit a candle at his head and took his photograph. I poured a glass of wine and called my husband. We wept together, my husband choking out, "I'm sorry! I'm so sorry I wasn't there!"

I sat with Basil for a long time. I cried. I stroked and kissed him. I pressed my face to his. I drank more wine as the rain pattered outside. Then I blew out the candle and went to bed. He lay in repose on the table until morning.

At dawn, I waded through wet grass to what was usually a damp spot beneath some trees, but that day was almost a pond. Among the rocks and fallen branches were some chunks of the local cream-and-rust-hued sandstone, the color of Basil's fur. The stones were mottled, freckled with lichen spores, some rippled from when they were sand at the bottom of some inland sea. I turned them over, hefted them, and chose several, juggling them in my bare arms back to the house. Out in the workshop, I found a thick piece of plywood, maybe two feet square. Coyotes live here; I wanted to at least deter their digging if I could. And in the woodpile was a perfect half-cylinder of elm, faded and split, frilled with luminous orange-yellow fungi called "witch's butter." Then I fetched the shovel.

In a sultry summer mist, I dug deeper and wider than I needed to. I scraped the sides of the hole smooth. Back inside, I kissed my cat one last time, covered his face and closed the box. I wrote all his names in thick black letters on the lid: Bingo Crepuscule, Basil, Beezer, Mr. B., Big Brown B, and just B. I carried him out.

This was only the second funeral I had attended in my life. The hardest part was to drop the first dirt on top of him. I did what people in television shows do: I sprinkled some in by hand. After that, it felt possible to spoon in the dirt with the shovel, leveling and layering it, tamping it down. Then I set the plywood square firmly on top. I spent some time arranging the stones in a way that pleased me, to display the ripples and the markings best. The brightly streaked elm log served as a headstone. And then it was done: a neat, small, rustic grave where butterflies and grasshoppers would flit, where Basil's cells, tissues and molecules would slowly return to the soil. I had chosen the place and dug the hole. I put someone I loved in it, filled it up, and set the markers with my hands. I had performed the right and necessary duties, and solace bloomed from the muscles of my sorrow.

The funereal trappings of mahogany and brass, flowers massed in crosses, silver hearses, organ dirges and black-clad processions are not for the dead. The dead do not care, and we should not pretend they do. The rites mark out the work that we do in their name.

Sitting up late, alone with the dead, I cleared space for memory because that was the only place Basil could be from then on. I did something that he never asked for, but I offered it anyway. Every bite of the shovel that morning felt deliberate and focused, with mindful attention fully paid. I walked the road with Basil all the way to the end. The simple energies of thought and labor had begun to frame the new path I would now walk without him and guide me into it.

I still go out to talk to him sometimes. The first snowfall on the grave wrung fresh tears, as I hated to think of him so cold. I do not show anyone the deathbed photo in my phone, but I do not delete it.

There is now a second neat, rustic grave next to his for another dearly loved cat, surrounded by an impasto of purple iris in the summertime. The house wrens raise their young in the elm overhead.

The day after Basil died, I learned the power of ritual.

—Julie Stielstra—

98

Toto's Last Christmas

Open your heart — open it wide;
someone is standing outside.
~Quoted in Believe:
A Christmas Treasury *by Mary Engelbreit*

S now fell softly on Christmas Eve as I made my final patient rounds. The old cat, fragile in his downy white coat, was sleeping. Days before, his owner had dropped him off to spend the holidays with us. Sadly, she had worried he might not make it to greet her in the New Year. Indeed, the day after she dropped off the cat, I called to warn her that he was failing. Her tear-choked voice let me know she understood. "No heroics, please, Dr. Foley, but let him rest easy and make him as comfortable as you can."

Soft blankets along with a heating pad were wrapped around his frail body to keep him warm. Puréed chicken and tuna had been offered and declined, and now he slept in the deepest of sleeps. Not wanting Toto to be alone in his condition on this holiday night, I wrapped him in a large wicker basket and carried him home.

A gust of wind blew the door from my hand as I entered the house. My cat, Aloysius, greeted us while my other cat, Daphne, peeked timidly from the corner of the room, sniffing appreciatively at the cold winter air. They both knew what a wicker basket with an electric cord hanging from it meant. Aloysius retreated haughtily across the room.

Rescued as an abandoned cat from a clinic I worked at previously, Aloysius has been with me for twelve years — through vet school, my first job and my first home. Other people see him as just a cat, but for me his presence has become a constant in my life. Aloysius is the one who listens to all my tales of woe. On the down side, he is possessive and has a low opinion of anyone, feline or other, who infringes on his territory.

Daphne had come to me a timid and yet ferocious feral tabby kitten that no one could tame. Ten years of love, patience and roast beef tidbits had paid off. Now a round and sassy butterball of a cat, her heart was mine. To keep the peace in the house, however, she usually agreed with Aloysius on the subject of uninvited guests. Sensing his disdain for the fellow in the basket, she politely hissed from the corner.

"Now, now, you big bullies," I said. "This fellow is old and may be leaving us soon. We wouldn't want him to be alone on Christmas Eve, would we?"

Unmoved, they glowered from beneath the Christmas tree.

Old Toto slept on in his basket. I placed him by the table in the kitchen and plugged the cord for his heating pad into the wall. My husband, Jordan, and I prepared our Christmas Eve dinner while Toto slept, and I checked on him every once in a while to be sure he was comfortable. Daphne and Aloysius, still resentful of our guest but moved by the smell of grilling steaks, crept into the room. I warned them that Toto was old and frail and to be good hosts, they must let him be.

Toto still slept.

Dinner was ready, and Jordan and I sat at the table. Relaxing after the long work day, soon we started teasing each other about what surprises were hidden in the gleaming packages beneath the tree. Then Jordan silently nodded toward Toto in his basket, and I turned my head slowly to look at the cats.

Aloysius first, and then Daphne behind him, slowly and cautiously approached the basket. While Toto rested, Aloysius sat up on his haunches, peered into the basket and gave a long, deep sniff. Gently, he lowered himself and walked to the corner of the old cat's basket. Then he rubbed his cheek against it, softly purring. Daphne followed, leaned into the basket and, sniffing Toto's face, placed a gentle paw on his soft blanketed body. Then she, too, lowered herself and purred as she rubbed his basket. Jordan and I watched in amazed silence. These cats had never welcomed any other cat into our home before.

Leaving my chair, I walked over and looked at Toto. With the cats still positioned at each corner of the basket, Toto looked up at me, breathed once and then relaxed. Reaching my hand beneath his blankets, I felt his heart slowly stop beating. Tears in my eyes, I turned to Jordan to let him know that Toto was gone.

Later that night, I called Toto's owner to let her know that he had died comfortably and quietly at our home, with two cats beside him, wishing him a fond farewell and Godspeed on his last Christmas Eve.

—Janet Foley, D.V.M. —

99

Sheba

What greater gift than the love of a cat?
~Charles Dickens

I first met Sheba in 1956. I was a third grade student at the Round Meadow Elementary School. She was a seven-week-old kitten in a pet shop window. She caught my eye immediately. I had always wanted a kitten, or at least that's what I told myself when I saw her there on display.

At first, she didn't even notice me standing there. I tried tapping on the glass, but her concentration remained elsewhere as she gave full attention to the task at hand. A thousand generations of hunting and stalking instinct were brought to bear as she successfully brought down her quarry — her sister's tail.

I tapped again. She stared at me for a moment, and the bond was made. Following a brief discussion through the glass, we concluded that we were made for each other. I vowed to return later in the day to take her home with me.

Unfortunately, I soon found that the road to kitten ownership was not without obstacles. Mom and Dad didn't think much of my plans. It seemed that they knew quite a lot about the subject of acquiring pets. "Who ever heard of paying money for a cat? A kitten is something that you can get for free at any barn. Besides, we're dog people."

I wasn't sure what that meant but, even at eight years old, I could see that the only true stumbling stone here was the finances. You see,

Sheba came with a stiff price tag, two dollars and fifty cents. "A lot of money for something that you can get for free anywhere."

Getting my own way this time was not going to be easy. However, I felt up to the challenge at hand and, after a day of typical little kid whining and a chunk of "birthday money" that came from Uncle Lou, Sheba was mine.

I was an instant hit with her, and the feeling was mutual. She slept on my bed every night. We had long and meaningful conversations when no one else was around. In fact, it was Sheba who was largely responsible for my deciding somewhat early in life to pursue a career as a veterinarian.

Through junior high, high school, college and veterinary school, she remained a close feline friend. Many important decisions regarding my career as well as my personal life were influenced by conversations, whether real or imagined, with Sheba.

Though she lived with Mom and Dad while I was busy getting married, raising a family and practicing the profession that she influenced me to join, she remained a close friend and seemed to enjoy visits from me, my wife and kids.

Undoubtedly, it was her influence once again that got me thinking about opening a veterinary hospital for cats only. She seemed to love the idea when we "talked" about it, and I knew from past experience that her judgment was flawless, so I set off down a new career path. In June of 1978, my new hospital, The Allentown Clinic for Cats, opened its doors.

Sheba was twenty-two years old on opening day when Mom and Dad brought her to see me and the beautiful new hospital that she had inspired. They hadn't warned me in advance that there was a second reason for the visit.

Sheba looked horrible. Apparently she had become quite ill that week. I did a thorough exam and was forced to a bitter conclusion. You see, I had been in practice long enough to know when a situation was hopeless.

It seemed fitting that in the new hospital, Sheba was the first cat whose suffering we could ease. We had the last of our long conversations as she fell gently asleep in my arms.

— Michael A. Obenski, V.M.D. —

The Cantor's Cat

It's really the cat's house — we just pay the mortgage.
~Author Unknown

I magine the head soloist, the music minister and the associate pastor of a house of worship. Now imagine one person taking on all those functions. That's about half of the job of a cantor.

Cantors commemorate every stop on the Jewish life-cycle. We chant the blessings that bring a child into the congregation; that celebrate the arrival of those children to young adulthood; that bind two lives together; and that pronounce a person's journey from life into death. We rejoice with the celebrants, as well as mourn with the bereaved. But how do we respond when somebody loses a loved one with four legs instead of two? And how do we handle this situation when it happens to us?

Some years ago, a silver tabby named Petey plopped into my life. We were a team from the get-go. Petey was large and cuddly and had the charming ability to hold hands with me, using a firm, tensile-pawed grip.

When I met my future husband, Mark, I was about to ask him the important question — did he like cats? — when he mentioned Julia, his own tuxedo puss. The first time Mark and I sat together on my sofa, Petey stretched out to his full length in order to sit on both our laps simultaneously. Then he looked at me with a face that said, "Can I keep this one?" And so our household numbered two cats, and two people who were allowed to live with them as long as they paid the rent.

On the first Sabbath in our first home, we suddenly noticed Petey and Julia sitting on the kitchen floor, watching our every move. We lit and blessed the candles together. They stayed at attention during kiddush and motzi, the prayers before the wine and food; and then they walked away. The following Friday, using the Yiddish word for Sabbath, we hollered, "Hey, Shabbos cats!" and they came into the kitchen and sat quietly during the blessings as they had the previous week.

Jewish law mandates caring for the animals in one's household, including feeding them before we feed ourselves. Being good Jewish pet lovers, we ran our household accordingly, and all of us thrived on the love that grew from this four-way relationship.

Many happy years passed. At fourteen, Petey started to lose his luster but none of his love. However, like an old man who doesn't quite understand why life doesn't continue on the way it did when he was young, he had his crabby moments. Still, he was my beautiful boy, and we all moved to Albuquerque from New York when I took a pulpit out West. Both cats seemed to thrive on the changed atmosphere and seemed extremely happy in their new home.

One Monday, some months after the move, I took Petey to the vet to try to find out why he couldn't keep his food down. The doctor prescribed an enzyme powder, and Petey valiantly continued to eat, but to no avail. By Friday night, he was miserable. No matter how hard we tried to make him comfortable, he cried like a baby with the effort of walking, of settling in my lap, of pressing next to the windowpane's cold glass. We ached for him and for ourselves. Clearly he was saying goodbye, but he wasn't about to go easily.

At last, too exhausted to fight any longer, he slept fitfully in our bed between Mark and me. He held my hand between the still-strong grip of his paws as I held him in my arms and whispered my thanks and my love. All night long, I struggled between fighting to keep him and facing the reality of letting him go. In the morning we rushed him to the vet, but Petey had other ideas. He died as soon as we got him inside the office.

His death destroyed us. The price of love just then was the deepest pain imaginable as we wept uncontrollably. To make matters harder,

Sabbath services would begin in two hours. How could I serve professionally when my heart had just been ripped in two? Only those who have had an animal in their home can fully understand that loss, no matter how much they sympathize with it. Would the rabbi and the congregation understand my sorrow over a cat?

But begging off was out of the question. We needed to be with our congregation in our spiritual home that morning.

When I arrived at the synagogue, Mark mourned in my study, calling friends and family who knew and loved Petey. I went to the rabbi and told him what had happened. His eyes were gentle and full of understanding, and I felt the genuine quality of his words of comfort. To my surprise, he said, "Do as much as you can this morning, and I will fill in when you falter. You need the support of your congregation today. And I think we should let people know what's happened after the service." His support buoyed me enough to manage through the service. My notes soared, but my customary ebullient sparkle was severely diminished. The rabbi knew that this would be noticed, and we would meet the consequent inquiries with honest answers.

Afterwards, I hesitated to greet the congregation one-on-one. I still wasn't sure how they would react to my grief over the loss of a cat. After all, I was their invincible cantor. With a slight sinking feeling, I noticed Mrs. Gold approaching me. For the last few months, I'd been directing her son in his religious studies and I found the Golds to be the most demanding, least flexible family I'd ever worked with. But as she got nearer, I saw compassion in her eyes. She took me gently into her arms, saying, "The rabbi told me about your Petey. I'm so sorry. It's hard to lose a dear friend."

When she released me, we smiled at each other, and both our faces were shining with tears.

And so it continued, members of the congregation clasping my hand or embracing me, as they spoke kind words of condolence. I saw that Mark was having the same experience. This wave of comfort poured over us like warm honey as we began to feel our grief over losing Petey.

And though we had lost a loved one, we'd found something,

too — the people in our congregation, a large and loving family to share our lives with. While Petey lived, he brought people together, and our Shabbos cat continued to do so — even with his passing.

— Jacqueline Shuchat-Marx —

The Christmas Angel

Let your tears come. Let them water your soul.
~Eileen Mayhew

When my daughter Rachel was six years old, we went to the local shelter, looking for the perfect cat. We liked a lot of the cats we saw there, but we were especially taken with a mother and her kittens. All the kittens were entirely jet black, except for one. She had a small white tip to her tail, like one bright light in the night sky. We brought her home and called her Star.

Starry was a charmer. Rachel admired her proud manner and enjoyed even more the secret knowledge that it was all an act. Starry could only appear aloof for so long before leaping into Rachel's arms to be cuddled and stroked. As time went by, Rachel and Starry adopted certain routines. At night when we watched TV, Starry crawled into Rachel's lap, and stayed there, purring contentedly. Starry always rubbed her face along Rachel's chin, ending the love fest with a gentle nip on Rachel's nose. Sometimes I couldn't help but feel the injustice of this. I was the one who took care of the cat, feeding, cleaning, grooming—yet, Starry was clearly Rachel's cat. Eventually, I came to love watching their cozy bond.

My little girl grew up, went to junior high and finally high school. Starry was ten and Rachel was sixteen. Starry and Rachel were still close, though Rachel spent less and less time at home. Starry spent most of her day sitting on the sideboard in the dining room, looking out the window into the backyard. I loved seeing her as I'd pass, her glossy black coat almost sparkling in the sunlight she loved to seek out, the white tip of her tail brilliant against the shining black of her curled body.

One Sunday morning, early in November, Starry got out the door before we could stop her. When Rachel's friend came over to study that evening, she came in the door with a worried expression. "Where's Starry?" she asked.

When we told her we didn't know, she had us come outside with her. There was a black cat lying in the street.

It was Star. The cat's body was warm and she didn't appear to be injured. There was no blood or wounds that we could see. It was after hours, but our vet agreed to meet us after our distraught phone call. Rachel was upset, but holding it together. My husband Burt and I told her to stay at home while we took Star to the vet.

Burt and I picked Starry up carefully and rushed her to the vet's office. The vet examined her briefly before looking up at us and saying, "I'm sorry, but she's gone."

When we got home, Rachel could tell by our faces that Starry was dead. She turned without speaking and went to her room.

It had been a hard year for me. My father had died not long before, and I hadn't totally come to grips with the loss. Rachel and I were in the midst of the delicate dance mothers and teenaged daughters everywhere find themselves performing — circling, pulling away and coming together in odd fits and spurts. I took a chance and knocked at her door. When she said come in, I sat with her on the bed and we cried together. It was a good cry, clearing out some more of the grief I couldn't face about my father and bringing Rachel and I closer as we shared our sadness about Starry.

Life went on. Thanksgiving came and went. Rachel and I both found ourselves mistaking black sweatshirts strewn on chairs or floors for our newly missing black cat. The sideboard looked desolate, empty of the warm presence glowing with life I'd come to expect there. Over and over, little pangs of loss stung our hearts as the weeks went by.

I was out Christmas shopping, when I saw it. It was a Christmas tree ornament in the shape of a "cat angel." A black cat with white wings and a red ball between her paws. I had to get it, but bought it wondering if it would be a happy remembrance of the cat we'd loved or a chilling reminder of our loss.

When I got home, I painted a white tip at the end of the angel cat's long black tail and hung the ornament on our tree.

That evening, when Rachel came in, she flopped on to the couch. She sat staring at the Christmas tree, "spacing out" after a long day at school and after-school sports. I was in the kitchen when suddenly I heard her gasp. "Mom," she called. "Mom, come here!"

I walked in and found her standing in front of the tree, looking at the cat angel with shining eyes. "Oh, Mom. It's Starry. Where did you find an ornament with a tail like hers?"

She looked about six again. I gathered her into my arms and wonderfully she didn't resist. We stood together, looking at the tree, feeling our love for Starry and for each other.

Our charming, nose-nipping cat was gone, but now Starry, the Christmas angel, would be a part of our family tradition for years to come.

Sometimes you can make your own miracles.

— Pamela S. Zurer —

Meet Our Contributors

We are pleased to introduce you to the writers whose stories were compiled from our library to create this new collection. If the story was published by Chicken Soup for the Soul in the past sixteen years, we have included the bio that was provided at the time of the original publication date.

Kristi Adams is a travel writer on a mission to explore as many European Christmas markets as she can. She lives in Germany with her husband, who is serving on active duty, and their cat Tiki. Kristi is a proud nine-time contributor to the *Chicken Soup for the Soul* series. Learn more at www.kristiadamsmedia.com.

Barbara Alpert lives in Florida with her hubby Dave. She's written books for children and adults. Her most recent, *Weight A Minute: God Cares About Your Body, Soul & Spirit*, was released in January 2020. She loves working from home turning writers' manuscripts into published masterpieces. E-mail her at comlish@aol.com.

Monica A. Andermann's writing has been included in such publications as *Woman's World*, *Guideposts*, and *Sasee* as well as many other titles in the *Chicken Soup for the Soul* series. When she is not writing, she can most frequently be found puttering in her garden, binge-reading magazines or taking long walks through her neighborhood.

Joe Atwater is a horseman who breeds, raises, and races Standardbred horses on his ranch in North Carolina. Horses have been an important part of his life since adolescence and they take up most of his time. The rest of his time is taken up by his devoted wife, Elizabeth.

Dr. Marty Becker has spent his life working toward better health for pets and the people who love them. He is the founder of Fear Free, which works to prevent and alleviate fear, anxiety, and stress in pets by inspiring and educating the people who care for them. Dr. Becker practices at VCA North Idaho Animal Hospital because he loves veterinary medicine, pets, and the people who care for them. Learn more at www.drmartybecker.com.

David L. Bishop and Boomerjax relocated to Montana following the fire. David continues to write amid the beauty of the mountains. He maintains his passions for reading, sports, and politics, while never missing a chance for good conversation with friends. Boomerjax has adjusted nicely, no longer suffering from fleas.

Theresa Brandt is a writer who lives with her three boys and lots of furry friends. She loves spending time with family and friends as well as reading, gardening, traveling, and crafts. E-mail her at tbbrandt1972@ yahoo.com.

Jean Brody is a national magazine columnist, Kentucky newspaper columnist, creative writing teacher and a public motivational/ inspirational speaker. She lives with her husband, a Newfoundland dog, three cats and a pet Nubian goat on their Thoroughbred horse farm, Jean & Gene Farm. Jean has published dozens of short stories, articles and *Braille Me*, a compilation of her published work.

Marcia E. Brown, of Austin, TX, has enjoyed sharing her family stories in magazines, newspapers and anthologies, including the *Chicken Soup for the Soul* series, for eighteen years. She especially loves writing about the dogs and cats that have graced her life. She is a member of the National League of American Pen Women.

Beth Bullard is an author, an award-winning photographer, a budding interior designer and an amazing personal shopper for her family and friends. Beth lives on a small acreage in Northern Colorado with her two children and their menagerie of animals.

Jill Burns lives in the mountains of West Virginia with her wonderful family. She's a retired piano teacher and performer. She enjoys writing, music, gardening, nature, and spending time with her grandchildren.

Eva Carter is originally from Czechoslovakia. She was raised in New York and resides in Texas with her husband Larry. In her past life she was a dancer in New York and Las Vegas. She enjoys photography, yoga and writing. She is a stay-at-home mom to a kitten named Ollie. E-mail her at evacarter@sbcglobal.net.

Harriet Cooper is a freelance writer and instructor. She specializes in writing creative nonfiction and articles. Her work has appeared in several Chicken Soup for the Soul anthologies, as well as in newspapers, magazines, newsletters and websites. She often writes about health, nutrition, family, cats and the environment.

E.M. Corsa is an artist and writer with a deep respect for nature. Her sketchbooks are her love letters from nature, filled with drawings and notes used as reference material for her work. E-mail her at ofcorsa3@gmail.com.

Suzanne Cushman lives in Carmel-by-the-Sea, CA with her husband Noel and cats Violet and Buddy. She earned her Bachelor of Arts in English at the University of Utah and Master of Arts in journalism at Pepperdine University.

Martha Deeringer writes for children and adults from her home on a central Texas cattle ranch. Her large, loving family provides endless material for her articles and stories. Visit her website at www.marthadeeringer.com.

Michele Dellapenta has been writing since childhood. This is her second publication in the *Chicken Soup for the Soul* series. She credits her sister, Jodi L. Severson, a writer, as her inspiration. Married since 1982 to Lou, Michele lives in Ohio and enjoys reading, writing, scrapbooking and cooking. E-mail her at mdellapenta@earthlink.net.

Sara Drimmie loves to hang out at the mall with her friends, go swimming, play her guitar and cello, and love her pets. Sara is a member of the local Air Cadets squadron. She hopes one day to become a fashion designer and share her love of designs and clothes with as many people as she can. Unita is still greatly missed, and her other cats are doing fine.

Steven Farmer was born and raised in Clarksdale, MS. He's currently attending college in pursuit of a degree in nursing. Steven enjoys hunting, fishing, kayaking and photography. He plans to become a Nurse Anesthetist one day. E-mail him at deltahuntersteven@yahoo.com.

Kate Fellowes' working life has revolved around being a words editor for a student newspaper, reporter for the local press, and cataloger in her hometown library. She's the author of four novels, and numerous short stories and essays. She and her husband share their home with a variety of companion animals.

Judith Fitzsimmons lives in Franklin, TN, and has been writing for personal enjoyment and professional use for over twenty years. It is with the fondest of memories that she dedicates this story to "my Ubu boy," who continues to warm her heart and spirit.

Peggy Frezon is author of the newly released book *The Dieting with my Dog Guide to Weight Loss and Maintenance*, and other books about dogs. She's also editor at Be the Change for Animals. Fetch her free newsletter, *Pawsitively Pets*, at peggyfrezon.blogspot.com/p/pawsitively-pets.html. Connect at her blog www.peggyfrezon.blogspot.com, Facebook www.facebook.com/PeggyFrezonBooks or Twitter @ peggyfrezon.

Kathleen Gemmell pens for an array of publications. Kathleen is also an animal rights proponent, a storyteller, and a psychology buff.

An avid animal lover, **Suzanne Gill** operated a pet sitting business most of her adult life. She discovered the art of screenwriting and, with her mother, composed five screenplays, one of which is currently under option. Suzanne also volunteers at the local animal shelter and loves to travel, especially to warm climates.

Amanda Ann Gregory, LCPC, is a trauma psychotherapist, national speaker, and author. She has provided trauma therapy for more than fifteen years in outpatient and residential settings and is currently in private practice. She lives in Chicago, IL with her partner and is raising a sassy black cat named Mr. Bojangles.

Bonnie Compton Hanson, artist and speaker, is author of thirty-seven books for adults and children, plus hundreds of articles, stories, and poems (including thirty-four for Chicken Soup for the Soul). A former editor, she has taught writing at colleges and writers conferences — plus loves cats! Learn more at www.BonnieComptonHanson.com.

Kaitlin Hodnett graduated from Louisiana State University at

Alexandria with a Bachelor of Arts in English. She was voted one of Louisiana's Best Emerging Poets in 2018 through Z Publishing House. Living with a chronic illness, she turns to writing as an escape from reality, and as an outlet for her unwavering faith.

Carol Huff, owner of Sudie Belle Animal Sanctuary in northeast Georgia, is a frequent contributor to the *Chicken Soup for the Soul* series, as well as a freelance writer for other well-known magazines. Aside from writing, she enjoys horseback riding and spending time with the animals. E-mail her at herbiemakow@gmail.com.

Rachel Katherine is a passionate Pentecostal, currently enrolled at Life Christian University. She enjoys learning languages, playing the ukulele, writing, and various other creative hobbies. E-mail her at rachelkatherine33@gmail.com.

Joyce Laird has made her living as a freelance writer/journalist since 1984. She has also published many human-interest essays and short fiction stories. Her artwork, photography and a house full of fur-babies round out her busy life, along with three great-grandsons.

Carole Marshall was a newspaper columnist and has written numerous features and health articles for *American Profile* magazine. Two of her stories were selected for the American Profile/HarperCollins book *Hometown Heroes*. She has written three books, poetry, and blogs at www.spiritexplored.com.

Adrienne Matthews is a previous contributor to the *Chicken Soup for the Soul* series and has also been published in both *Mysterious Ways* and *Guideposts*. She is enjoying retirement alongside her husband Greg and is proud mom to Eric. She feels led by God to share her stories of blessings and to offer joy and hope to others.

Jane McBride has loved to write ever since she was a small child when she entertained her friends with her stories. Writing for the *Chicken Soup for the Soul* series is a dream come true for her.

Jan Penton Miller graduated with honors from the University of Southern Mississippi. She is the mother of three wonderful children and grandmother to two beautiful grands. Jan is a remarried widow whose heart's desire is to honor God and encourage others with her writing. E-mail her at lilsisjan@yahoo.com.

Sue Mitchell swapped her teacher's desk for a writer's desk. Her short stories have appeared in several publications, but her tribe of cats remains in luxurious isolation, declining publicity. Sue has a growing Twitter following @pagancatmommy.

Courtney Mroch writes fiction in addition to blogging about travel, health and fitness. When she's not writing, it's a safe bet you'll find her on a tennis court somewhere. She lives in Nashville, TN with her husband and their two cats, Mr. Meow and Lady Tabitha Tabernathy Tabberkins Pryor (or Tabby for short).

Kathleen M. Muldoon is a freelance writer who lives in San Antonio, TX. She is the author of *Princess Pooh*, a picture book, as well as many other children's stories and articles. The original Ralph died in August of 1996, but she continues to babble to Prissy, a four-year-old black-and-white stray who came to stay last year.

N. Newell, a longtime skeptic, discovered his own psychic ability at age forty-seven — since that "awakening" he has helped several people with messages from the spirit world. He considers himself a reluctant psychic.

Diane C. Nicholson is a professional photographer, photo artist (specializing in animals and nature) and writer. This is her sixth story published in the *Chicken Soup for the Soul* series. She lives in beautiful British Columbia with her menagerie and long-suffering husband. E-mail her at mail@twinheartphoto.com.

Connie Kaseweter Pullen lives in rural Sandy, OR, near her five children and several grandchildren. She earned her Bachelor of Arts degree at the University of Portland in 2006, with a double major in Psychology and Sociology. Connie enjoys writing, photography and exploring nature. E-mail her at MyGrandmaPullen@aol.com.

Donna L. Roberts is a native upstate New Yorker who lives and works in Europe. She is an Associate Professor and holds a Ph.D. in Psychology. Donna is an animal and human rights advocate and when she is researching or writing she can be found at her computer buried in rescue cats.

Sallie A. Rodman's stories appear in various *Chicken Soup for the Soul* anthologies. She loves writing about the foibles of her crazy pets. She enjoys reading, writing, and raising Monarch butterflies. Sallie also teaches writing at Cal State University, Long Beach's OLLI campus. E-mail her at writergal222@gmail.com.

Angela Rolleman is a social worker, writer, speaker, trainer, entrepreneur, wife, daughter, aunt, sister and friend. She is founder of Mission: Empowerment, a company that provides personal and professional development seminars and events. Angela loves animals, travelling, reading and spending time in nature. To learn more, visit www.angelarolleman.com or www.missionempowerment.ca.

Catherine Rossi adds creative flair to everything she touches. She loves cooking, floral arranging and cake decorating. This is her first writing adventure. She has also just illustrated her first children's book called *Katie's Smile*.

Alexis Sherwin attends University of Massachusetts Amherst, pursuing an education in environmental law. She shares a home with her parents, her younger sister, three cats, and a dog. Her pets were her inspiration for writing her story. Alexis also enjoys traveling, fitness, and spending time with her friends.

Sheila Sowder's stories and essays have appeared in anthologies and literary journals. She received an Indiana Arts Commission Individual Arts Grant and the Rose Voci Fellowship for Indiana women writers. Currently, she and her husband travel and occasionally work at resorts from New England to Death Valley. E-mail her at sksowder@aol.com.

Julie Stielstra lives in the Chicago suburbs but escapes regularly to central Kansas. She is the author of over a dozen published short stories and essays, and two award-winning novels: *Pilgrim* and *Opulence, Kansas*. She blogs on animals, books, writing, the prairie and whatever else strikes her fancy at juliestielstra.com.

Nancy Sullivan holds multiple degrees and has written extensively over her career in the disability arena. She just completed a mystery novel with plans to write many more. She volunteers in animal rescue and is a Reiki Master Teacher and certified Laughter Yoga leader. Contact her at nancy.writes@sbcglobal.net.

E. Sutton has a Bachelor of Arts degree from the University of North Texas. Her hobbies are writing and art. She belongs to a small writers' group where the members help hone each other's craft. E-mail her at eas.paint@gmail.com.

Dawn Turzio is an award-winning writer whose work has been featured in many publications including *The New York Times*, *MSN Lifestyle*, *Yahoo! News*, and *Salon*, which can be found at www. dawnturzio.com.

Samantha Ducloux Waltz offers people inspiration, courage and a fresh perspective on life as the writer of more than fifty creative non-fiction stories published in *Chicken Soup for the Soul*, *Cup of Comfort* and other anthologies. Naomi, her feline accountability partner, keeps a close eye on her.

Nemma Wollenfang is an MSc Postgraduate and prize-winning short story writer who lives in Northern England. Her fiction has appeared in several venues, including four of Flame Tree's bestselling *Gothic Fantasy* series. She enjoys rambling around ancient ruins and is currently working on several novels.

Meet Amy Newmark

Amy Newmark is the bestselling author, editor-in-chief, and publisher of the *Chicken Soup for the Soul* book series. Since 2008, she has published 198 new books, most of them national bestsellers in the U.S. and Canada, more than doubling the number of Chicken Soup for the Soul titles in print today. She is also the author of *Simply Happy*, a crash course in Chicken Soup for the Soul advice and wisdom that is filled with easy-to-implement, practical tips for enjoying a better life.

Amy is credited with revitalizing the Chicken Soup for the Soul brand, which has been a publishing industry phenomenon since the first book came out in 1993. By compiling inspirational and aspirational true stories curated from ordinary people who have had extraordinary experiences, Amy has kept the thirty-one-year-old Chicken Soup for the Soul brand fresh and relevant.

Amy graduated *magna cum laude* from Harvard University where she majored in Portuguese and minored in French. She then embarked on a three-decade career as a Wall Street analyst, a hedge fund manager, and a corporate executive in the technology field. She is a Chartered Financial Analyst.

Her return to literary pursuits was inevitable, as her honors thesis in college involved traveling throughout Brazil's impoverished northeast region, collecting stories from regular people. She is delighted to have come full circle in her writing career — from collecting stories "from the people" in Brazil as a twenty-year-old to, three decades later, collecting stories "from the people" for Chicken Soup for the Soul.

When Amy and her husband Bill, the CEO of Chicken Soup for the Soul, are not working, they are visiting their four grown children and their spouses, and their five grandchildren.

Follow Amy on Twitter @amynewmark. Listen to her free podcast — Chicken Soup for the Soul with Amy Newmark — on Apple, Google, or by using your favorite podcast app on your phone.

Thank You

We owe huge thanks to all our contributors and fans. Here at Chicken Soup for the Soul we want to thank our Associate Publisher D'ette Corona for reviewing our story library and presenting us with hundreds of cat stories to choose from for this new collection. Publisher and Editor-in-Chief Amy Newmark made the final selection of the 101 that are included here, all personal favorites, and D'ette created the manuscript.

The whole publishing team deserves a hand, including Senior Editor Barbara LoMonaco, Vice President of Marketing Maureen Peltier, Vice President of Production Victor Cataldo, and our graphic designer Daniel Zaccari, who turned our manuscript into this beautiful, entertaining book.

About American Humane

merican Humane is the country's first national humane organization, founded in 1877 and committed to ensuring the safety, welfare, and wellbeing of all animals. For more than 140 years, American Humane has been first to serve in promoting the welfare and safety of animals and strengthening the bond between animals and people. American Humane's initiatives are designed to help whenever and wherever animals are in need of rescue, shelter, protection or care.

American Humane is the only national humane organization with top ratings and endorsements from the key charity watchdog groups. The organization has earned Charity Navigator's highest "Four-Star Rating," the Platinum Seal of Transparency from GuideStar USA, and is one of the few charities that meets all of the Better Business Bureau's Wise Giving Alliance's 20 Standards for Charity Accountability.

American Humane's certification programs that help verify treatment of animals are wide ranging, covering animals in film, on farms, in zoos and aquariums and even those in pet retailers. The iconic "No Animals Were Harmed®" certification, which appears during the end credits of films and TV shows, today monitors some 1,000 productions yearly.

Through rigorous, science-based criteria that are independently audited, American Humane's farm animal welfare program, Conservation program and Pet Provider programs help to ensure the humane treatment of more than one billion animals living on certified farms and ranches, in zoos and aquariums, and at pet provider locations. Simply put, American Humane is the largest certifier of animal welfare in the world.

Continuing its longstanding efforts to strengthen the healing power of the human-animal bond, American Humane also pairs veterans struggling to cope with the invisible wounds of war with highly trained service dogs, and also helps reunite discharged military working dogs with their former handlers.

To learn more about American Humane, visit AmericanHumane. org and follow them on Facebook, Instagram, Twitter and YouTube.

AMERICAN★HUMANE
FIRST TO SERVE˙

Editor's Note: Chicken Soup for the Soul and American Humane have created *Humane Heroes*, a FREE new series of e-books and companion curricula for elementary, middle and high schoolers. Through thirty-six inspirational stories of animal rescue, rehabilitation, and humane conservation being performed at the world's leading zoological institutions, and eighteen easy-to-follow lesson plans, *Humane Heroes* provides highly engaging free reading materials that also encourage young people to appreciate and protect Earth's disappearing species. To download the free e-books and learn about the program, please visit www.chickensoup.com/ah.

Sharing Happiness, Inspiration, and Hope

Real people sharing real stories, every day, all over the world. In 2007, *USA Today* named *Chicken Soup for the Soul* one of the five most memorable books in the last quarter-century. With over 110 million books sold to date in the U.S. and Canada alone, more than 300 titles in print, and translations into nearly fifty languages, "chicken soup for the soul®" is one of the world's best-known phrases.

Today, thirty-one years after we first began sharing happiness, inspiration and hope through our books, we continue to delight our readers with ten to twelve new titles each year, but have also evolved beyond the bookshelves with super premium pet food, a podcast, adult coloring books, and licensed products that include word-search puzzle books and books for babies and preschoolers. We are busy "changing your life one story at a time®." Thanks for reading!

Share with Us

We have all had Chicken Soup for the Soul moments in our lives. If you would like to share your story, go to chickensoup.com and click on Books and then Submit Your Story. You will find our writing guidelines there, along with a list of topics we're working on.

You may be able to help another reader and become a published author at the same time! Some of our past contributors have even launched writing and speaking careers from the publication of their stories in our books.

We only accept story submissions via our website. They are no longer accepted via postal mail or fax. And they are not accepted via e-mail.

To contact us regarding other matters, please send an e-mail to the webmaster@chickensoupforthesoul.com, or write us at:

Chicken Soup for the Soul
P.O. Box 700
Cos Cob, CT 06807-0700

One more note from your friends at Chicken Soup for the Soul: Occasionally, we receive an unsolicited book manuscript from one of our readers, and we would like to respectfully inform you that we do not accept unsolicited manuscripts, and we must discard the ones that are sent to us.

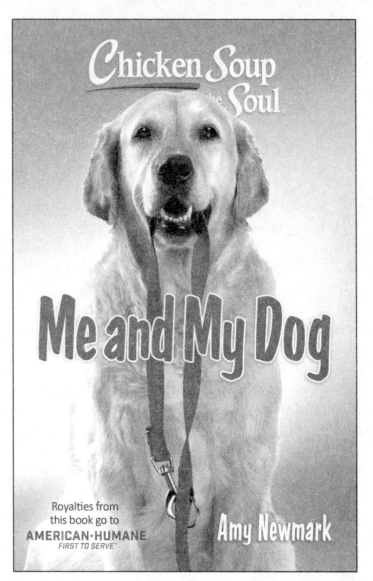

Paperback: 978-1-61159-110-1

eBook: 978-1-61159-345-7

More fun with pets,

Paperback: 978-1-61159-099-9
eBook: 978-1-61159-336-5

our furry family members

Paperback: 978-1-61159-101-9
eBook: 978-1-61159-338-9

Add some sunshine to your day

Chicken Soup for the Soul

Read, Laugh, Repeat

101 Laugh-Out-Loud Stories

Amy Newmark

Paperback: 978-1-61159-075-3

eBook: 978-1-61159-315-0

with these hilarious stories

Changing Your World One Story at a Time®
www.chickensoup.com